THE
PAUL HAMLYN
LIBRARY

DONATED BY

Peter Williams

TO THE
BRITISH MUSEUM

opened December 2000

RINGS OF STONE

The prehistoric stone circles of Britain and Ireland

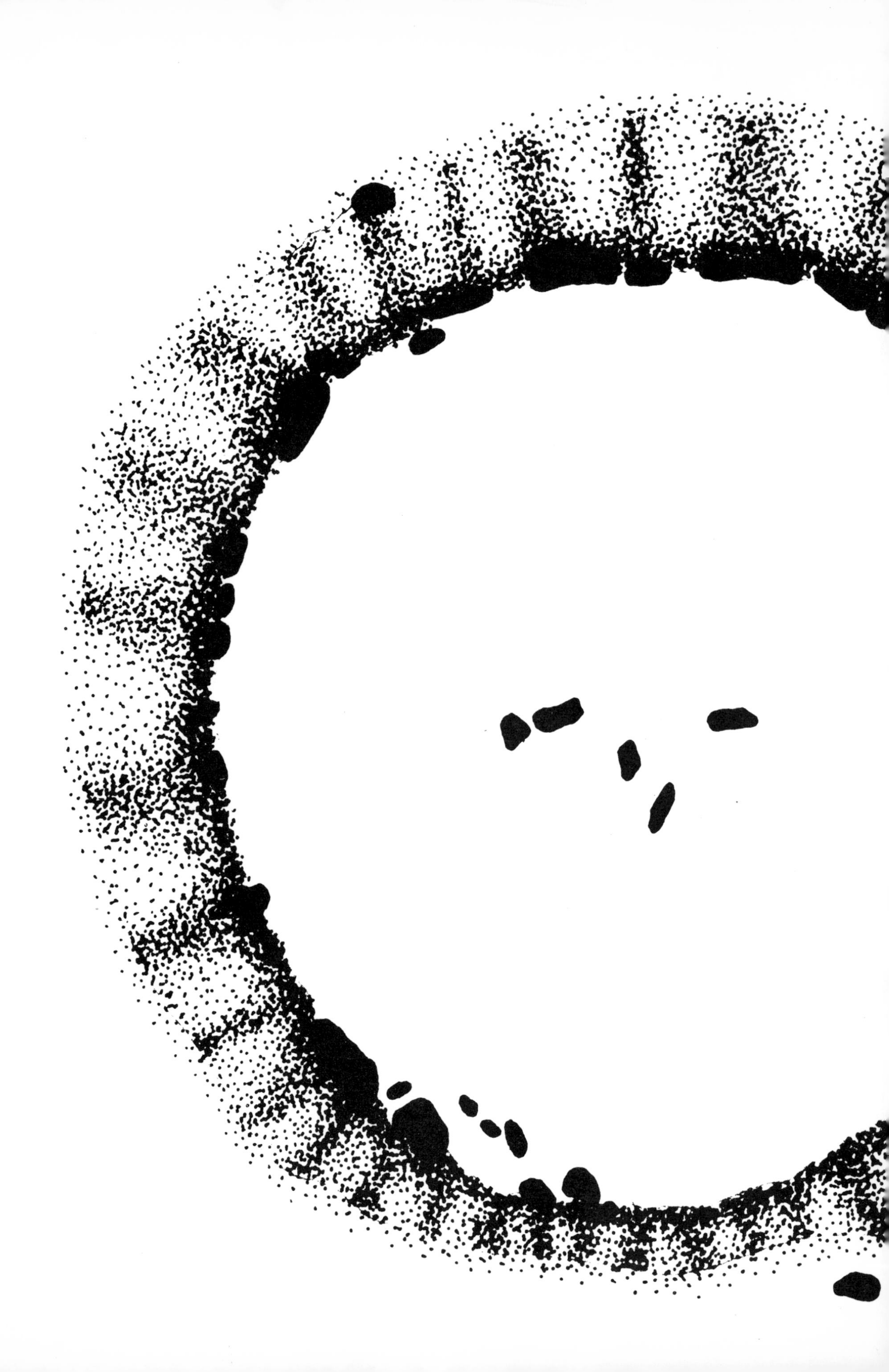

RINGS OF STONE

The prehistoric stone circles of Britain and Ireland

Aubrey Burl

with photographs by
Edward Piper

Frances Lincoln
Weidenfeld
& Nicolson

To
Stanley Thomas
an inspired teacher
who opened antiquity to me.

Atque, in perpetuum, frater,
ave atque vale.

936.1
BUR

Editor: Josephine Christian
Art director: Sally Smallwood
Designer: Tim Foster
Assistant editor: Karen Hearn
Assistant designer: Caroline Hillier

Text © Aubrey Burl 1979
Photographs © Edward Piper 1979

First published in Great Britain 1979 by
Frances Lincoln Publishers Limited,
Mortimer House, 37–41 Mortimer Street, London W1N 7RJ
in association with Weidenfeld and Nicolson Limited,
91 Clapham High Street, London SW4 7TA

All rights reserved
No part of this publication may be reproduced, stored in any retrieval system, transmitted in any form or by any means, electronic, mechanical, photocopying, recording or otherwise, without the prior permission in writing of the Publishers

ISBN: 0 906459 03 6

Filmset and printed in Great Britain by
BAS Printers Limited, Over Wallop, Hampshire
Colour separations by Newsele Litho Limited, Italy

Contents

Preface

In the years when Egypt was young, long before the pyramids, at a time when the earliest forms of writing and numbering were being developed in the Near East and when pathless forests and swamps obscured most of Western Europe, at this time a group of people in the British Isles, somewhere, built a stone circle. Its very simplicity hinders our understanding of it. Upright stones as tall as a man around a space a person could stroll across in half a minute, a few bits of human bone, patches of charcoal, these are all that remain of a place that people struggled to build many years ago. It is not surprising that conjectures about such an enigmatic monument are as many as the clues are few.

The words of Macbeth, who lived in the region of the most tantalizing of all these rings, the Scottish recumbent stone circles, describe their nature very well:

That palter with us in a double sense;
That keep the word of promise to our ear,
And break it to our hope.

This book is not an exhaustive review of stone circles. Other works, listed at the end, provide detailed information. Here there are very few diameters, astronomical computations, or tables of measurements, just enough to make the explanations intelligible without confusing the reader with a bewilderment of mathematical calculations – most of which would be irrelevant anyway. What the book does offer is a personal statement of what I believe stone circles were and what happened inside them. It is an opinion based on years of enjoyable field visits to the stones, of reading old journals and older manuscripts, and of several worrying and wearying excavations in these rings that entice and frustrate like rainbows' ends.

After the sections about stone circles and the strange things that went on in them there is a gazetteer describing fifty rings that a visitor should enjoy seeing. It is not definitive any more than a list of the world's most beautiful women would be. But it may lure the reader to look at some of these centres of forgotten cults that are so peaceful now in the fields, stooks of corn propped against the stones where once a living corn dolly may have been sacrificed.

Except for Wales, the pre-1974 county names have been retained in the text, as these are more familiar to most people. For ease of reference the new names have been added in brackets in the gazetteer.

No one helped me with the text and I can avoid no blame for it. But June Buckland did type it. And Margaret, my wife, once more accepted absences, preoccupations and stony silences with grace and encouragement. My thanks to both of them.

Introduction

Because it is obscured by the trees, the circle is seldom seen by the people in the cars that hurtle by. Long after the stones were raised, the clearing in which they stood was abandoned, became so overgrown that the pillars were almost hidden from the Iron Age peasants stepping warily around them. For thousands of years the ring was ignored. Neither medieval pilgrim nor Tudor merchant bothered with it, and few people cared when other circles were torn from the ground in the nineteenth century by farmers intent on clearing their fields.

Dorchester, near the south coast of England, the Casterbridge of Thomas Hardy, is an old town. Long before Hardy's time the elegant eighteenth-century houses in the main street were built there, and centuries before that masons and guildsmen created the tall-towered church with its Easter sepulchre. Older still were the ruined walls of the Roman town. Yet even these reached less than half-way back to the age of the prehistoric stone circle a few miles away.

Outside Dorchester the Roman road extends westwards, straight, passing the ancient hill-fort of Maiden Castle, older by eight hundred years than the road but, even so, younger than the round barrows that fringe the road two miles on. Under one were three skeletons, dumped there by Bronze Age people who heaped the burial-mound over the bodies. Beyond the barrows the road curves down to a stream, glimpses a huddle of thatched cottages, bends through Winterborne Abbas and straightens again among the hills whose sides are shadowed with outlines of ancient fields. Here, in a thicket of oaks, the circle stands, in the shade of the trees, iron railings around it, the long silence of four thousand years destroyed by the cars and lorries that echo against the branches.

It was not always noisy. When John Aubrey, the first English archaeologist, saw the Nine Stones, as the ring is called, three hundred years ago, it stood 'a little within the hedge', with only the peaceful lane alongside it. Sixty years later William Stukeley, another antiquarian, sketched it, and there were no trees, no railings, only a hedged lane with round barrows scattered on the hills behind, nine stones 'of a very hard sort full of flints' in a misshapen circle, the two tallest stones at the exact north of the ring. Stukeley called it a 'Celtic Temple'. Aubrey said nothing about its age and purpose, and today one could find a dozen guesses as to why it was built.

Wherever in the north and west of prehistoric Britain there was plentiful stone and good earth, people settled, felled trees, planted crops and built a stone circle, but left little inside it except a lasting mystery that teases our modern minds and imaginations. Who erected the stones, how old they are, how they were moved, what drove people to such efforts, these questions are easy to ask. But the answers are not always obvious, indeed remain elusive.

They are, all the stone circles, mysterious. Even when they are not spoilt by fences and explanatory notices, by entrance tickets and custodians, the rings are remote and still as though life has been chilled out of them. And the silence has encouraged speculation. The fragments of skulls and long bones have been interpreted as evidence for sacrifices, as the remains of battles, as a sign, more simply, that a circle was the burial-place of a chieftain. The rings have been called temples. They have also been called meeting-places where people gathered to debate tribal problems. Quite differently, but appealingly, some astronomers have claimed that the rings of upright stones were a form of calendar, and others that the sites were celestial observatories for the prediction of eclipses. Mathematicians have supposed that they were designed on rigorous geometrical principles by people who were aware of the properties of right-angled triangles. Other, more mystical, researchers have suggested that these rings were spiritual generators linked to each other by lines of psychic energy radiating across the countryside in a network of invisible rays.

At such a distance of years, looking at the handiwork of people who could neither read nor write, examining the ruins of circles in which all the movement has been concealed by the mouldering stains of time, it seems impossible ever to know what they were built for, impossible to select any one of the many suppositions about them and decide that this was the correct explanation, the others wrong.

Below From William Stukeley's *Itinerarium Curiosum* II of 1776, the Nine Stones. 'Within an inclosure, near the London-road, there stand certain stones, nine in number, in a circular form. The stones . . . seem to be petrify'd lumps of flints.'

In the extreme north of the British Isles, between two lochs in the Orkneys, the high slabs of Stenness rise around the inner edge of a rock-cut ditch. There used to be a holed stone near them. John Tolund, a contemporary of Stukeley, thought this was the sacrificial stone to 'which criminals and victims were ty'd'. A similar claim was made for the Athgreany circle in the foothills of the Wicklow mountains in Ireland. Today its squat granite boulders sit comfortably under the trees, but there survive folk-memories of sun-worship and death in this ring, and someone years ago carved a Christian cross on a stone outside the circle to exorcise the evil that lingered there. A thousand-year-old poem preserved the legend of sacrifices:

Their god was he –
That Cromm, all misty, withered, wan –
Those whom he ruled so fearfully,
Are dead – and whither have they gone?

To him – oh, shame!
Their children, piteous babes, they slew,
Their blood they poured out in his name,
With wailing cries, and tears, and rue.

It is noticeable that Athgreany stands in a pasture known as Achadh Greine, the Sun-Field, and it is easy to imagine offerings to the sun in this ring, quiet now but once fire-lit and tense as the midwinter sun was setting. It is sometimes called the Pipers Stones because it is said that the stones are the petrified bodies of men condemned for taking part in a pagan dance.

Other writers about stone circles, however, have explained the presence of human bone in them differently. Avebury, the biggest megalithic ring in the British Isles, with an enormous bank, even deeper ditch, and stones vast and heavy enough to crush a bus, was thought to be a graveyard in which King Arthur had buried his warriors killed in the battle of Mount Badon. A few miles away, its neighbour, Stonehenge, was believed to be a cenotaph. After the treacherous Saxon Hengist had massacred nearly five hundred British nobles, the King of Britain commanded that his magician Merlin should bring great stones from Ireland to build Stonehenge as a memorial to those brave men. Later the King himself was buried there.

Less dramatic, and perhaps therefore more plausible, are the claims that the stone circles were family burial-places. In Aberdeenshire the wrecked stones of Old Rayne lie in the arable fields, a wire fence separating the one remaining upright from a great recumbent block still in position at the south-west. The circle overlooks the plain where the whale-backed mass of the holy mountain, Mither Tap, the Mother of the Top, heaves and juts against the skyline. A hundred years ago diggers found a pit inside the ring, filled with charcoal, broken pottery and burnt human bones. To the Victorian excavators it seemed obvious that sites like Old Rayne should be 'regarded as the graves of chiefs, or sometimes, it may be, family sepulchres'. We are less certain today.

It was an explanation feasible for those rings where there were bones, but quite inappropriate for other circles such as the famous Rollright Stones in Oxfordshire, in which no skeletons or cremations have been discovered. The limestone pillars of this ring have been so ravaged by the weather that Stukeley described them as 'corroded like worm-eaten wood by the harsh jaws of Time'. Standing on an exposed ridge above the Oxford plain and the valleys surrounding the Cotswolds, this plain, uncluttered ring defeated the ingenuity of Stukeley, who could write only that it was 'a curious and ancient monument: the first kind, and most common of the Druid Temples, a plain circle'. And temples for ritual activities are what many other stone circles have been thought to be. Some are even named the 'Druids Temple' or 'Druids' Circle', though they were built almost two thousand years before the first Druidical bard emerged in Britain.

Such a vague description as a 'temple' did not satisfy other writers, who rejected all thoughts of worship and offerings and instead pointed out how convenient the shape of a circle was for assemblies. A community could use a ring as a moot-place for the settlement of disputes over boundaries, livestock, dowries and blood-feuds. The Nine Ladies, at the edge of a wood on Stanton Moor in Derbyshire, was just such a site. The stones were set in a pleasant low bank of earth and rubble on which the people could sit around an open area, ample for the chief and his wise men as they pondered on the problems brought before them. Nowadays, with an ugly wall enclosing it, the Nine Ladies has little resemblance to a court of justice, perhaps never did, but the widely dispersed cemetery of cairns and earth circles on the moor nearby makes it a place worth visiting.

These assumptions about the use of stone circles have been 'romantic', investing the rings with men, women and children anxious to protect their lives from the world's perils by engaging in unknown rites, even burying the bodies of respected ancestors inside the circle. But there are also 'scientific' theories in which the stones become components of logically constructed instruments for computations of calendars and eclipses. As long ago as the eighteenth century William Borlase, an enthusiastic Cornish antiquary, having cantered across the granite austerity of Land's End inspecting the old monuments there, observed that there were four stone circles within eight miles of each other, every one with nineteen stones in its ring, 'expressing, perhaps, the two principal divisions of the year, the twelve months, and the seven days of the week. This conjecture will not seem strange and groundless, when we reflect that the Priests were the only Chronologers and Registers of Time.' When one thinks of the Merry Maidens ring, a dainty and entire setting of stones on its hillside near a stone-built tomb with magical markings at its entrance, it is difficult to believe it was no more than a sundial and calendar, particularly as these stones also are reputed to be girls who had been caught dancing on the Sabbath. Science and superstition conflict here.

More impressive than Borlase's conjectures, because the analyses were made by trained astronomers, are the claims that rings like the Standing Stones of Callanish in the Hebrides were used 'to reckon the seasons and perhaps to predict eclipse seasons'. At Callanish, just above the black, seaweed-slippery rocks of the shore, there is a little circle, hardly big enough for six people with outstretched arms, its stones slim and tall, with a dominant central pillar that looms over a tiny tomb in which cremated bone was found a hundred years ago. Rows and avenues of stones extend roughly towards the cardinal points from the ring. The landscape of rock, mottled peaty grass and sea-filled loch is lovely in the shifting lights and shadows across the circle, whose lines of stones may have been aligned towards important movements of the sun and moon. 'Callanish seems to have been used primarily to establish a calendar, though it may possibly have been used for predicting eclipses as well.' This may be true. But the existence of the human bone at the heart of the ring must not be forgotten.

It would have been possible to align a setting of stones towards the place on the horizon where the sun rose in midsummer without the builders having any knowledge of mathematics, but other scholars have contended that all the rings were designed geometrically. On the exposed upland moor above Conway Bay the Druids' Circle is silhouetted against the sky, its leaning pillars embedded in a bank of white quartz stones blurred by the grass that blows and quivers in the persistent breeze. One has no impression of precise measurements or careful design here, and yet, according to Professor Alexander Thom, this ring was planned as an ellipse based on two right-angled triangles, 'one of the almost perfect triangles . . . . It would have been quite impossible for the builders to detect the discrepancy in the hypotenuse . . . . From their point of view the perimeter was also perfect.' Inside the neatness of this meticulous oval people had buried the burnt bones of young children.

As well as the 'romantic' and 'scientific' interpretations of the British megalithic rings there are also the mystical explanations, made by people who do not analyse but sense the significance and purpose of these rings. The Cornish rings, in particular, have attracted them, perhaps because they lie in the Lands of the Blessed where in the mists above the surf-crashing shores figures of ghostly knights and hags may be half seen. One such enchanted ring is Boscawen-Un, hidden in a gorse-thick hollow with an overgrown wall bristling around it. A tapering column of granite leans at its centre. The sceptical archaeologist is perplexed to learn that lines of kinetic force, the leys that emanated from the forgotten extrasensory powers of prehistoric people, radiated from Boscawen-Un, connecting with other sites. One ley that pointed towards the rising of the Pleiades in May passed through a stone cross, then through another large standing stone a mile away, extended beyond the submerged forest in Mount's Bay and terminated at Perranuthnoe church, 'a centre of local legends and folklore', although the local guide-book more prosaically advises the visitor that 'the excellent beach will probably provide a stronger attraction.' The fact that Perranuthnoe is eight miles away from Boscawen-Un, and quite invisible from it, does nothing to diminish the convictions of the devout ley-liner.

There has even been an explanation for the quartz pillar at the west of the ring. As anyone with a digital wristwatch knows, quartz particles produce an electric current when placed under tension, and it has been suggested that such force might be produced by people whirling and twisting in dances around the stones, or by pouring water over them. 'If quartz and other minerals have vibrating potencies that can restore a natural harmony to tissues and cells that are diseased then using pure well-water as a medium for conveying the healing properties would make good sense.' The stones of Stonehenge were also supposed to imbue water that had been poured over them with medicinal virtue.

So many are the meanings given to stone circles and so few are the sensible books written about them, that it is no surprise to find people fascinated but frustrated by the mystery of the rings. Probably the most complete explanation ever provided as a catch-all to account for all their features came from the zealous William Borlase. He had been looking at a strange and inexplicably interlocking complex of rings at Botallack, near St Just in Cornwall. Endeavouring to sort out the medley of overlapping rings and lines, and attempting to explain why any group of Druidical priests should have needed so many different rings, he provided a comprehensive explanation. He perceived that 'in the seeming confusion I cannot but think that there was some mystical meaning, or, at least, distinct allotment to particular uses. Some of these might be employed for the Sacrifice, and to prepare, kill, examine and burn the Victim, others allotted to Prayer, others to the Feasting of the Priests, others for the station of those who devoted the Victims: whilst one Druid was preparing the Victim in one Place, another was adoring in another.'

Such desperate ingenuity was entirely unrewarded. The unfortunate Borlase, like others after him, had been inspecting not stone circles but the wreckage of an Iron Age village in which cattle had been stalled in crude compounds and where the smell of cooking had drifted from the turf-roofed circular huts. Its resemblance to a group of megalithic rings was quite accidental.

In 1861 James Bryce was digging in one of the splendid, ruined rings on Machrie Moor on the island of Arran. Near the rain-grooved pillars his labourers dug through the peat until they came to the top of a ponderous slab, a ton of thick sandstone that they slowly prised up. 'A white object like a blanched human skull loomed out from the deep obscurity of the cist. We had come at last to a veritable human grave.' It is the presence of human bones and cremations in many of the prehistoric stone circles of Great Britain that provides one of the clues to what these mysterious rings once were.

Opposite Stone circles in the British Isles.

Clues to the past: recumbent stone circles

Not long ago there were many unanswered questions about stone circles. We asked when they were built, by whom, what their history was, and, above all, what happened inside them. To some extent we now have answers. For the empty, plain rings of southern England we can reconstruct their purpose only by reference to circles in other parts of Britain, and it is simplest to begin by looking at the most informative group, the recumbent stone circles of north-east Scotland.

These rings are rich in promise. Closely grouped together along the outskirts of the Grampian mountains in a largely isolated region, and overlooking the coastal plain which in prehistoric times may have been so heavily forested that it was almost uninhabitable, the recumbent stone circles of Aberdeenshire and Kincardine tantalize the archaeologist and

Below Recumbent stone circles in north-eastern Scotland.

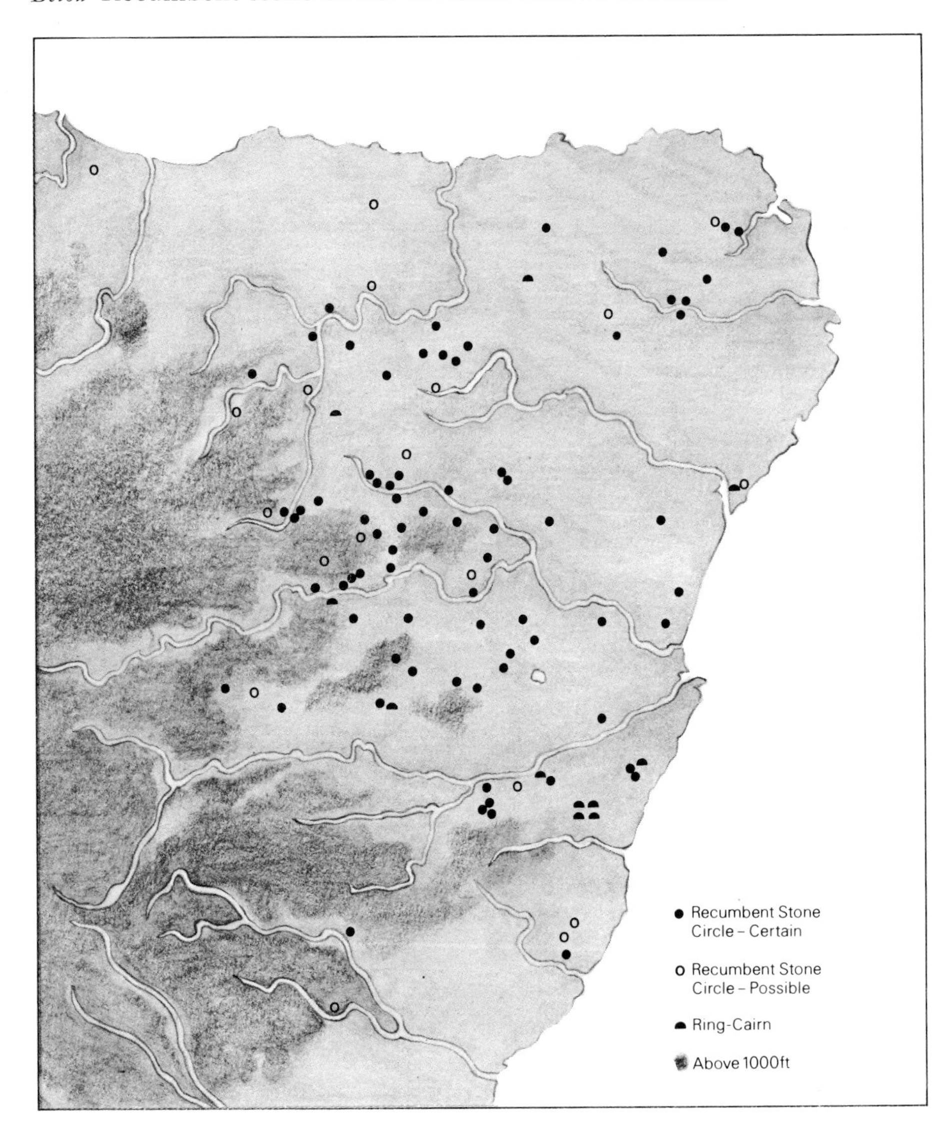

astronomer. Circles elsewhere contain so little that it seems impossible ever to know what they were used for. But excavators of the recumbents have discovered charcoal, quartz, flint tools, bronze daggers, archers' wristguards, a variety of pottery, burnt human bone, a mass of material left inside monuments with peculiar architectural features and with astronomical alignments built into them, such treasure-houses of information that it seems it would be a straightforward matter to decide what the circles were used for. A recumbent stone circle, however, is not a treasury but a tantalus. As in a dance of the veils, one by one the coverings are removed, a little more of the mystery is disclosed until everything is about to be revealed, and then, as the last veil falls . . . the lights go out.

It is disappointing but not disastrous. With effort we can learn still more and claim, in the words of John Aubrey, that we 'have gonne farther in this Essay than any one before.' Much of this section, for instance, is based on my own fieldwork, which included the total excavation of one of these unusual monuments. Well-preserved rings like Castle Frazer or Easter Aquorthies, the Field of the Pillar-Stones, in central Aberdeenshire show what strange features a typical site possesses. At first they seem to be rough and ready structures, 'rude stone monuments' James Fergusson called them in 1872, but examination shows that they have unsuspected subtleties in their design. They were engineered as nicely as the techniques available to their builders allowed, and every excavated ring has revealed precise planning. The circle itself is not an ordinary ring of stones but has pillars that rise noticeably in height towards the south-western part of the circumference, where the two tallest flank a huge, prostrate block, many tons in weight, the recumbent stone laid there when the circle was built.

On it, or on the stones nearest it, one can sometimes make out artificial depressions about the size and depth of an ash-tray. These are called cupmarks, ground out with a piece of harder stone. Not every circle has them. Where they do exist they are frequently indistinct until the rising or setting sun casts shadows into them, but these enigmatic cavities have excited speculation, some investigators seeing in them astronomical patterns of the stars while others have claimed that they were basins intended for the dripping blood of Druidical victims.

Near the recumbent in the interior of several rings fragments of brilliant white quartz have been scattered, lying starkly on a rectangular setting of earth-fast stones that formed a platform between the recumbent and the central ring-cairn that was the heart of the monument. Ring-cairns are unknown in other stone circles. They are, as their name suggests, low circular mounds of cobbles with an open central space a few metres across and lined with upright slabs. It is in this space that pits have been discovered, almost always holding broken pottery, charcoal, traces of fire and cremated human bone. This combination of circle, quartz, ring-cairn, bone, pottery and cupmarks, in rings built on hillside terraces with views for miles around, appears sufficient for us to reconstruct the ceremonies that went on in them.

The lack of domestic equipment and rubbish, such as burnt-out hearths, flints for scraping animal skins, grinding-stones for making flour, tells us that these were not places where people lived. Equally, they were not industrial sites, for there is no sign of flint- or metal-working in them. Despite their hillside position they could not have been used defensively, for they have no substantial banks or ditches around them. Nor are they cemeteries. The number of 'burials' is small and the burnt bones have usually been only portions of cremations, less like the reverent interments of chieftains than offerings of human bone made when the circle was put up. This negative argument against dwelling, work-place, refuge or burial-ground leads to the conclusion that these were ritual centres, an interpretation which the carefully designed architecture, the quartz and cupmarkings, and the positioning of the recumbent itself support.

Below The artificial depressions known as cupmarks have excited much speculation. These cup-and-ring carvings are on a red sandstone cist-slab which may originally have formed part of a stone rectangle at the centre of the recently excavated circle at Balbirnie, Fife.

One question that had to be settled was how old the rings were, for once that was known they could be related to a particular prehistoric society, among the hunters and wanderers of seven thousand years ago, or with the farmers of the New Stone and Bronze Ages, or with the more aggressive tribal warriors of the Celtic Iron Age. Early excavators could not date the rings. Charles Dalrymple, digging up four of the circles in the mid-nineteenth century, had to be content with vague comments that 'three fragments of small urns were found burned red' at the wrecked recumbent of Old Rayne, where a lovely greenstone wristguard that once had protected a man's forearm from the whiplash of his bowstring was unearthed by Dalrymple's labourers.

Few other recumbent stone circles were dug into. In 1904 Fred Coles made an unexpectedly good excavation at Garrol Wood, and in 1910, after a decade of studying these challenging sites, he observed that 'no evidence . . . is yet forthcoming which points to their purpose and use, earlier than or more recent than the Bronze period.' Nor did he believe in the wild astronomical speculations that scientists like Sir Norman Lockyer were making about the rings.

In the 1930s Gordon Childe, an Australian, great prehistorian, and professor of archaeology at Edinburgh University, dug into the ruined ring at Old Keig with the specific intention of deciding how old it was. This was at a time twenty years before the development of the radiocarbon method of assessing the age of decayed organic material and Childe was forced to examine his finds of pottery and other artefacts in the hope that he could place them accurately in a general chronological framework for prehistoric Britain. This was a time-honoured approach and often quite reliable. Unfortunately, he was misled by the resemblance of the pottery he found to other vessels that belonged to the beginning of the Iron Age and he suggested that 'Recumbent Stone Circles may have been erected in Late Halstatt times.' Shortly afterwards, following his own excavations at the vital ring of Loanhead of Daviot, another archaeologist, Kilbride-Jones, found himself with the same problem, which he solved by suggesting that the ring itself had been built in the Bronze Age but that the 'Centre Pit was re-opened apparently in the Iron Age, and the people of that period deposited their dead therein.'

Childe and Kilbride-Jones were mistaken in identifying the pottery with Iron Age vessels, but it is only from later excavations in other parts of Scotland that we now realize that crude bucket-shaped pots, known as flat-rimmed ware, were being made as early as 2900 BC, probably fashioned by women in their own homes, and continued in long, tedious vogue until as late as 1700 BC, deep into the Bronze Age. They are of little value for precise dating.

This teasing result is characteristic of recumbent stone circles. One can visit magnificent rings like Dyce, its tapering flankers looking out towards Aberdeen airport, or Auchquhorthies, where the ring-cairn is still well preserved despite Dalrymple's depredations, one can admire the shaping of the stones at Cothiemuir Wood, undisturbed in the quietness of a forest, one can wander around Loanhead of Daviot, tidied and lawn-cut by the State, examine the central area where children's bones were found, look at the cupmarks, see the later enclosed cremation cemetery alongside the circle, but the questions remain as many and the answers are still as few. Arnhill, seen in a downpour, raindrops slithering down the rubble that farmers have dragged from the field and piled against the recumbent, has a grandeur that impresses the imagination with the labour that must have gone into the building of the ring. Balquhain, often barred from the enthusiast by ripening barley, is just as intriguing, with its cupmarked stones and with a giant pillar of quartz just outside the circle.

Below The recumbent stone circle at Dyce. Surrounded by a romantic plantation of trees, it lies close to Aberdeen airport.

It is not that there has been no speculation or writing about these sites that survive in the stone-walled fields of north-eastern Scotland. As early as the sixteenth century the Scottish historian Hector Boece described the rings as 'the old temples of the gods' in which 'the new moon was hailed with certain words of prayer', an intriguing remark. James Anderson, in 1777, suggested that the platform between the recumbent and the ring-cairn was a stage from which priests conducted their ceremonies. Christian MacLagan rather eccentrically believed the rings to be the collapsed wreckage of brochs, the tall stone-built towers of western and northern Scotland built well into Roman times, but never explained how the tons of rubble that would have tumbled from such lofty constructions could have vanished from every ring. Fred Coles thought the circles were burial-places. Hadrian Allcroft argued in huge detail and quite wrongly that they were post-Roman meeting-grounds. Until recently, in spite of the field researches of Coles and of Alexander Keiller, the rich amateur archaeologist who in the 1930s bought and rescued Avebury from its state of deteriorating neglect, quite what these rings were was still unclear.

How they came to be built is not so uncertain. Seventy miles to their north-west, a journey of a week or two in prehistoric times straggling along the mild coastline of the Moray Firth, there are the Clava tombs near Inverness. These are impressive monuments, probably earlier by several hundred years than the recumbent stone circles but having so many similarities to them that they must be related. Built by Neolithic farming families on the easily worked sandy soils at the head of Loch Ness, they are cairns surrounded by stone circles, also graded in height towards the south-west, with scatters of quartz in some of them, and with cupmarks on their stones. Sometimes the central mounds are ring-cairns like those in the recumbents. Alternatively, they may be passage-graves like Corrimony, twenty miles west of Inverness in the meandering Enrick valley, a great circular cairn with a stone-lined passage leading to a round central chamber which once was roofed. Although every one of the Clava passage-graves has been damaged Corrimony has been partly restored, and one can crawl along the passage, stand up in the chamber and look at the massive capstone of the tomb where the sightless dead were laid.

It is wrong to think of all these Clava cairns simply as graves. Many of them were places that the living used as shrines, perhaps as centres of ancestor cults where the human bones were instruments to protect the living from the dangers of their everyday lives. For as long as a thousand years these great mounds were visited time and again by generations of farmers, but only one or two bodies have been found in them, none at all in some mounds, and it is unlikely that every bone could have been removed for rites elsewhere or by scavengers. The one body discovered at Corrimony had dissolved into a mere stain on the turf-stripped sand, yet people had come to the chamber on several occasions after the 'burial', scattering sand in thick layers and trampling it down. At other ring-cairns and passage-graves there were one or two pockets of cremated bone, never more. Yet burnt bone is not susceptible to natural erosion. We have to assume that these deposits of burnt bone were all there ever were in the cairn. In one the bones had been deliberately smashed into small pieces after burning. It is the practices of the Clava communities that we must expect to find repeated in some form in the recumbent stone circles that were built in later years.

The finest Clava site to go to, because it has several cairns close together, a small cairn-circle, two passage-graves and a ring-cairn off-centre between them, is the Balnuaran of Clava 'cemetery', a few miles to the east of Inverness and just south of Culloden battlefield. Little has been found there, but the persistent visitor will observe cupmarks on all three cairns: at the entrance to the chamber of the south-west passage-grave and on its western circle-stone; on the eastern kerbstones of the ring-cairn; on the eastern stone of the tiny cairn-circle to its west; and in the chamber and on the northern kerbstone of the north-east passage-grave. The significance of these positions should not be overlooked. The pattern of north, east, west, so consistently repeated, cannot be accidental. An astronomical explanation is likely, though the question is unresolved.

Farmers built the earliest Clava cairns on low-lying land, but over the centuries, as the population increased in this region of valleys and mountains with only limited patches for crop-growing, many people were compelled to move out to the higher slopes overlooking the Spey, and ultimately farther out still to the south-east, wandering along the coasts, avoiding those territories already occupied by other farmers and the miners of the good red flint of Buchan, pushing cautiously inland along the rivers until they came to the rounded hills of central Aberdeenshire overshadowed by the massive, upthrusting ridge of Bennachie granite known as Mither Tap, the Holy Mother mountain. Here they settled, men, women, children, old and young, with the precious seed grain, a few cattle, struggling against the wild land and dangerous beasts, the men labouring to cut down trees, clearing the ground, dragging away stones, planting crops, building sturdy timber cabins and cattle-stockades, women tilling the broken soil, weeding, children food-gathering at the dappled fringes of the forests, all of them engaged in the effort to establish the family on terrain that yielded nothing without day-long work.

These first generations of pioneers would not have had leisure or energy to erect a circle of heavy stones and it may have been this enforced lapse of years between the earliest settlements and the construction of any recumbent stone circle that led to the incorporation of the recumbent stone itself into the monument. No Clava cairn had a recumbent stone. Nor did it have anything resembling it. But in Ireland they were known, superbly decorated supine stones outside the entrances to some of the most magnificent passage-graves in the British Isles, in the chambered tombs of the Boyne valley twenty-five miles north of Dublin. Here, colossal mounds like New Grange and Knowth had prostrate stones marvellously engraved with lines and spirals, obviously of deep importance to their makers. We know, from the discovery of Irish pottery and of axes made of Irish stone, that there were trade-routes between Ireland and Aberdeenshire during the New Stone Age, and it seems that the intermingling of people, quite possibly by the marrying-out of women to forge stronger trade bonds, led to an acceptance that such supine stones would enhance the traditional Clava cairn and make it even more potent.

Other cairns with recumbent stones lie along the routes that Irish traders followed across Scotland in these early prehistoric centuries, paddling their loaded, lightly built boats along the calmer seas between the Mull of Kintyre and Arran where Auchagallon cairn with its supine stone still looks out across the Kilbrennan Sound; overland to Loch Awe, humping their packs and canoes along the trackways near Kintraw and Culcharron cairns with their prostrate stones; until they reached the lovely waters of Loch Tay, at whose northern tip the stone circle of Croft Moraig has a south-western supine stone plentifully cupmarked; then northwards through the low-lying, shadowy woodlands or over the high and arid mountain passes that led to the river Dee and Aberdeenshire. Evidence for a supine-stone cult manifests itself all along this old route. At the nearest point to Ireland there is the strange recumbent stone circle of Torhousekie, standing with its diminutive ring-cairn on the sandy soils near Wigtown Bay.

One should not imagine a sudden burst of circle-building. The forests were heavy with stands of oak and birch, light-loving hazels and alders growing at their edges. Willows spread over rivers and burns. The people avoided the most hostile countryside and it is noticeable how expertly they picked out the places where the earth was best and settled there. A map of AD 1696 showed that crofters then lived where the soil was deep, fertile and well-drained and where the hill-slopes were not over-steep. Some localities are named: Kirkton of Bourtie; Meldrum; Daviot; Old Rayne; Insch; Dunnideer – and these are all names of recumbent stone circles, put up in the same rich districts four thousand years before the Scottish highlanders built their crofts there. It is a sudden insight into the skills of those prehistoric farming people.

In a fascinating letter written in June 1692, the Reverend James Garden of Aberdeen told John Aubrey that there was a local belief that ancient priests had compelled people to carry good earth to the recumbent stone circle of Auchquhorthies, 'which is given for the reason why this parcell of land (though surrounded with heath and moss on all sides) is better and more fertile than other places thereabout.' One wonders what folk-memory lies behind this reminiscence.

It is unlikely that over eighty stone circles were built at the same time, but it is just as improbable that they were put up one after another, each used for only a few years. The most reasonable explanation is that there was an early colonizing period by about half a dozen families who settled on the gentle hills near modern Inverurie where their cattle grazed by the middle waters of the rivers Don and Urie.

These early rings were quite close together, as could be expected if the families looked to each other for help and protection, each with a territory of some four to six square miles which inevitably included unworkable hillsides, rivers, forest, stone-littered ground and swamp. If we also make allowance for land not yet under cultivation or lying fallow, then we might assume – realizing that all these figures are conjectures – that as little as half a mile square was under crop in each territory, about one hundred and fifty acres of arable land. Had such a tract been used solely for cattle it would have provided food for no more than two or three people, but cereal-growing would have yielded enough to nourish twenty to thirty members of the family of men and women, grandparents, children and infants, and this is probably the size of group that a recumbent stone circle was meant for.

Twenty able-bodied men and women could have built such a ring. There were, it seems, three requirements when a site was selected. It had to be level. It had to provide long views. And common sense demanded that it be near a source of glacial stones that required no quarrying but could simply be dragged the few hundred metres to the circle.

The chosen stones, thin cylindrical pillars, selected for their symmetry and differing lengths, were first keeled by having their bases bashed into a parrot-beak shape to make the task of heaving them upright easier. The stones picked out to flank the recumbent were also sometimes 'dressed' by pounding with heavy stones to make them smoother and more elegant. Each stone was then lashed with ropes of leather to a tree-trunk sledge, and, as even the heaviest of these granite pillars, the tall flankers, weighed no more than six or seven tons, a score of adults could have hauled it to its prepared stonehole quite quickly. Already the perimeter of the ring had been scratched out on the ground and the places where the stones would stand had been marked by stakes. Using picks of antler, people hacked and prised out deep sockets. Then each stone was levered into its hole, the keeled, curved base acting as a fulcrum on which the stone could be tilted upwards until it stood erect, held steady by ropes and wooden props while packing-stones were jammed into its pit to fix it firmly in position.

There is a contradiction. Although any one family might have been able to cope with the erection of the circle-stones, they could not have moved the recumbent itself. Because this stone necessarily had to be bulkier and longer than the others, and because, if possible, it had to be level-topped, a property which the local granite boulders did not normally have, it was very often a different type of stone that had to be dragged from another locality some distance from the site. An average recumbent weighed about twenty tons, a fearsome block to be shifted over a mile or two of uneven countryside by several scores of people. The monstrous recumbent of gneiss at Old Keig, five metres long, as high as a man's shoulder and thick as a full-grown oak, was fifty tons of dead weight to be manhandled from its riverside position six miles away. Oxen were not used. They were too slow, too stupid and too valuable to be risked in dragging this murderous slab over the dangerous slopes and bends that had to be faced. It is hardly possible that fewer than two hundred people combined in transporting the Old Keig recumbent, straining at the ropes, gasping as the sledge jammed in softer ground or jerked dead against a half-buried stone, slowly hauling it forwards up the slopes, children keeping at a distance, hour by hour moving gradually onwards until at last the site was reached and the recumbent inched and levered into place and its flankers raised alongside it.

Families must have co-operated in the building of these stone circles. Such times were solemn undertakings that demanded days of careful, ceremonial preparation before the first stone could be touched. Every omen would be regarded, the casual flight of a bird, a glimpse of an inauspicious animal, an illness, for it was only at propitious times that the building of a circle could be undertaken. Contemporary primitive societies have tabus and embargoes that seem illogical to our conditioned, 'rational' minds, but to such people the natural world is an entire one from which man is not excluded. He is bound by its laws and constraints as snow is affected by sunshine or flowers and leaves by drought.

In this way, bound by custom and superstition, the people raised their stone circle, heaping a low bank of smaller stones around the circumference when the standing stones were up, laying down the platform against the inner face of the recumbent, each stage of the work done as, traditionally, it had always been done. At many sites the turf had been stripped off before the ring was laid out. In some cases the ground had been levelled. At Castle Frazer crude terraces had been piled up to compensate for the slope on which the ring was to stand. At Druidsfield a similar artificial bank was over a metre and a half high. At Loanhead of Daviot the slope had been cut into, rubble laid and soil spread about to make an even surface, and such efforts reveal how important the choice of a particular site must have been. Otherwise the people could have used another, flatter place where no levelling with wooden spades, shoulder-blades of oxen and antler picks would have been needed. We can guess that the need for a distant view was the fundamental requirement when the men searched for a suitable spot on which their ring could be built.

The results can still be seen today, the circle, the grassed-over bank, platform stones almost buried in the earth. What cannot be seen, and what this book must explain, are the events that followed. A recumbent stone circle was a ritual monument and rites had to be performed to give it power. It seems that pottery, deliberately broken, was sometimes set down in the holes where stones were to stand, beaker sherds and Irish vessels with round bases and incurving rims that we know were being made around 2500 BC. Pieces of flat-rimmed ware have been found in the interior of some rings, and shattered urns of the Bronze Age, several hundreds of years later than the Irish pots. Some of these could have been casual breakages but it cannot be accidental that where circles have been thoroughly excavated signs of fierce fires have been noticed in their interiors, the ground burnt red with the heat. As, in nearly every ring that has been investigated, cremated bone has been discovered, one thinks of the people building a pyre on the bared earth in the middle of the ring, laying a corpse upon it, and watching as the flames consumed wood and flesh down to the flecks of bone and lumps of charcoal that time after time have been unearthed in these circles.

It was only then that the ring-cairn was built, after the people had raked away the ash and smouldering wood and gathered up the bits of bone. At Loanhead of Daviot someone neatly buried one chunk of charcoal, one bit of pottery and one piece of burnt bone near the area where the fire had been, as clear a dedicatory offering as one could expect to find. Some of the remaining charcoal, some of the broken pottery, was placed in little holes by the circle-stones and covered with small cairns. But never any human bone. This was kept for the open ring in the middle of the ring-cairn. Here the people dug out pits, sometimes lining them with stones, and set the cremations deep down in the earth.

At Hatton of Ardoyne, a circle still in good condition on a farm within sight of Mither Tap, interrupted now by a hedge but with a remarkably flat-topped recumbent, the men had dug a grave-like shaft over a metre into the earth and rock, long enough to lay a body in, paved it with cobbles and then laid just one cremation on the stones with the broken bits of a fire-reddened urn alongside it. In other circles the pits were usually shallower, but always had cremated bone in them. When Childe excavated Old Keig he found the earth 'baked to a bright brick-red by the intense heat'. A large pit had been dug through this patch and people had thrown in broken bits of pot and 'numerous but minute fragments of cremated *human* bone' belonging to a young adult. In such practices no family aped another, nor was there a supervising priesthood. Every family buried the bones differently, in hollows, in deep shafts, in stone-lined pits, but they all made these offerings to the forces of Nature that they were invoking.

At Loanhead of Daviot the whole of the central area was covered with a layer of earth, charcoal and bone, some fragments of which had come from the skulls of children. Commonly, as in the Clava cairns, there were only two or three cremations at most, sometimes spread out as though they had been thrown all over the central space. Dalrymple reported that at the cupmarked ring of Sunhoney he found 'deposits of incinerated bones, with some charcoal and black mould, but in no great quantity', and at Ardlair 'a small quantity of incinerated bones, with the usual deposit of black burnt mould and charcoal'. These, surely, were offerings, not burials, put there when the circle was new, and concealed beneath piles of small stones. Whether they were the burnt bones of some respected member of the family or, just as possible, were sacrifices, is one more of the problems that the builders of the recumbent stone circles have left us.

The earliest rings, constructed from about 2500 BC onwards, although they varied from site to site, had many features in common. They were clearly intended to be imposing. They were circular and quite large. Ten people with outstretched arms could have stood comfortably side by side in any of them. The stones were noticeably graded in height, were big, the flankers higher than a tall man, the recumbent many tons in weight and always placed between south-west and south-south-east, with a platform that extended about a metre between it and the ring-cairn. These circles built in the central regions, whatever their diameter, usually had ten standing stones set out in five opposing pairs with no stone opposite the recumbent. It was only in the next phase of circle-building that an eleventh stone became fashionable, perhaps to mark the place from which observations were to be made across the ring. This standardization of numbers has only recently been recognized, but it does reveal something of the elementary numeracy of these people whose need to count was probably limited to checking the size of their scrawny herds. The fact that they repeatedly included ten stones in these first rings, whether at Cothiemuir Wood or at Midmar, now oddly hallowed in a country churchyard where the visitor can hear the sounds of hymn-singing as he takes photographs of this pagan sanctuary, demonstrates the conservatism of these primitive and heathen people.

The very last rings, maybe built as many as eight hundred years later, were different. Expectedly, they are mainly to be found at the outer limits of the recumbent stone circle region, to the east near Aberdeen where the nine stones of Binghill, a ring barely big enough for half a dozen children to play in, poke out of the long grass; to the south where the sixteen quartz pillars of North Strone once stood. Sometimes they are distorted into sub-oval shapes, as at Garrol Wood. They are ungraded, small, with recumbent stones more often placed between south and south-south-east, as though there had been some change of belief among these later people.

In the very north-east of Aberdeenshire, a few miles from Peterhead, a fishing village now thriving on the proceeds from North Sea oil, there was a separate group of recumbent stone circles, a dozen of them in a rough triangle of about twenty square miles, each near well-drained, fertile land. One of them, Berrybrae, had lost many of its stones, and the soil-filled stoneholes could be examined without any fear of an archaeologist being crushed under an unstable granite pillar. There was no record that it had ever been dug into. It was this promising site that we chose to investigate in 1975. It proved to have a quite unsuspected history.

The countryside to the south of Fraserburgh, another fishing village on the north coast, is unremarkable but pleasant, a patchwork of arable fields in an undulating plain from which Mormond Hill rises smoothly. In AD 1700 a white horse was cut in its southern slopes and in the nineteenth century a stag was added, contrasting sadly with the ironmongery of NATO early-warning equipment that litters the hilltop. Like Mither Tap, Mormond Hill is a commanding landmark, and one wonders, quite hopelessly, whether the people who built the stone circles looked on such hills as the dwelling-places of powerful spirits. Whether among the Peruvian Indians who set out so many straight lines in the Nasca desert towards mountain crests, or among Australian aborigines, or Burmese tribesmen who worshipped hill-spirits and would not cultivate land near the hills for fear of causing offence, natural eminences have often been treated with awe. In Europe Mount Parnassus in Greece and Mount Ida on Crete were also thought of as the homes of the gods. It is a matter mentioned here because the builders of the British stone circles were without writing or any form of art which can be interpreted, so their beliefs are now irrecoverably lost. Yet without knowing their beliefs our understanding of the monuments they left behind can never be complete, and we must sometimes flesh out these architectural skeletons with knowledge obtained from comparable primitive societies even though this is an imprecise and unreliable process.

Berrybrae stands a few metres from a country lane in the corner of an extensive field, protected from the plough by a low wall inside which a nature-loving landowner planted a spacious coppice of trees. Of the circle, the recumbent stone, its west flanker and one other stone still stand but the rest have gone, leaving only a grassy bank on which cattle browse, their hoofs kicking up the loose stones.

When Charles Dalrymple dug into his circles around 1860 he used three or four labourers for a day on each, delving into the centre, hoicking out the pots in a form of instant archaeology that horrifies today's archaeologist. It is, of course, unfair to criticize a Victorian digger for not observing the rigorous standards of the later twentieth century. But in contrast to his speed we spent three seasons at Berrybrae, 1975, 1976 and 1978, usually with about twenty people working all day for ten weeks altogether. For those who truly believe that all British weather is bad it should be added that out of over five hundred hours spent at the site we lost only two because of rain.

Americans did most of the work. Intrigued by the prospect of excavating at this remote and attractive ancient circle, they came year by year, paying for the privilege of hard but rewarding work, gathered together by the Earthwatch organization of Belmont, Massachusetts, who advertised this and other projects in a nationwide brochure. To guide these volunteers there were experienced supervisors, usually my own graduate students, who knew that we were likely to find pottery, quartz, cremations and, probably, charcoal that would provide the first scientific date ever obtained from a recumbent stone circle in Scotland. We could also anticipate some relatively modern interference by treasure-seekers, and we found it. Three large pits had been dug inside the ring, luckily missing everything of importance. Elsewhere, a dog had been buried beside the recumbent by the farmer's young son (who was amazed that we were able to find it), and the skeleton of a horse was uncovered when we were digging some sondage pits well away from the ring to establish what the soil layers in undisturbed ground looked like.

We began in the belief that the damage to the ring had been caused by some tenant-farmer who wanted to remove the obstructive stones from his land. This was a common-sense explanation. Similar destruction had occurred at the recumbent of Strichen, seven miles away, about 1830, and the owner of the land, Lord Lovat, was so angry that he ordered the stones to be put back, which his tenant duly did, replacing them wrongly so that Strichen became the only circle to have a recumbent stone at the north of its perimeter. The nearby ring of Upper Crichie had been destroyed a little earlier and the uprooted stones were sold by the tenant. 'Not long after it was noted that his family were visited by illness, one after the other dying. The superstition of these days was at no loss in assigning a cause.' But superstition often failed to stop vandalism. Another ring in the district, Gaval, was blown up by young apprentice masons in 1869. One stone survives. The recumbent at Auchmacher was shattered in the 1830s by the lighting of a Hallowe'en fire on it. Another of its stones was embedded in a wall. A second was used for a bridge, and a third was taken to support a threshing-mill. All this had happened in the past two hundred years, during the Age of Reason, and there was no reason to believe that the history of Berrybrae was different.

In consequence I anticipated that we would find the spread-out debris of the stony bank with earth-filled holes in it where the stones had stood, and, if we were fortunate, flecks of bone, charcoal and a few sherds of broken pottery.

The first minor surprise came when we examined the ground on which the circle stood, for it soon became clear that this little ring also had been built on an artificial platform, made up with clay and rubble where the ground sloped away. Then, as day after day the bank was cleared of roots and grass and soil, the base of a drystone wall appeared, its upper stones fallen outwards into a ditch that some eighteenth-century farmer had dug to drain off the rainwater that turned the site into a pond in wet weather. This wall had stood exactly where the bank should have been but had been about a metre high, far taller than any bank known in other recumbent stone circles. It had been laid out in straightish sections of varying length and was prevented from collapse into the interior by a wide, sloping bank of clay topped with little stones. Showing their understanding of the infirm nature of such a bank, the builders had stabilized it by first driving a hedgehog pattern of stakes into the ground and then packing down the clay over them. These short, pointed stakes had long since rotted, but their stains showed darkly in the clay with a yellow penumbra where rainwater had run down their sides.

In contrast to the survival of such delicate marks, not one hole for the missing circle-stones was visible in the wall or the bank, suggesting that the great stones had either been propped insecurely against the wall or even had never existed. Neither answer seemed likely. All that we found were some small flint scrapers and knives, poorly shaped pebbles from the seashore three miles away. These would have been the implements used by women in their everyday work of preparing food and dressing skins for the family clothing.

A well-run dig is peaceful, with only the clink of trowels against the stones as each participant concentrates on the work to be done in his or her area, the whole site meshed out with orange plastic string into a chessboard of two-metre squares so that any find can be pinpointed to within half a centimetre. In this case the divisions were all the more valuable as the prehistoric land surface was reached beneath half a metre of earth left by years of grass rotting, leaves falling and wind blowing soil off the ploughed fields nearby. Very exact planning of the features was necessary and the squares were indispensable.

A ring-cairn should have appeared. Instead, we found its ghost. Where stones should have been piled high in a ring as large as a traffic island and where there should have been a small central space . . . there was nothing, only bare, hard earth. Just here and there a pebble showed. And then, very, very slowly as the earth was trowelled away, there, as on tissue paper pencilled over a coin, an outline emerged, a thin single ring of small stones, cobbles, bits of quartz, with a smaller circle of pebbles at its centre,

Below A section of the site of the Berrybrae recumbent stone circle, under excavation, clearly showing part of the underlying stony bank. Photograph taken by the author.

the outer and inner rings of the ring-cairn with no cairn of bigger stones between them. Indeed, these rings were so frail that a heavy-handed excavator could have swathed sections of the lines away with one swing of his trowel. They were certainly nothing like the substantial ring-cairn of a recumbent like Loanhead of Daviot. Yet cremations lay there at Berrybrae, two in the vestigial central space, one at the edge of the outer ring.

These were not complete bodies but deposits about the size of a plate, with the whitened spikelets and flakes of bone coagulated in the clay, one with a leaf-shaped flint arrowhead underneath it, another with a Bronze Age urn sherd, unburnt, alongside it in a pit a couple of centimetres deep. Rough cubes of quartz lay like broken necklaces around all the cremations. Each deposit was removed entire and later analysis showed that they were indeed only parts of original cremations. Two that could be analysed were the remains of very young people.

At this stage, like most excavations organized to solve problems, Berrybrae was providing no answers but, to the contrary, was presenting extra questions unconsidered when the work began. The wall and bank were still unexplained, the circle-stones and their holes were still missing and the 'ring-cairn' looked like something in the first stages of building rather than a completed structure. Yet, if it had never been finished, it was difficult to understand why there were cremations in it. Better and worse was to come when on the last afternoon of the second season a beaker lying on its side, its upper half dissolved by years of rain, was revealed in the bank, surrounded by a mass of charcoal. Worse, because of the time when it was found, as we were leaving the site; better, because it gave us a date and a clue to what had happened at Berrybrae.

This crude little pot had little similarity to the beautiful beaker vessels of earlier years, when their makers had first arrived in Britain. Its fabric was thick and coarse, its incised herringbone decoration sprawled drunkenly around the body, and its ill-formed shape proclaimed that it belonged to a very late style that was made mainly along the coasts of the Moray Firth at a time when Beaker people there were being driven out by newcomers from the Scottish lowlands.

The charcoal confirmed the period. Two radio-carbon tests provided 'dates' of 1500 ± 80 bc and 1360 ± 90 bc, averaging 1430 bc. Nowadays it is accepted that such Carbon-14 'dates' are somewhat inaccurate, perhaps because of fluctuations in the earth's atmosphere, and need recalculation. 1430 bc should really be about 1750 BC, late in the Early Bronze Age and just about the time when beaker pottery was going out of fashion. During the 1978 season we came upon a further clue, a neat stack of urn sherds hidden in the wall.

Perhaps a hundred and fifty years before the beaker was made, in the years around 1900 BC, people had raised a recumbent stone circle at Berrybrae. They had built a level foundation and dragged the heavy recumbent and nine other stones on to it. The sockets for the stones were dug around the perimeter of an ellipse, not a circle, with the recumbent at the west-south-west end of the short axis. The people then rammed down a fairly wide setting of stones as a ground-level bank that passed around the circle-stones, enclosing the whole ring in an unbroken ellipse.

An interesting point emerged from a study of this ellipse. Professor Alexander Thom has claimed from a statistical examination of nearly two hundred stone circles in Great Britain that the makers of these rings used a standard unit of measurement, his 'Megalithic Yard' of 0.829 metres. In circles, multiples of this determined the radius but, according to Thom, 'Megalithic Man' sometimes preferred to design an ellipse because this non-circular shape permitted circumferences made up of lengths of $2\frac{1}{2}$ Megalithic Yards, the Megalithic Rod of 2.07 metres. Thom has provided tables to calculate the length of the perimeter.

Berrybrae's ellipse had a long axis of 13.0 metres and a short one of 10.7 metres. Neither of these corresponds to a multiple of the Megalithic Yard, but Thom's formula showed that Berrybrae's circumference measured 37.26 metres, an error of less than 4 centimetres from exactly 18 Megalithic Rods. More will be said about the Megalithic Yard elsewhere, but its apparent confirmation at Berrybrae must be mentioned here.

After the erection of the circle-stones a ring-cairn was built, linked to the recumbent by a platform of very heavy stones. Cremations were deposited in the middle of the ring, and for a hundred years or more people came to the ring for their ceremonies. Then, around 1750 BC, other people arrived, people who did not build stone circles but preferred ritual centres of continuous banks of earth with wide open central spaces. Archaeologists know these inconspicuous sites as enclosed cremation cemeteries. One of them was built alongside Loanhead of Daviot after that splendid ring had been abandoned.

Excavation can never recover all the story. Nevertheless, it seems that at Berrybrae some band of people had violently wrecked the stone circle. The tops of most circle-stones were smashed off. Only the stumps were left, leaning over, half out of their sockets, the jagged fractures in the granite weathering smoother and smoother as centuries of rain wore down the sharp edges. Almost every stone of the ring-cairn was taken to build a wall that hid the low bank and the broken stones. Just a skin of trampled earth was left over the cremations. Then, as if fearful of angering the disturbed spirits, the despoilers of this ring placed some freshly broken pieces of an urn in a niche in the new wall, stood a beaker upright beneath a plank and covered both offerings with the clay bank they heaped up to form their new enclosure. The beaker toppled, the wood disintegrated, Berrybrae was deserted for a second time and for over three thousand years it was left neglected and undisturbed.

Destruction like this was almost commonplace. The bluestones of Stonehenge were ripped up when the massive sarsens were brought there. Early prehistoric times were not always peaceful and there were keen, sometimes fierce differences of belief between communities. There is very little evidence of national accord.

Many stone circles were changed into burial-grounds by people of alien cults who almost cynically used the sanctity of these shrines for their own purposes, turning them into cemeteries with little respect for the ancient stones. Often they openly damaged them. Strangers picked out the stone circle of Callanish in the Hebrides for the site of their passage-grave even though it meant that the chambered tomb had to be abnormally small. Inside the circle-henge of Bryn Celli Ddu on Anglesey another group built a large burial-mound that completely engulfed the standing stones. In the bleak and picturesque Butterlope Glen in Northern Ireland the stone circle of Clogherny was transformed when people put up a wedge-grave inside it, taking up nearly half of its interior. Stone-lined graves or cists were packed into the nearby ring of Dun Ruadh. A three-sided Cove was removed and a gigantic round barrow inserted into the circle-henge of Cairnpapple outside Edinburgh. Cists and a cairn filled the space inside the Balbirnie circle in Fife. And Moncrieffe near Perth was in turn altered from an open henge into a stone circle with a ring-cairn and then had the ring-cairn destroyed by people who used the site for metal-working.

Many more examples could be given of disturbances and alterations to British stone circles. Berrybrae's history is only one of many instances of the schisms and antagonisms that were part of the Bronze Age, when differing customs were just as liable to create suspicion and physical hostility as they are today. Theories of a national priesthood are denied by this evidence of destruction. One is also warned against the danger of supposing that what one sees today is what the monument looked like originally. So many modifications have taken place and so much earth has accumulated, obliterating the minor features, that what now appears above ground may be no more than the coarser parts of a complicated and meticulously contrived structure.

The excavation of Berrybrae had three important results. It provided the first Carbon-14 date for a recumbent stone circle. Because this ring seems to be one of the latest of these monuments, it is likely that the first were being built as early as 2500 BC. The excavation also emphasized that vandalism in antiquity was not unusual, and this suggests that prehistoric societies during the age of stone circles were not in any sense unified. Thirdly, it became clear that Berrybrae was not merely a roughly built ring of stones but was very well designed.

This is generally true of recumbent stone circles. We know nowadays how well built they were, but it was by good fortune, when making a plan of Loudon Wood not far from Berrybrae, that we noticed that the huge recumbent there, twelve tons of ponderous granite, was perfectly horizontal. Any observant visitor will perceive that all these vast recumbents are fairly level, but it was not until a metre-long boxwood spirit-level was casually laid on the stone at Loudon Wood that we realized how exactly true this levelling was. It is obvious that if one moves a spirit-level about on a recumbent stone then somewhere or other it is likely to be in a horizontal position. To overcome this, when we went to other circles we placed a long ranging-pole along the top of the stone to establish its general level and then rested the spirit-level on the pole. At nine of the ten rings we examined the flat upper edge of the recumbent stone was absolutely horizontal. Only at Easter Aquorthies was there a slight inclination, probably because that stone had tipped forwards. Even the awesome recumbent at Old Keig, all fifty tons of it, was horizontal.

One asks how this was achieved, and why, even as one's admiration for the aboriginal builders of these mysterious rings increases. The answer to the first is easy. Where the undersides of these gross blocks have been inspected they have been found to be not flat but shaped to an off-centre point on which they were balanced in their prepared pits. They had a longer end sloping upwards, usually towards the east, and underneath this several heavy packing-stones were inserted, and moved to and fro until the workers were satisfied that the flat top of the recumbent was level. At Aikey Brae, one of the circles in the region of Berrybrae, the chockstones can still be seen, some of them half a ton in weight. On these the tapering bottom of the recumbent rested.

There was no mystery about the way in which the prehistoric engineers decided that their recumbent was correctly balanced. All that was necessary was a water-filled trough on top of the stone. As long as the water spilled out at one end or the other the recumbent was not level. It only needed men to lever with sturdy timbers while other men shifted the chockstones and eventually they would be able to manoeuvre the stone into its proper position. One circle which shows how the bottoms of these stones were shaped for this purpose is Sunhoney near Echt in the shadow of the Hill of Fare. The marvellous cupmarked slab there has fallen outwards and its flat top and triangular base are exposed to view. The penetrating question – and one so relevant to this inquiry into the rituals that took place there – is why prehistoric people thought it vital to balance the stones so nicely. The answer to this question seems to lie with the astronomy of the rings.

Prehistoric astronomy could have had one of two aspects. It might have been 'scientific', with observations made by highly trained priests who were aware of the complex movements of the sun and moon and stars. Knowledge like this would have enabled them to construct a calendar and to predict eclipses, an ability that would impress the simple, untutored peasants who had laboured to manhandle the stones of the observatory into place. Alignments for such purposes would have had to be very accurate, precise within a few seconds of arc.

Alternatively, astronomical observations could have been a form of symbolism, the sun and moon being regarded as gods, or purveyors of warmth and cold, light and dark, as the homes of the dead or the sources of life. For this kind of imagery sight-lines directed only approximately towards their targets would have been adequate. These problems will be considered in another section, but recumbent stone circles, as in so many other matters, do offer an insight into the thinking of their builders.

Although Fred Coles dismissed the likelihood of observations having been made in these rings, he was probably mistaken. The position of the recumbent is so consistently between the south-west and the south-south-east of the circumference that it cannot be fortuitous. It must have been decided upon after long observation of a heavenly body. Some researchers have denied this. Allcroft, intent on proving that the rings were places of assembly, said there was 'no regard for any systematic orientation', and Alexander Keiller condemned the 'verbose fatuities, concerning sunrise on Midsummer's Day' that supporters of the astronomical theory, such as the Reverend G. F. Browne, Bishop of Stepney and Bristol, had put forward. Keiller exuberantly described Browne as 'a certain unconscious archaeological comedian', which, considering Browne had been Disney Professor of Art and Archaeology at Cambridge, seems somewhat severe. Browne did choose to inhabit the rings with living people, pointing out that 'there were ... positive attractions in their ceremonies which appealed to them strongly in their state of nature. Such were in the intercourse of the sexes, at some of their annual feasts, and the great excesses of eating and drinking.' This could be true. Rites of fertility may well have been enacted in the rings. The circles could have been the centres of orgies, scenes of sexual activity, if we use 'orgy' in the true sense of a secret rite in honour of a god.

Keiller, who believed the rings were burial monuments, would have none of it. Yet the fact is that these orgiastic men and women positioned the recumbent stone carefully, and it should be possible for us to discover upon which celestial object it was aligned. People have tried. The first thorough analysis, in 1906, was by Sir Norman Lockyer, Director of the Solar Physics Observatory. Over a couple of years he studied twenty-nine of the rings, although, inexplicably, he took his bearings from the centre of the recumbent to the other side of the circle instead of choosing the more obvious alignment from the lowest stone to the recumbent with its tall flanking stones.

Assuming that the builders had been concerned with the rising of heavenly bodies, he was disconcerted to find that the recumbents were scattered so widely between south-west and south-south-east that neither sun, moon nor any star could account for all of them. He accordingly decided that fifteen of the rings were directed towards rising stars, either Capella between 2000 and 1200 BC or Arcturus between 950 and 250 BC. Neither set of dates would appeal to archaeologists today. Of the fourteen remaining sites, two, Lockyer calculated, were aligned on May Day sunrise, three on midsummer sunrise, four were 'special cases' that faced north, one was another 'special case' towards the east, and four were unfortunate rings in which the recumbent must have been moved. A sceptic might suggest that if enough targets are provided a dedicated searcher must find something that fits.

This was true of the only other group of recumbent stone circles in the British Isles, those of south-west Ireland. Although not identical, the positions of their recumbent stones generally match those of their counterparts in Scotland. Here, after three years of meticulous fieldwork, John Barber, who worked with us at Berrybrae, examined the hypothesis that the recumbents were 'oriented upon the rising or setting points of significant heavenly bodies'. The results were little different from those of Lockyer. No one target fitted all the alignments. Barber chose the more plausible sight-line towards the recumbent, but, even so, of the thirty circles three were apparently aligned on sunset, nine on settings of the moon, five on the settings of the sky's third-brightest object, the planet Venus, and three on nothing at all. As if this were not bad enough, the ten other sites might have been orientated towards any one of twenty-two stars with no means of anyone today deciding which one was correct.

Following this interesting and highly unsatisfactory result, I turned my own attention to the Scottish rings. Although I was able to leave out all the stars, I was still left with a multiplicity of solar, lunar and Venusian alignments more appropriate to the improbabilities of a von Däniken than to the well-built recumbent stone circles of prehistoric Scotland. It is proper to add that Alexander Thom, having planned nearly thirty of these rings, failed to find more than four sunset lines and one moonset line in them.

The solution to this puzzle of the recumbents is embarrassing in its simplicity. Our obsession with risings and settings had led all of us in the wrong direction. The rings were not aligned on these quite difficult positions that would often have been obscured by morning mist or evening clouds. The builders of these circles had, instead, placed the recumbent stone on an axis that pointed to the moon itself when it was raised in the sky.

Below Recumbent stones and positions of the moon. It can be seen that most of the recumbents were carefully placed between the directions where the moon rose and set.

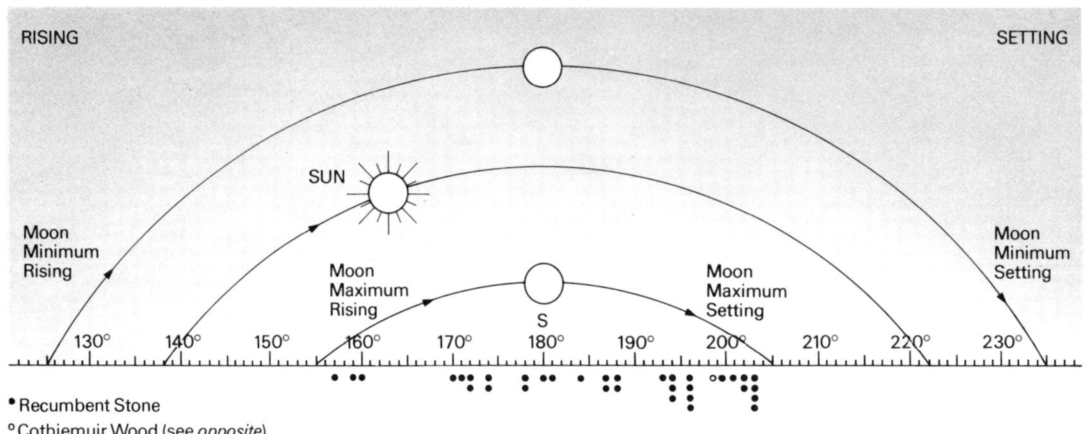

A short explanation is necessary. Unlike the sun, which at midwinter or midsummer always rises and sets at fixed points on the horizon, the moon's movements are more variable. At her extreme or 'maximum' on the southern horizon she will rise at the south-south-east and set at the south-south-west. Next year she will rise and set a very little to the north of these positions, and for some nine years she will rise and set steadily further away from the south until she reaches her 'minimum' rising and setting at the south-east and south-west respectively. Then she will begin her slow return to her maximum positions. The whole cycle from maximum back to maximum takes 18.6 years to complete. The exact compass-bearings depend upon the latitude of the observer and upon the height of any hills or mountains on the horizon.

In Aberdeenshire, with a mean latitude of 57°30′, the moon, at its maximum, will rise at about 155° (south-south-east) and set at 205° (south-south-west). Of the forty-eight recumbent stone circles where it is possible to plot the axis, no fewer than forty-five have recumbent stones placed between these limits, far too many for this to be chance. The remaining three were placed at 230°, 231° and 232°, just at the place where the minimum moon would be setting. Berrybrae, of course, with its recumbent at west-south-west, was one of these errant rings.

Whenever the moon was full during its course across the southern night sky in any year, it would have passed above the recumbent, the tall flankers silhouetted against its brightness, a spectacular event to prehistoric observers. There is more. In these northern latitudes the midsummer moon at its maximum only just rises above the horizon and must have skimmed the very top of the recumbent stone. As Wood has remarked, 'at the major standstill the moon's movements are at their most

Below The recumbent stone circle at Cothiemuir Wood. This diagram shows the exact positioning of the stones, and indicates the path of the full midsummer moon above them.

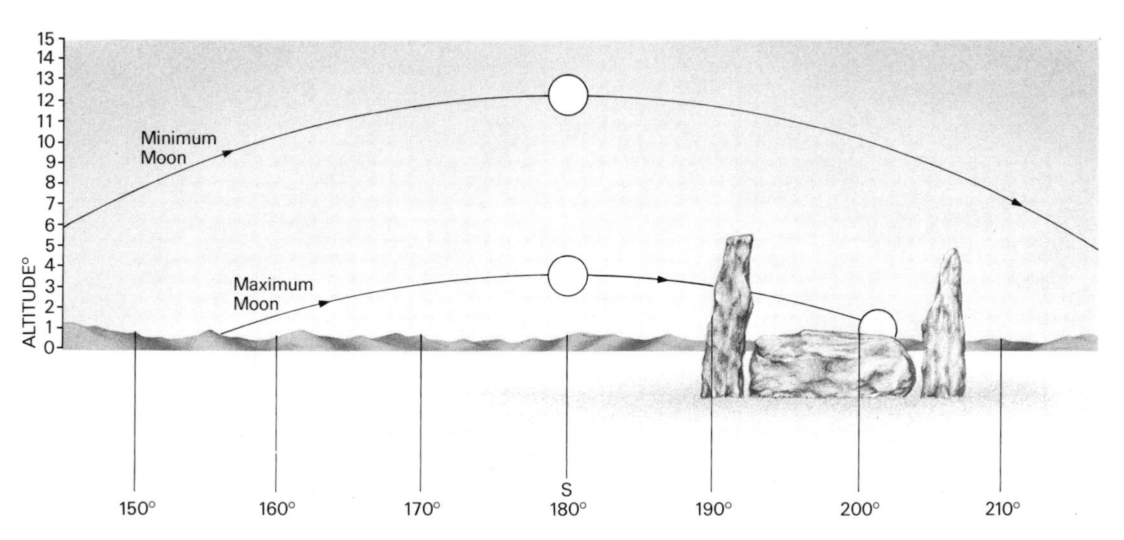

dramatic. Not only does it reach its highest possible elevation each month, but two weeks later it is very low in the sky . . . These movements would have been very conspicuous to early man!'

So remarkable is this relationship of the moon to the recumbent that it is of interest to show what the effect was at a specific ring. The axis of Cothiemuir Wood points towards the south-south-west at 198°. The slight upward slope on which the circle was built – like Easter Aquorthies, Loanhead of Daviot and some other early sites – caused the flat top of the recumbent stone to be on a level with the skyline. Because of the height of the mountainous horizon the midsummer moon would appear to sink on to the western end of the stone, something hardly likely to have happened by chance. Cothiemuir is typical of the first circles, which were directed towards the declining moon, whereas the latest rings faced it as it rose in the sky or when it was setting at its minimum position.

This rising and falling in the sky, the declining down almost to the horizon itself at midsummer, were probably the times of intense ceremonies by people to whom the wanderings of the moon were the heart and spirit of their religious beliefs. They wanted to 'catch' the essence of the moon as it moved between the highest pillars of their ring.

For people living in the unhurried days and nights of the countryside, working in the light, sleeping in the darkness, the moon was always easier to see than the blinding sun, and its constant monthly cycle was more obvious than the sun's slow yearly journey. Its waxing and waning symbolized for many early peoples their concepts of fertility, the growth and decay of plants, the health of young children, pregnancy in women. Because of its rapid rising and falling it was believed to be the cause of crops flourishing, and many American Indians worshipped the moon that brought dew and moisture to their ripening maize. Eskimos believed that to bring snow into their igloos at the time of the new moon would help them catch seals in the spring, because the rising moon would give strength to the melting waters of the seas. The natives of New Guinea thought that the waxing moon was beneficial to their children, and other societies regarded the waning moon as too dangerous for their children even to look at.

Other people have seen the moon as the source of life. At one time in Greenland the islanders believed that when the moon was full in the sky it sometimes came down to earth in the form of a young man and impregnated women. No wife 'dare sleep lying on her back without she first spits upon her fingers and rubs her belly with it. For the same reason the young maids are afraid to stare long at the moon, imagining they may get a child by the bargain.' All these beliefs about the fecundity of the moon merged together in the image of Diana, the Greek moon-goddess of hunting, who lived in everlasting celibacy, giving the earth strength to nurture grain, bringing pregnancy to women and protecting women in childbirth. Whatever the particular images the people of the recumbent stone circles attributed to the moon, we can be fairly sure that the rites enacted in the rings were closely connected with the flourishing and dying of plants, crops, animals and human beings in the short-lived world of four thousand years ago.

We can now understand some of the complexities of these intriguing sites and realize how much they tell us about the prehistoric mind. The locations of the circles with their long views were chosen to give the most vivid effect to the phenomena of the moon's movements. For this same reason sites were if necessary sometimes levelled so that the perfectly horizontal top of the recumbent stone could become an artificial skyline above which the moon would swing. The circle-stones rising in height towards the recumbent probably symbolized the rising and waning path of the moon, the recumbent being the 'door' through which the moon could enter the ring with its dead bones. It could also be that the pieces of white quartz near the recumbent were themselves symbols, the bright fragments shining in the light of the full moon seeming to be particles fallen from the moon itself. This might explain why so many prehistoric burials, like the Berrybrae cremations, have little bits of quartz interred with them, deposits of life-giving stone.

Below No one has yet interpreted the cupmarks and the cup-and-ring marks on this recumbent stone at Rothiemay, Banffshire. From a retouched photograph published in Sir James Simpson's *Archaic Sculpturings* in 1867.

The cupmarks in the vicinity of the recumbent have an equally persuasive explanation. Bishop Browne thought they might be patterns of stars shown back to front, and he even explained how he thought this unlikely project might have been fulfilled. 'The magician had some material . . . perhaps of the nature of deerskin on which he planned the stars as he saw them, with plenty of opportunity to make corrections as need arose. Having got his plan to his satisfaction, he marked each star with some adhesive coloured matter, and then laid the skin on the (recumbent) stone face downwards, and so marked on the stone the place for each star.' As these cupmarks sometimes appear on stones which were subsequently set upright, tipping the back-to-front constellations on their sides, or were carved on bases which instantly vanished into their sockets, it may be that Keiller's opinion, after all, was justified.

If, instead, the cupmarkings were roughly shaped representations of the moon, there may be no way in which we can ever fully understand their significance. Perhaps someone will try to decipher the distribution of carvings on stones at Sunhoney, Balquhain, Loanhead of Daviot or the incredible sarsen at Rothiemay where over a hundred cupmarks almost magically emerge in the oblique light of the rising sun. These may be lunations recording the yearly shifting of the moon from maximum to minimum. In Argyll two pillars at the centre of a row of stones at Ballymeanoch are both covered with cupmarks and are said by Thom to point to the 'Moon setting in its extreme northerly position'. No one, as yet, has been able to interpret these clusters of cups, some with rings around them and with grooves pointing to the south-south-east.

What is clear, however, is that recumbent stone circles were in no sense scientific observatories. The great length of any recumbent stone presented too wide an arc for any precise sight-line to be taken across it. The rings were built by families dependent for their livelihood on good harvests, and the people were always at the mercy of sunshine and rain. A drought condemned them to starvation. Deer could ravage their growing crops. Wild animals could trample down the harvest. In the unending insecurity of their lives they built a stone circle in which they communicated with the terrible forces with which they had to live. They burned great fires, gave 'dead' things, the deliberately broken pots, the incinerated bones of their own people, as offerings to give strength to their temple. Whether the moon to them was the land of the dead, whether it was the mother of life, we shall never know, but we do know how the quartz and the cupmarks and the recumbent stone were blended together in the area where anyone in the ring would see the moon shining down in the short midsummer nights of the ceremonies. These were times of hope and fear. The people had cause to be fearful.

Opposite Time chart, showing the ages of principal sites. The dates of the sites underlined have been confirmed by Carbon-14 dating. Italics indicate radio-carbon 'dates' before recalculation.

YEARS BC		PARTICULAR CIRCLES AND HENGES	GENERAL EVENTS IN BRITAIN
3300	MIDDLE NEOLITHIC		Native farmers on light
2500 bc	Earliest stone	New Grange	soils of British Isles
	circles and henges	Llandegai I henge	Tradition of native, round-
3200	– large open rings	Arminghall henge	based pottery
	in Lake District and		
	along Atlantic	Carles	End of long barrow building
3100	coasts	Ballynoe	
3000			
		Stenness	First grooved ware
2900			
2250 bc	LATE NEOLITHIC		
2800		Stonehenge I	
2700			
			Beginning of single-burial
2600		Avebury stone circles	tradition
	Middle period of		Early copper working
2500	stone circles –	Early recumbent stone	First Beaker people
2000 bc	rings on western	circles	
	coasts		
2400		Arbor Low	
		Merry Maidens	
2300		Rollright Stones	
		Woodhenge timber ring	
2200	EARLY BRONZE AGE	Stonehenge II	First bronze implements
		Llandegai II henge	Round barrow building
		Druids' Circle	First food-vessels and urns
2100		Stonehenge IIIA	Rise of Wessex chieftains
1700 bc	Late stone circles –	Stonehenge IIIB	
	small family rings		
2000	on uplands	Callanish	
1900		Berrybrae recumbent stone circle	
1800			
1475 bc			
		Beaghmore rings	
1700			
	MIDDLE BRONZE AGE		Beginning of a
			deterioration in the climate
1600			
		Stonehenge IIIC	
1500		Sandy Road	
1200 bc			

The people

By the middle of the New Stone Age, around 3300 BC, which may have been the time when the first stone circle was built, people in the British Isles had been farming the land for almost a thousand years. In the pleasant climate that succeeded the chilling wastes of the Old Stone Age, great forests of oaks and elms had reached across the hills and the valleys, encouraged by the rains and the warm summers, and these endless woodlands with their packs of wolves and foraging wild boars were as dangerous as the spreading swamps and choked rivers of the south and the rock-littered highlands of northern Britain, where bears and snakes went unhindered except for the swooping and calling of birds in their untiring scavenging for food. It was only in the regions of the chalk plains where the land could be cleared that men could move easily, separated by perhaps a hundred miles of wilderness from the next area of population.

Scattered about these territories, on Salisbury Plain, on the Yorkshire Wolds, in Ulster and a dozen other parts of Britain barricaded from each other by the forests, there were farmhouses, buildings strongly constructed of logs, much like the homesteads of early settlers in the American West, big enough for a family and standing alongside the cultivated patches where strains of wheat and some barley grew. A bull, three or four cows useful mainly for the leather they would give, were all the stock that most groups owned. Because they knew little about the need to replenish the cultivated soil, the ground they tilled lost its goodness after ten or twenty years and the family moved to another clearing in the territory that they had claimed, cleared away the weeds, planted more crops, and eventually travelled on again until, finally, they returned to their first home.

These were self-sufficient people whose possessions were few, simple and homemade. Their pots were shaped from local clays by the women and girls, who squeezed out tiny thumb-pots and made larger bag-shaped vessels for storing grain, burnishing them with pebbles or bones when the clay was leather-hard, standing the pots in hollows alongside the cabin. Other girls crushed wheat into flour on flat grinding-stones, or scraped and cut animal skins with razor-sharp flints to make thonging, pouches and clothes. The men, dressed in scuffed garments of leather, worked the land with axes and hoes of stone, dug drainage ditches with antler picks and levers, day after day returning to the drudgery of forcing a living from the reluctant land, sometimes hunting the red deer with bows and arrows if food was scarce. Their meals were often lukewarm gruels. The pottery would not sustain direct heat without cracking, and meat was too rare a luxury for it often to be baked in a fire.

These were small people, lightly built, with skulls longer and narrower than our own; sinewy people whose only ornaments were necklaces of wolves' teeth or boars' tusks or the hollowed-out bones of birds and small animals. Malformation of some of the ankle-bones found shows that they squatted around the fires, and in some cases the inward bending of a bone in their feet tells us that they had worn strapped sandals.

Their lives were hard in existence, short in duration. In skeleton after skeleton there are signs of severe arthritis. Men suffered from fractures. Many children died of malnutrition or were deformed by rickets. There were other bone disorders, some congenital, some induced by under-nourishment, especially among the women and girls. Most men were dead by thirty-five, women by thirty. A majority of infants and children never reached the age of four. In the whole of the British Isles there may have been no more than fifty thousand of these Neolithic farmers whose need for protection was so great.

As though compelled by their own insecurity to intercede fanatically with the natural forces against which they were helpless – famine, blizzards, disease – they built gigantic mounds in which the bones of the dead were laid. Every region had its own style: long mounds with a timber mortuary house built into one end on Salisbury Plain and, rather differently, in Yorkshire; long mounds with stone-built chambers in the Cotswolds, with variations in Ulster and south-west Scotland; round chambered tombs with internal vaults in Ireland and northern Scotland. Yet all these had one thing in common. As the Scottish recumbent stone circles later were aligned on the moon, these earlier monuments were directed towards the sun. New Grange, the passage-grave in Ireland, had its entrance exactly aligned on the place where the sun rose at midwinter. Maes Howe, an Orcadian tomb, faced the midwinter setting sun.

It is possible then that these, like the Clava cairns, were shrines rather than burial-places, sanctuaries where the living took the powerful bones of their ancestors for rituals of intercession with sun, moon, rain, water-hole, whatever force of nature was being invoked. The rites were complex. In some of the Irish mounds the passage-stones were engraved with triangles, lozenges, meanders and spirals, in compositions impossible to interpret but clearly of vital significance to their makers.

That sexuality formed part of these rituals can hardly be doubted from the evidence of male organs carved out of chalk found in ritual enclosures in southern Britain, in long barrows, in mines, in those places where sexual activity might be thought to affect, by sympathetic magic, the fertility of land, the production of flint, the awakening of the dead. In Somerset, at the point where a wooden trackway was wearing away, someone had buried a little ashwood figure with pronounced breasts and erect penis. This bisexual carving could have been a child's toy but, if so, in the words of the excavator, 'it was for a rather strange child by our standards.' More probably it was a fertility figurine set down to give magical strength to the track.

Increasingly, after about 3300 BC, in the later New Stone Age, circular enclosures of earthen banks were constructed by families who banded together to build these henges that were to be the centres of their ceremonies. As one might expect, these rings were dug out where the soil was deep and soft, in well-populated areas that could supply sufficient labour for the projects. In regions to the north and west smaller groups were erecting some early stone circles. By now there was more co-operation between families, encouraged by the network of routes along rivers and hill-ridges where traders carried fine-grained stone for axes from 'factories' in the Lake District, in Cornwall, in Wales and Ireland. Bartering may have gone on in the circles and henges where the families assembled at special times, reminding us that neither a stone circle nor a henge was a centre restricted to one function, and that trade, arguments over land-ownership and the marrying-out of girls may have been activities as normal inside them as the religious ceremonies.

Reflecting the more permanent fittings of benches and shelves in the round houses of the time, more and more flat-based pottery was produced, still made locally by the women, introduced into regions of

Below New Grange, County Meath. When this passage-grave was built, the dawn sun shone through the entrance on midwinter's day.

traditional round-bottomed vessels by shadowy people whose bucket-shaped grooved ware remains one of the enigmas of British prehistory.

It was around 2600 BC that one of the few immigrations to be recognized in these islands occurred. Beaker people, so-called from their finely shaped and decorated drinking vessels, entered the country from the continental mainland. These stockily built incomers, whose round skulls contrasted oddly with the long, narrow heads of the natives, were farmers and archers who soon became involved in the manufacture of Britain's first metal objects, minute gold ornaments and daggers made from Irish copper. There cannot have been many of these newcomers. Of the earliest beaker pots only about two hundred and fifty have been recovered from graves and occupation sites in the whole of the British Isles, and as these vessels could have been made at any time over the three hundred years between 2600 and 2300 BC it is likely that the first Beaker people were to be counted in scores, perhaps hundreds but certainly not thousands, small bands settling among the natives and maybe gaining a supremacy over them.

New ideas were introduced. One Beaker innovation may have been Britain's first alcoholic drink. What seems to be the sediment of mead has been found adhering to some pots. Single burials in pits became fashionable, gradually replacing the communal 'tombs' of the Neolithic Age, and as the Neolithic blurred into the beginnings of the Early Bronze Age more and more people were buried with grave-goods that were to accompany them into their Other World. This was the great time of circle-building and some of Britain's finest megalithic rings were erected in the centuries around 2400 BC.

Death and the sun were still associated as they had been in the great mounds of the New Stone Age. Although the dead now lay in prepared graves underneath round, stone-piled cairns or earth-made barrows without entrances, they still looked towards the sun. A fascinating study of Beaker burials in Yorkshire has revealed that most men were laid on their left sides, their heads to the east, facing south where the sun would always pass during the day. Yet the dead man, his beaker behind his head where it would not obstruct his view, could only have 'seen' the sun symbolically. Women lay on their right sides, heads to the west, but also facing south. In Wessex, that vast expanse of southern England centred on the chalk uplands of Wiltshire, Beaker men and women were placed with their heads to north and south respectively, gazing either to east or west where the sun rose and set. In Scotland the stone-lined burial-cists, blocked from the living world by monstrous round cairns, had similar alignments, and it is obvious that, among the creeds of the Early Bronze Age, death, the sun and ritual monuments were all parts of a complicated but understandable symbolic framework.

The clearing of much of the countryside permitted great herds of cattle to be maintained, and the emergence of pastoralists led to the development of chieftains as these energetic herdsmen took over large tracts of land from crop-owners who could not abandon their fields. Flocks of sheep grazed on the downs, offering more wealth. Britain may have had forms of 'heroic' societies, aristocracies of leaders and their warriors with great bronze axes and daggers, men flamboyantly and lavishly apparelled in soft textiles, displaying gold ornaments, wearing necklaces of jet and shale and powder-blue beads of glass known as faience. Round barrows in linear cemeteries are still a feature of the Wessex landscape around Stonehenge and from them the skeletons of these Wessex chieftains have been unearthed, some of them cremated and buried in urns alongside their valuables in pits or cists, others in coffins hewn out of the trunks of massive oak trees.

Elsewhere similar forms of urn burial and cremation were common. People making thick-rimmed pots known as food-vessels mingled with late Beaker groups in Yorkshire and Derbyshire, spreading out to the north and west of Britain in a kaleidoscope of shifting, blending or warring societies.

As early as 2000 BC the cooling but drier climate encouraged the more adventurous of the growing population to occupy parts not previously settled, uplands like Dartmoor, the less well-drained areas of the Peak District and the present-day moorlands of Wales, Scotland and Ireland. Better husbandry, manuring, the walling of fields, cross-ploughing, the winter feeding of stock, enabled these Bronze Age farmers to work the thinner soils for decades at a time. The ruins of their round, stone-built huts survive on many of our moorlands. For more than six hundred years families lived on these bleaker lands, felling the trees, impoverishing the ground, putting up little rings of standing stones in which burnt human bone is almost always found. But as, during the Middle Bronze Age, from about 1700 to 1300 BC, the climate worsened, becoming wetter, the pattern began to change to one of a search for land, of a struggle to exist on it, when the water would no longer run away, where trees no longer provided irrigation, as bogs formed, seeping and growing against the stones, creeping up their sides. Gradually the people left their homesteads and went down to the overcrowded lowlands. By 1200 BC the cult of the stone circle was ended, abandoned under the grey, raining skies of the Late Bronze Age.

The stone circles

We shall never know where the first stone circle was built, but we do know that it must have been at some time late in the fourth millennium BC, long before the Beaker people came to the British Isles. Many big and impressive circles of stones had been erected by the time of their arrival, put up by the New Stone Age native farmers in the Lake District and along the north-western coasts of Britain from Ireland up to the Orkneys.

It was a time when the tradition of the rectangular farmstead and the long rectangular burial-mound was giving way to a preference for circular houses and barrows. What folk-movement, if any, lies behind this change archaeology cannot yet tell. It may have originated in the passage-graves of Ireland, their great round cairns lined with kerbstones. These kerbstones and the stone-built passage and chamber were put up before the overlying cairn, and the half-finished site must have looked like a henge or a circle of closely set stones. There were rather similar monuments in eastern Scotland and Yorkshire and these, too, may have been the forerunners of henges and stone circles, because some of their mounds covered huge circular ditches or rings of stones or posts at the centre of which there was a timber mortuary house in which the bodies of the dead were laid. Such rings were presumably intended to demonstrate the 'sacred' precincts of these shrines, which may have stood exposed to the open air for years. Like the uncompleted passage-graves, these were enclosures whose appearance would alter only when the cairn or barrow was finally piled, basket-load by basket-load, over their interiors.

Not all these round mounds contained burials. In 1974 we excavated one built of sand at Fochabers, near Elgin on the Moray Firth. Despite the distraction of seven Iron Age skeletons and a Bronze Age cremation, we found that this monument was in fact Neolithic, built around 3750 BC by a community of farmers to cover four small cairns that in turn covered thick layers of charcoal and pottery which appeared to have been deliberately broken. But at another recently excavated site, Pitnacree in Perthshire, built within a century of Fochabers, the people had put up a plank-roofed mortuary house of cobbles in which they placed several cremations. This 'shrine' stood in the middle of a large oval enclosure whose heavy stones separated the area from the profane world. The oval wall did not follow a perfect curve but was laid down in a series of straight segments, perhaps by individual work-gangs, a technique anticipating by several centuries the methods used to dig out the ditches of henges.

In Yorkshire there were others of these Neolithic ditched enclosures. At Callis Wold, a Neolithic family built a wooden mortuary house at the centre of a vast ring-ditch, and at Whiteleaf Hill in southern England, a similar hut received the bones of an old man whose skeleton, apparently, had been dug from its grave when the flesh had rotted, then carried to this place. Again, a circular ditch surrounded the area in which the people lit fires and dug pits to receive offerings of which all trace has gone, and at both Callis Wold and Whiteleaf Hill it may have been many years before the sites were closed off by having huge round barrows built over them.

It can be seen that the sacred circle, whether of earth or of stones, had a long tradition behind it in prehistoric Britain, linked to cults in which human bones were used in rites so powerful that there had to be a barrier between them and the ordinary world of the living. But it was only when people ceased to cover such sanctuaries with cairns or barrows that the open circle became the monument that archaeologists recognize as a henge or a stone circle today.

From this point of view it is interesting that two of the earliest henges yet known, Barford in Warwickshire and Arminghall in Norfolk, were close to areas where earlier Neolithic round barrows were constructed. They were built around 3200 BC. And the circle of towering rough stones that surrounded New Grange's passage-grave belongs to the same period, so that we can be confident that by the late fourth millennium BC societies in several regions of the British Isles were laying out enormous rings, whether of earth or standing stones, for their ceremonial occasions.

Nowadays the wreckage of over a thousand stone circles, some magnificently preserved, others so ruined that they are almost indistinguishable from the natural boulders among which they lie, are to be found in the British Isles, the survivors of perhaps three times that number. Whereas the earliest may date back even before 3300 BC, the latest may be as much as two thousand years younger. When we contemplate this passing of century after century after century of time, and when we also realize that the rings were built as far to the north as the Shetlands where the Fairy Ring of Haltadans with its two central slablets crouches inside a wild grassy ring, and as far south as Land's End where Boskednan, over seven hundred miles of sea and storm from Haltadans, leans in tall disorder, a cairn slumping on to its southern rim, common sense tells us that such lengths of time and such distances make any single comprehensive explanation for these rings impossible. The earliest were communal centres. The latest were for individual families.

Unlike the Scottish recumbent stone circles with their rich assortment of evidence, however, most of the early rings provide few clues to their purpose. Any attempt to understand them must be composed of hints of information from a lot of different sources.

Hardly anything has been recovered from what are probably the very earliest circles, the impressive and austere rings of the Lake District, their heavy granite stones grey as snow-filled skies, their wide interiors as empty as our understanding of them. Rings like Grey Yauds or Elva Plain, as much as ten miles apart, can be found on stretches of fertile land among the mountain valleys, their stones closely set together with a gap left for an entrance. These rings are usually circular. Sometimes they have one flattened arc, perhaps caused by the same method of construction as that used at Pitnacree. Some of them also have shallow banks or ditches around them, a reminder of their ancestry.

These are big enclosures, wide enough for a grown man to take twenty seconds or more to stroll across, nothing in the middle to impede him, and they must have been intended for large numbers of people. There are, admittedly, the faintest signs of a cairn inside the Carles, the Castlerigg ring near Keswick, and it is also true that John Aubrey, who collected information about stone circles from correspondents all over Britain, learnt from Sir William Dugdale's notes that two cairns once stood at the centre of that colossus of rings, Long Meg and Her Daughters. 'The Diameter of this Circle is about the diameter (he guesses) of the Thames . . . In the middle are two Tumuli, or barrowes of *cobble-stones*, nine or ten feet high.' And Aubrey added, '*Quaere*, Mr. Robinson, the Minister there, about the Giants bone, and Body found there', but if he did he received no reply. It is likely, however, that such cairns were later additions to these spacious rings. A cairn inside the Studfold circle was well away from the centre, as were the five cairns inside Brats Hill, high up among the squelching tussocks of Burn Moor.

Ballynoe, near Dundrum Bay in Northern Ireland, is a good example of a Neolithic ring having Bronze Age burials insinuated into it. This is one of the finest megalithic rings in the British Isles. Typically, it is a true circle, very wide, standing in a buttercup-rich field behind which the mountains of Mourne rise crookedly. Its perimeter is crowded with tall, unevenly spaced pillars and there is a conspicuous entrance of outer stones at the west-north-west. It may also have a silted-up outer ditch. One sherd of Neolithic pottery was found somewhere inside the ring, where, well east of the centre, there is an untidy mound. This is a Bronze Age cairn in which there were several cists, quite out of context inside the stone circle which may have been standing for a thousand years before peasants chose to build a family vault inside it.

The Ballynoe ring with its entrance and its outlying stones to north and south was, perhaps, built by people engaged in the stone axe trade. There was a 'factory' sixty miles to the north on Tievebulliagh mountain, but probably even more important were the Lake District centres, only eighty miles across the often-travelled sea, a voyage made easier in rough weather by the landfalls of the Isle of Man and of south-west Scotland. It is not surprising to discover a ring almost identical to the Irish circle, Swinside, at the head of the Duddo Sands, just where a trading party passing to the south of the Isle of Man would have landed on their way to the Lake District. Swinside is as well preserved and attractive as Ballynoe, and also has many stones, including a thin, tapering pillar at the north, but no cairn spoils its interior. In 1901 Dymond discovered that each stone had been bedded on a layer of rammed pebbles, but otherwise he found only a piece of charcoal and a 'minute fragment of decayed bone'.

It is easy to imagine assemblies of people there, the local families, traders of stone from farther away, the time of the meetings decided by the position of the sun on the horizon. This may be the reason for the north and south stones at Ballynoe, the splendid northern entrance at the Carles, and the gargantuan blocks that stand, if that is the word, at the exact east and west of Long Meg's circumference, set in a worn-down bank. This flattened circle, one of the very largest in our islands, also has a double-stone entrance, with Long Meg, a thin decorated outlier, rising above the skyline at the south-west where the midwinter sun would have set.

All these features are embodied in the Carles on Chestnut Hill, with its entrance of two tall granite pillars, its bank, its outlying stone. But inside the ring at the east is a perplexing stone-lined rectangle, big enough to accommodate a bus, unlike anything in any other ring. It may not be part of the original circle. An excavation in 1882 did nothing to explain it, for all Kinsey Dover found was one pit with charcoal in it. According to Anderson the rectangle was directed east-north-east towards the far-away cone of Great Mell Fell, its summit rising a third of a mile high. On it Anderson discovered an earthen circle with a single gap that pointed back to the Carles six and a half miles away. Yet if the rectangle defined an astronomical line in the Carles it was towards sunrise early in April, an indifferent time of year to choose. Once again, having offered us a glimpse of their beliefs the circle-builders fade back into the dimness of prehistory.

There are other rings of this early period, far from the Lake District, at a time when people travelled more easily by water than through the trackless, ominous forests. In the Orkneys, close to Maes Howe chambered tomb, which may well have been built by people from Ireland, is the circle-henge of Stenness, once a ring of twelve steepling stones set along the inner edge of a rock-cut ditch which, even if quarried by as many as a hundred people, would have taken three months to complete, an immense effort for the gathering of families who laboured there. In this ditch were the jaw-bones and limb-ends of dogs or wolves, oxen and sheep, which could be 'the unwanted refuse from food, sacrifice, clothing or artefact manufacture'. The first two of these cautious explanations seem to be the most likely.

One causeway was left across the ditch, in whose corner lay a grooved ware pot. On the central plateau only four stones remain entire, but near the middle of this evocative circle, standing as it does between two lochs with the stones of the Ring of Brodgar in sight, the excavator, Graham Ritchie, discovered the postholes of a crate-sized mortuary house linked by slabbed paving to a square, stone-lined 'hearth' in which flecks of burnt bone and seaweed lay. A heavy timber upright, perhaps carved like a totem-pole, once rose from its centre. Beyond, to the south, were five pits filled with earth mixed with barley, nuts, seeds and fruit-stones. Two Carbon-14 dates averaging the equivalent of about 2950 BC show how early in the history of stone circles the Standing Stones of Stenness were erected. One can only speculate about the nature of the ceremonies, but any person entering the ring would have come first to the mortuary house, and here cremated bones may have been laid until the people were ready to carry them ceremoniously to the central square with its towering pole. Perhaps the bones of animals were thrown on to smouldering seaweed as offerings to the spirits, the people asking in return for a bountiful harvest symbolized by the grain and the fruits deposited in the pits nearby.

Dancing and singing may have taken place, just as they may in another very early site eight hundred miles to the south on the half-submerged hillock of Er Lannic in Brittany. A long time ago two rings, both very large, stood side by side here, but the rising of the sea since Roman times has covered one and almost swallowed the other in the Gulf of Morbihan. The close-set, high stones were set in a rubble bank, with a wide gap at the north-east. At the foot of stone after stone there were cists filled with Neolithic pottery, flints, axes, grinding-querns, quartz, animal bones, all broken, many of the cists reddened by intense fires. These barbaric offerings can be understood. To the primitive mind if something is broken it is 'dead'. If it is dead it can reach the Other World, to be accepted as an offering by the spirits and ghosts whose protection the prehistoric people of the circles so badly needed.

Some of the Clava cairns were built in this early period, but most were probably constructed in the middle phase of circle-building. Between 2700 and 2100 BC, the centuries which saw the end of the Late Neolithic Age, the arrival of Beaker groups and the beginning of the Early Bronze Age, some of the finest of our stone circles were built along the western coasts, eye-catching monsters like the Twelve Apostles near Dumfries, and the gentle, river-cut Girdle Stanes, more rings in the Lake District, the huge central circle at Stanton Drew in Somerset, other open rings around the rim of Dartmoor, and in Cornwall as far down as Land's End.

Circles were put up around the Wicklow mountains of Ireland, although in that green, rich island henges were more common. Even in the west the ring of the Lios, perhaps visited by Beaker men prospecting for copper, had stones supported by a heavy earthen ringwork. People raised other circles along the coastal fringes of Wales. With the expanding and hastening of trade there was more contact between regions. Distinct architectural styles developed, yet almost everywhere that there were people there was a ceremonial enclosure: henges of earth in the south and east; or stony banks at the foot of the mountains, where a bank like that of Mayburgh near Penrith, composed of over five million back-breaking stones, defies the imagination with the steady fanaticism that went into its building; and then, in the west and north where glacial boulders were plentiful, stone circles.

This simplified picture is misleading. At many megalithic rings, especially in Scotland, the circles have been found to stand on the sites of earlier settings of posts. At the Sanctuary in Wiltshire four consecutive timber rings may have been put up and rotted before the concentric circles of stones were raised around 2300 BC. Elsewhere in England other wooden rings have been discovered, at Woodhenge on Salisbury Plain, at Arminghall in Norfolk, and at Bleasdale in Lancashire. Others lie undiscovered, their postholes invisible beneath the grass. Others are known in Ireland. In central Scotland the stone circle of Croft Moraig was preceded by a horseshoe of posts. Not far to the east Moncrieffe also had a ring of upright timbers. The damaged circle-henge at Balfarg in Fife, its bank levelled, nearly every stone dragged away, is now known to lie on a site where 'a massive timber circle . . . was entered by means of a porch, was probably associated with a number of rings of palisade fencing . . . and was directly associated with late Neolithic sherds.' Evidence like this again warns us not to accept as complete what can be seen today.

There are other complications. Along the central hilly spine of Britain, from the Cheviots, along the Pennines and right down to the Stripple Stones on Bodmin Moor, wherever the henge-building tradition of the east overlapped with the stone circle regions of the west, there are circle-henges, stone circles erected on the central platform of a henge. In many cases the circle was a later addition, as it was at Balfarg and at Stonehenge to which in 2200 BC Beaker prospectors were transporting bluestones from south-west Wales. Some centuries before then the vigorous inhabitants of the Marlborough Downs had put up two fantastic free-standing rings at Avebury near the Sanctuary, sixty or seventy tremendous blocks of sandstone. They had even started to erect a third ring when the work was suddenly discontinued. The two existing rings were then enclosed within the largest of any of the stone circles in the British Isles, a hundred giant stones in a ring a quarter of a mile across. And around that the natives constructed a cliff-like bank and ditch approached by two avenues of stones, making Avebury the most complicated prehistoric monument in Britain. It was immense. In the Egyptian Fifth Dynasty of the same period each pyramid occupied a vast average area of over eighty metres square. Thirteen of them could have stood inside Avebury.

Remembering the vanished timber rings, the varying sequences of circle-henges, and the restructuring of rings like Berrybrae, the reader will appreciate how difficult it is to understand the history of even one stone circle. Regions generated their own forms of ritual centre. In the south-west peninsula of England there were a few multiple sites, two or three rings alongside each other. After Avebury, Stanton Drew is the biggest, but there are others, in Cornwall, at the damaged Hurlers on Bodmin Moor, and at the splendidly re-erected Grey Wethers on Dartmoor. Some Cornish circles had internal stones that perhaps marked central burials. Avenues of stones led to occasional rings in Wales and Westmorland. Elsewhere there were concentric circles, rings within rings, and many of the Scottish recumbent stone circles must have been built at this time.

Another, less obvious, regional variation was in the number of stones preferred for the circles. One might assume that this depended on the lengths of the circumferences, but one would assume wrongly. It will be recalled that the early recumbent stone circles of north-east Scotland often had ten standing stones. In north-west England many rings were built of twelve stones, whereas in Galloway, hardly a hundred miles of the Solway Firth away, nine stones were usual. On Dartmoor thirty to thirty-six stones were used, on Bodmin Moor twenty-six to twenty-eight, and at Land's End nineteen or twenty.

Such choices may have been based on the different counting-systems of these primitive societies. Without knowing the date of each ring and what interference has taken place inside it one has to be cautious, but there are indications that the circle-builders had only very basic counting-systems of threes or fours or fives, so that if they wished to check a herd of seven cows then those communities that numbered, for example, in fours would have counted: 1, 2, 3, 4, 4+1, 4+2, 4+3. It was tedious, restricted and liable to mistake if large numbers had to be computed. Nevertheless, such limited numeracy seems typical of other early societies without writing and it appears true of the people of Neolithic and Bronze Age Britain.

Most of the rings of this middle phase were still either circles or circles with one flattened arc. Yet their widely differing architecture, the cremations in some, the absence of deposits in others, the varied styles of pottery and flint implements, the destruction of rings by newcomers, all conflict with the suggestion that every one of these rings was planned by people using the same unit of measurement, the Megalithic Yard. It is hardly conceivable that this yardstick could have been current from the Orkneys to Land's End. It is far more probable that people used body-measurements, the distance between outstretched arms, or the body-yard measured from the nose to the fingertip. Natural measures like these were normal among many primitive communities. Such lengths would vary slightly from region to region and from circle to circle, something that Professor Thom's own data reveal. Statistical analysis has demonstrated that regional differences do exist. One's confidence in a national Megalithic Yard is not increased, moreover, when one learns that the flattened Cornish ring at Goodaver has a diameter of almost exactly thirty-nine Megalithic Yards, producing, in Professor Thom's own words, 'a circumference of 122.52 (for 122½) Megalithic Yards'. This seeming proof contradicts itself, because the Ordnance Survey correspondent has written of Goodaver, 'forty years ago these stones were lying about on the moor and a local farmer supplied labour for erecting them in their present position.' The Reverend A. H. Malan, who directed the work in about 1906, cannot have been aware of the Megalithic Yard. It is more likely that body-measurements were used to lay out the ground plans of our stone circles, and that the country-wide Megalithic Yard is a chimera, a grotesque statistical misconception.

However they were designed, the circles were meant for rituals. Fires burned inside Brisworthy and Fernworthy on Dartmoor, both circles with stones graded in height to north or south. Across the Bristol Channel Gors Fawr also was graded, again to the south, reminding us of the cardinal point alignments in many of these rings. Other circles display their associations with death. Three-sided Coves in the monuments of Avebury, Stanton Drew, Arbor Low and Cairnpapple, maybe even at Er Lannic, seem to have been imitations of the entrances in Neolithic long chambered tombs to which human bones were brought. Rites descended from the practices there may have been mimed around the Coves.

The final stage in the history of stone circles probably saw the construction of most of them, small rings erected by families for their own use on the marginal uplands from Cornwall to Caithness and the sombre hills of northern Ireland. In the years between 2100 and 1500 BC, deep into the Middle Bronze Age with its clouding skies, hundreds of rings were built, different in every region. Dozens of them, a cairn inside, and approached by a wavering row of lightweight stones, can still be seen on Dartmoor. On the millstone soils of the Peak District herdsmen embedded the stones in rubble banks, again around a central cairn. In central Scotland ovals of six or eight stones were customary, but there were also rectangles known as Four-Posters with urned cremations at their centres. Similar 'rings' with a recumbent stone added, the five-stone settings of south-west Ireland, stand in the Boggeragh mountains. Not far away are the Irish recumbent stone circles, which perversely have their tallest stones not alongside but opposite the recumbent. Ring-cairns lie by some of them.

Below Arbor Low circle-henge, with Gib Hill beyond the bank. One stone of the central Cove can be seen lying on the right.

In the north of Ireland there is a concentration of rings in the hills of the Sperrins. The stones are low and numerous, the rings are small, often with cairns inside them and with a short row of tall pillars standing at a tangent to the ring. In south-west Scotland there were similar small, many-stoned circles with a centre stone added, fallen at Lairdmannoch where bulls slumber by sun-warmed gateways, but heavy and proud at Glenquickan on the moor where Claughreid and Cauldside Burn are also to be found.

Rows, avenues, centre stones, concentrics, cairns, pairs of rings, everything intermeshed. At Bryn Cader Faner in Merioneth, a splendid circle by a trackway was half-buried under a cairn from which the standing stones now lean outlined like a coronet against the sky.

It is in this late period that many oval rings were designed. Some are so small that it is difficult to know if one is looking at a good oval or a poor circle, but often the stones are thin enough to show that the ring is indeed elliptical. One naturally asks how and why this was done. Professor Thom has suggested that the design was achieved by the use of right-angled triangles so that the builders could have a circumference which was a multiple of his Megalithic Yard. His theory provides answers to both how and why, but has seemed too involved for some other researchers. In 1970, Thaddeus Cowan, an American professor of psychology, put forward an alternative method for planning these non-circular rings that required only two anchor stakes and two pivot stakes at right angles to them around which a rope could be swung to lay out flattened circles, ovals and egg-shapes as the people wished.

Later, Ian Angell, a mathematician at London University, remarked that the real constructional methods might never be identified because there were so many possibilities. He demonstrated that one only needed two stakes and a loop of rope to plan an oval, three stakes for flattened circles, and four for an egg-shape. Although simple, this was not, he added, necessarily the way in which prehistoric people did design these later rings and he devised yet another method, using a shadow cast by a pole from day to day, to plan eggs, flattened circles and ellipses. Angell expressed his scepticism unequivocally. 'What is more interesting about the new method is . . . simply that it differs from Thom's construction. The fact that there are two incompatible methods which give good fits to the same megalithic sites . . . highlights the ever-present danger of projecting the experience of modern mathematics and technology onto the artefacts of what must be considered an alien culture.' It is an opinion with which I wholeheartedly agree. Mathematics have been misapplied in the remeasuring of these rings. Geometry has been misapplied in the search for their design. And astronomy has been energetically misapplied in some of the investigations into the 'meaning' of stone circles.

There was no need for this, and it has misdirected research into our past. The tiny, late rings of the British Isles, whose stones could have been moved by a few men and women, were not observatories but centres of supplication. Death is even more apparent in them than in the circles of the earlier phases. In the late rings of central Scotland it is commonplace. At Cullerlie, fifteen miles away from Loanhead of Daviot, the central area was reddened by heat and a second fire had burned in a central pit where cremated bone lay. At Tuack, seven miles north of Cullerlie, Dalrymple found that each of the six stones had a deposit of cremated bone by it. Around the centre stone were more pits with bone and charcoal in them. Urns were discovered by the northern stones. At the nearby Fullerton a pyre had scorched the interior. Other fires had burned within the two rings of Fowlis Wester across the mountains in Perthshire, and at Monzie in the same area a furious blaze of hazelwood had eaten into the ground. Bones of an adult and a little child lay in a cist by the north stone.

Fires had blazed and a cremation burned at the Druids Temple in Lancashire and in many others of the later rings of northern England and Wales. Even on the heights of Lacra, high above the sea, one of the tiny rings contained a cairn built on top of an area of burnt earth in which cremated bone and charred birch and ashwood still lay. And, perhaps in the very years when the sarsen structure of Stonehenge was being rearranged for the last time, two unmemorable rings were being put up at Sandy Road in Perthshire. One has been destroyed. In the other, excavated in 1961, a pit was found. Charcoal from it gave a date of 1200±150 bc, about 1500 BC, making this the latest known circle in the British Isles. A broken urn, upside down in the pit, held incinerated bones. 'The cremated contents were only a token deposit.' Lumps of charcoal lay on top of the bones. To understand stone circles we need to know the significance of deposits like these.

Bones and burials

In 1855 workmen were ordered to clear away the scratching thickets of broom and bramble that were growing against the Perthshire cottage known as Tigh-na-Ruaich, the House of the Heather. Among the bushes upright stones could be seen, and as they hacked and cut, the labourers exposed an oval of six rough blocks, the longest lying overgrown at the south. Digging the ground over, the men 'turned up wood charcoal, or cinders, generally mixed with the remains of burnt bone.' A little deeper they unearthed four huge urns, every one of which they broke. John M'Gregor, who watched the work, went on, 'the soil in the place is a light sand, but inside the Circle the sand was of a dark brown colour, such as it would assume if saturated with blood.'

The idea of stone circles being cemeteries, whether of chieftains or sacrificial victims, was not new. In 1851 Daniel Wilson pointed out that although Scottish highlanders going to church would ask each other, 'am bheil thu dol do'n chlachan?' ('are you going to the stones?'), this did not prove that the ancient stone circles were ritual centres. 'It has already been shewn that some of these were not temples but sepulchral monuments.' Deceived by the bodies found in them, researchers, even in the twentieth century, continued to interpret the megalithic rings as burial-places.

This is no longer acceptable. Whether in the Clava cairns or in recumbent stone circles like Berrybrae or Gingomyres, destroyed 'by one Dick', a farmer, around 1875, there are simply too few bodies for these to be cemeteries. At Gingomyres, the Reverend Cowie, who dug there, found only a layer of charcoal and a few animal bones. In the centre of another recumbent at Ardlair, Dalrymple came upon 'a small quantity of incinerated bones' in a single pit, not enough for even one body, let alone a graveyard.

Yet the fact that bones do lie inside the rings has to be explained, and the most plausible theory is that these were token offerings made at the time that the circle was built. An ancestor cult is possible. It would explain the incomplete cremations at Berrybrae and Sandy Road, and it would account for the somewhat gruesome care of the skeletons in the strange Irish ring of Millin Bay, where a dozen or more bodies lay in a long cist. The skulls were neatly stacked and when the teeth fell out they were replaced, sometimes in the wrong jaw. Clearly, the living were tending the powerful spirits of the dead, not simply burying them.

There are several reasons why the 'sepulchral' interpretation of such rings should be abandoned. The mortality rate among these primitive societies was probably some forty deaths annually in a population of a thousand individuals. An extended family of twenty-five persons, the kind of group that used the later rings, could expect on average one death each year. Had one of these little circles been a burial-ground for as short a while as a century it would have had to accommodate a hundred or more cremations rather than a mere two or three. Even selective burial, the discriminating interment only of chiefs or priests, would have resulted in more cremations than are found in these rings.

That circles were not burial-grounds is also shown by the fact that some of them actually stand in or against an obvious cemetery of the same period. Stonehenge was surrounded by clusters of long and round barrows. The Sanctuary near Avebury stood only a few steps from a line of fine barrows on Overton Hill. In the Peak District, on Stanton Moor, a veritable hill of the dead, over seventy cairns are scattered about the plateau and from the score that have been excavated archaeologists have recovered over eighty cremations. It is possible that altogether as many as three or four hundred people were buried there, the remains of perhaps two family groups who occupied the moor for a couple of centuries during the Bronze Age. This is a reasonable supposition because there are two stone circles here, both on the outskirts of the cairn-field, Doll Tor, and the Nine Ladies three-quarters of a mile away to the north-east.

The Nine Ladies, whose stones are reputedly maidens turned into millstone grit for irreligious dancing, is a typical Derbyshire ring with its stones set in a rubble bank. To its south-west is the outlying King Stone, sometimes known as the Fiddler, and inside the ring is a damaged cairn from which a tiny 'pygmy' cup, a funerary pot, is said to have come. The circle is delightful but small, and Doll Tor is smaller, six great stones enclosing an area no bigger than a boxing-ring. Bateman excavated there in 1852 and the Heathcotes in 1931–3, finding several cremations in urns with pygmy vessels by them, and as many again in a cairn which was built over the edge of the ring during the Bronze Age. At that time a wall was added between Doll Tor's stones much like that at Berrybrae, and it is arguable that the burials inside the ring were the work of latecomers who modified the site to their liking.

The Heathcotes encountered a mystery. 'A peculiar thing happened during the excavation – when returning to the site one day, the excavators found that [the north and south stones] were smashed into fragments . . . This was put down to unknown vandals, but one wonders who would take a large sledgehammer up onto the moor for this purpose. Should they have considered a paranormal explanation?' It is quite appealing, this vision of a malevolent spectre shattering the stones of an antique Derbyshire ring, the work, one might say, of a Doll-Tor-geist.

More seriously, it is apparent that our understanding of stone circles has been confused by the later introduction of cairns, cists and burials, particularly by Food-Vessel people. Whether at Studfold with its off-centre mound, or at Arbor Low where a barrow was superimposed on the bank, there are many instances of such interference. The confusion is magnified by the fact that in their latest phases many stone circles and burial-mounds were intentionally built together, integrated into one monument. The encircled cairns on Dartmoor or in Derbyshire, or the circles with above-ground boulder-tombs in County Kerry, typify these late 'burial' circles. Yet even in them the number of interments is few. At Lakehead in Devon the little six-stone ring was approached by a long row of stones that made it an impressive monument, but there was only one cist inside the circle. The reader may remember that when Bryce was excavating on the island of Arran in 1861 he uncovered a cist in one of the circles on Machrie Moor.

Two of the seven rings there are formed of weather-worn and majestic pillars of sandstone that glow luminescently in the sunlight, small rings that rise impressively on the moor. People must have gone into them over many years for their ceremonies. Yet there were just two cists in each, one cist being empty, others having food-vessels with minute fragments of cremated bone in them, 'all', Bryce philosophized, 'that remained of the great chief in whose honour, and for whose last resting-place, these huge monuments had been reared'. Another cist contained no cremation, but a skull and some bones so tidily arranged that all the flesh must have decomposed and the skeleton itself decayed into loose bones before they were stacked here. They were, it seems, the ribs and leg-bones of a young woman, set down with some animal bones and a deer antler. However, the presence of food-vessels in the rings of Machrie Moor may mean that these were cist-burials inserted into existing rings.

Bones must have been considered to add potency to the rings and this is one explanation for the urns with their cremations that are found at the foot of so many circle-stones. Even more convincing are the bones that have been discovered actually underneath the stones. Several Beaker 'graves' were located along Avebury's Kennet avenue and at least one of them had a sarsen erected over it. And at Balbirnie in Fife cremated bones were deposited in several holes before the stones were set upright above them. Similar deposits have been noticed by careful excavators elsewhere. It seems that like the little bits of quartz found in the disturbed stoneholes of Berrybrae bones were believed to add strength or sanctity to the ring.

There are so many small deposits of human bone like these, either beneath the stones or in small pockets at the centre of stone circles, that we must assume that these were intended as dedicatory offerings. Many of them are the remains of children. The blazing fire and the little cist with an adult and a child cremation at Monzie is one example. In Ireland at the circle of Castle Mahon, magnificently situated on a mountainside, people lit a fire in a pit at the ring's centre and later scattered charcoal all around it. Just to the north of the pit they lined a neat hole with cist-slabs and put the intensely burnt bones of a little child in it. The body of a child, the skull split open, lay under a cairn of flints at Woodhenge.

It is natural to wonder whether these dedicatory offerings were not also sacrifices, although the condition of most of them makes this impossible to decide. Marks of blows or cuts, except at Woodhenge, have disappeared and one can only guess what may have happened. It can hardly be coincidental that both at Avebury and at Marden, seven miles away, the skeleton of a young woman was buried in the ditch, right against the causeway as though guarding the entrance. Over fifty fragments from the skulls of children lay among other burnt bone at the centre of Loanhead of Daviot. In North Wales the ear-bones of children have been discovered in barrows and cairns. In one ring-cairn there was the skeleton of a child. It had no skull. At what may be the most dreadful of all the megalithic rings, the Druids' Circle on the headland overlooking Conway Bay, there is other evidence. The ring has a stark and splendid setting alongside an old trackway. The thirty stones once stood in a bank of boulders and rubble, broken by an entrance at the south-west emphasized by cumbrous portal-stones. Today the interior is empty and quiet, the grass blown by the ceaseless moorland wind, but under it there lay a cist around which quartz stones had been dropped. In the cist were the cremated bones of a child. Near it was a pit holding the remains of another child. A third child cremation was found nearby. It would be remarkable if these were simply burials of children, isolated from parents and other adults, laid to rest at the centre of an important ritual circle, and as one looks down on the Druids' Circle from a ridge of harsh rock one wonders what rites had been performed inside it.

High above I stand
In a bitter, bleak-blown land,
Ragged with rocks, crag-cruel,
Under the buzzard's wing
Of yore,
With grim grappling they reared
This wind-worn, rain-racked ring.
Of late
Someone, digging, found
A drift of white pebbles,
A bronze knife
And children's fire-charred bones.

Redemptive sacrifice.

These words, part of a poem by R. D. Ray, express the feeling of the ring. Proof is lacking. But what evidence we have today argues against circles like these being burial-places, while the existence of cremations in them suggests that these were in many cases dedicatory offerings in ceremonies for which human bones were required. Sometimes the bones were consumed on a pyre inside the ring itself and then raked out without particular care and buried near the centre of the ring. Indeed, the tall 'centre' stones in some rings may be slightly off-centre because they were put up to one side of such offerings to mark them. Conversely, at the henge of Longstone Rath in County Kildare a stone as high as a house stood 'in the exact mathematical centre' of the earthwork. Two adult cremations were found in a cist at its foot. The bodies had been burnt in the cist, 'which bore marks of a severe fire', before the monolith was raised, and it was only after this that the encircling bank was 'traced out by means of a rope tied to the standing stone at one end and swept round as a radius', forming an unbreakable barrier between the ritual site and the profane world. A circle of stones had the same purpose.

The ring needed human bone to give it meaning. When people replaced the last of the timber rings at the Sanctuary near Avebury they dragged long sarsens off the Marlborough Downs to build a stone circle. First, though, they carried the body of a Beaker girl to the site, putting the corpse into a shallow pit. She lay crouched on her right side, head to the south, facing east. Her arms were crossed, her hands touching her face. Just below her knees the people set down a beaker. Over her body they spread some inedible bones from the hoofs and jaws of an ox and a pig and part of an antler from a deer. And then they heaved the eastern stone of the ring upright on top of her grave, half-burying her beneath it, exactly at the east where she would look towards the rising sun. It is an interment which exemplifies the 'burials' in stone circles. Death and the sun and the moon were linked in the minds of the people and they buried bodies in their rings to make the association stronger. It is similar symbolism that is hinted at in their art.

Below Corrimony passage-grave. This displaced slab once roofed the burial chamber within. The cupmarks, originally on the underside of the stone, would have faced down on to the bodies lying in the dark chamber.

Art and the Other World

Carvings of axes in the chambers of megalithic tombs in Brittany; cupmarkings in the Irish passage-graves; and the cupmarked slabs in the blackness of cists in the north of Britain are further evidence that the primitive societies who built stone circles regarded the sun and moon as symbols of death and fertility. The imagery itself and the astronomical positions of the decorated stones emphasize this.

In 1954, while he was photographing a seventeenth-century name engraved on one of the sarsens of Stonehenge, Professor Richard Atkinson, the authority on this strangest of British stone circles, noticed other deeply weathered carvings there, of a dagger and four axes. They looked very like the real weapons used by Wessex chieftains and their warriors during the Early Bronze Age.

Ever since the twelfth century people had been visiting Stonehenge, yet for eight hundred years no one had noticed that this pillar of the lintelled trilithon standing on the south axis of the monument had such markings. Prehistoric artists had chipped them out, and the significance of the carvings was fairly clear. Axes of chalk, quite useless as tools, had been ritually buried with cremations at Stonehenge and in postholes at Woodhenge, and it is likely that these objects were symbols of the sun and its life-giving warmth. The axe has been portrayed as a sun symbol in other cultures. Prehistoric rock-carvings in Scandinavia show men holding up axes underneath the wheel-disc of the sun, and in Brittany many passage-graves have carvings of axes in the chambers where the dead lay. These tombs were related to the passage-graves of Ireland, although the art is quite different, none of the Irish carvings being as obviously representational as the Breton axes and archers' bows. Some of the clearest axes can be seen at Gavrinis, a lavishly decorated tomb near the rings of Er Lannic. Elsewhere in Brittany there were deposits of precious axes, of rare stone or bronze and in mint condition, at the entrances to these tombs that looked towards the autumn and winter sunrises. To any Breton trader the Stonehenge axe-carvings would have seemed entirely familiar and appropriate in this great monumental temple of the dead.

It was not surprising, then, that other 'Breton' carvings were discovered on the sarsens. A fallen pillar at the west had a badly worn rectangle pecked out on it. This, with its rounded upper extension, may have represented a ship. In Brittany there are several variations of this motif, and Professor Giot has speculated that 'perhaps these alleged ships were ceremonial vessels carrying away the souls of the dead.' It is an interpretation quite in keeping with the associations between death and the sun noticed in other stone circles.

More carvings appeared. Another dagger was noticed on the south trilithon. At the west on the underside of a fallen lintel there was a second 'ship', just a few paces from the first, and as both of these were carved on western stones they may have been boats sailing with their cargo of the dead towards the setting sun and the night.

At the east on the outer faces of three circle-stones were more axe-carvings. Interestingly, remembering the links between Breton and Irish chambered tombs, there is also a faint lattice-carving on the eastern stone, very like the trellis patterns on kerbstones at New Grange. The positions of all Stonehenge's decorated stones support the claim that this art was based on solar symbolism, for they stand at east, south and west, where the sun rose, reached its zenith and set. That Stonehenge was a temple in which the dead were paramount is a belief a long way from modern assertions that it was an astronomical observatory, but it is probably a lot closer to the truth. It holds good for other stone circles with carvings.

Much of the inspiration for such art may have originated in Ireland, not in the later, lovely geometrical compositions but in the simpler, rougher cupmarks. There are relatively few stone circles with any sort of art, fewer than one in twenty-five, and most of these have a remote connection with Irish passage-graves. They also have burials in them and the carvings are on astronomically significant pillars. One of the nearest to Ireland is Temple Wood in the Kilmartin valley of Argyll, where there is also a long line of cairns, one of them with a crowd of cupmarks and axe-carvings on the underside of a cist-slab that only the dead could have seen. In 1974 while looking at the Temple Wood circle I noticed a crude double spiral scratched out on its north stone. Spirals are a characteristic motif at New Grange and neighbouring tombs. Since 1974 Jack Scott has dug quadrant after quadrant at Temple Wood, patiently uncovering cists, one with a slab in line with the shadow cast at midsummer sunset. He has taken up cremations, excavated cairns, and he discovered that the ill-fashioned spiral descended to another magnificent double spiral, carved low on the stone, out of sight of the world, exactly at the north of the ring.

Other stone circles with carvings nearly all belong to the Clava cairn – recumbent stone circle tradition with their cremated bones. The Irish connections of these rings have already been remarked on. It will also be recalled that the Clava cupmarks were on stones at cardinal points and that the carvings in the recumbent stone circles were always on or near the recumbent itself with its orientation towards the full moon. Cupmarks can even be found on much later rings which seem to be shrunken versions of these great circles, the small ovals and Four-Posters of central Scotland. These little rectangles were built as far south as Northumberland, where the Goatstones near Bellingham has thirteen cupmarks on its hip-high east stone, and even in central Wales, where the Four Stones in Powys has at least one cupmark low down on its squat south-west pillar.

The rare decorated circles outside the Clava tradition also display Irish associations. In Cumberland the dominant outlying stone at Long Meg and Her Daughters has a spiral on it. A carefully treated photograph in Sir James Simpson's *Archaic Sculpturings*, published in 1867, reveals a collection of concentric circles, several with grooves extending from them, cupmarks at their centres, on the east face of this weather-beaten outlier. It stands in line with the midwinter sunset.

From such celestial associations cupmarks seem to be symbols, interchangeably, of the sun or moon, although these heavenly bodies themselves may have symbolized life or death or some other aspect of prehistoric cosmology. Attempts at further interpretation lead quickly to rash, unproveable conclusions and the lunacy of moon-madness. Some stones have just one cupmark. Some have rings surrounding cupmarks. Similar carvings occur on rocks and cists and standing stones, singly, in pairs, in lines, or in frenzied collections like an outburst of action painting. If – and there is no proof even of this – the cupmarks were a record of the moon's movements, then they might indicate its monthly risings, or its phases, or its highest and lowest positions above the horizon, or its nineteen-year journey from maximum back to maximum, or the occasions when a member of the family died. They might have been carved on the stone one at a time or have been the result of one energetic composition when the stone was erected. There may be others out of sight below ground level. And they might not even be symbols of the moon. Reason suggests an acceptance of their association with death and the sun or moon, and

Below Two retouched photographs from *Archaic Sculpturings* by Sir James Simpson, 1867. *Left* The enigmatic carvings on Long Meg, in Cumberland, no longer appear as clearly today. *Right* These carvings from New Grange and Dowth have been interpreted as symbols of a Great Goddess whose eyes watched over the dead.

sanity demands that someone else should undertake any further research.

There are carved stones in some Irish circles. The recumbent stone at Drombeg in County Cork has two cupmarks on its upper surface, one inside the outline of an axe. At Kiltierney in County Fermanagh there is another decorated stone, aligned on the midwinter moonrise. These rings have the same associations with astronomy and death. Inside the concentric ring of Castledamph in County Tyrone a low cairn covered a cupmarked cist where the cremated bones of a youth rested.

Of the other rings perhaps the most instructive to consider is the devastated circle at Beltany in County Donegal, perched on a small but conspicuous hillock near Raphoe. It is a large ring but nearly all of its sixty stones, placed as they were just below the crest, barely rise above the interior. The exception to this is one giant pillar at the west-south-west. Looking from this across the ring, one sees a triangular stone opposite, cupmarks all over its inner face, exactly orientated on the May Day sunrise. The association between the carvings and the sun seems clear. Yet for those who would have Beltany as an example of an observatory it must be pointed out that this ring of stones probably once encircled a cairn quite high enough to obstruct any sight-line between opposite stones. In the rubble of the cairn one can still see the wreckage of a cist. Admiral Boyle Somerville, who surveyed Beltany in 1909, remarked that there was an outlying stone set up in line with the midwinter sunset.

The name of the ring is important, for it must derive from Bealltaine or Beltane, the Celtic Iron Age festival that celebrated the pastoral god Belenus, the Shining One, on the night before 1 May. Sunrise on May Day signalled the end of the festivities. That such a name should be given to a ring that must be at least as old as the Bronze Age suggests that some Celtic festivals were of an antiquity long before the Iron Age.

Although the astronomical settings of cupmarked stones in the circles are too consistent to be accidental, yet the lowness of some of them and the intervening cairns in other rings argues against these ever being meant for astronomer-priests. Two cupmarked kerbstones of the ring-cairn at Balnuaran of Clava, although they were at the east, were out of sight from the central space of the ring. At Tordarroch, another Clava ring-cairn inside a stone circle, there was a kerbstone with over thirty cupmarks on it in line with the maximum midsummer moonset. But Audrey Henshall, author of two magisterial volumes on the chambered tombs of Scotland, commented, 'the slab appears to have fallen outwards from the kerb. If this is so the cupmarks must have faced inwards and been hidden by the cairn material.' Only the dead could have seen through it.

In this apparent conflict between astronomical sight-lines and the impossibility of anyone's looking along them we must ask not how we would use such alignments but what they signified to the prehistoric people who laid them out.

Astronomy: science or symbolism?

The belief, once widespread, that stone circles were observatories has largely been discredited, although it is occasionally resurrected by devotees who write about the astronomical temples of Megalithic Man without mentioning his natural cousins, Timber Man of the post-rings and Earth Man of the henges. In reality, if there were observatories in prehistoric Britain they were probably lines, not rings, of stones or wooden pillars, and in his latest book, *Megalithic Remains in Britain and Brittany*, Alexander Thom has said of stone circles that 'most of them seem to have no astronomical significance.' It is a pity that other investigators have not been as objective and disinterested.

Stone circles did have astronomical alignments built into them. In the case of the Scottish recumbent stone circles these were directed towards the moon. In the majority of other rings, built by people with different beliefs, the orientations were towards the sun. The question is what the people intended when they laid out these sight-lines.

If prehistoric people fabricated calendrical devices for recording the seasons of the year, or composed megalithic computers that enabled their priests to predict eclipses, then these structures were scientific instruments. If, on the other hand, orientations were built into cists and circles to bring the moon or sun into association with the dead, such lines would be not scientific but symbolic. Precision in them would not be of the first importance.

Stonehenge is central to this question. Two hundred years ago Dr John Smith realized that the midsummer sun rose in line with the Heel Stone outside the entrance to the henge. 'The Arch-Druid . . . looking down the right line of the temple, over the stones II and I [the Heel Stone] his eye is bounded by Durrington field, (a charming horizon about two miles distant,) he there sees the sun rise from behind the hill; the apex of the stone I, points directly to the place . . . .' This is not strictly true, but from Smith's slim paperback of 1771 Stonehenge's astronomical literature has grown into a whole library of paperbacks. A look at some current theories may help the reader to see the problems facing archeo-astronomers.

The complexity of the three phases of Stonehenge and its prison-window architecture offers a multiple-choice answer to the problem of its astronomy. There have been multiple answers, some sensible, most silly. One writer claimed that the first henge was devised to predict tides off the south coast. Someone else argued that its cremation pits were arranged for eclipse prediction. Another ingenious and unsupportable hypothesis stated that Stonehenge was an Egyptian eclipse observatory and that it had been remodelled by Greek priest-scientists from Delos who preserved 'the original astronomical sight-lines wherever they could'. Disagreeing with this, another person suggested that the second Stonehenge contained an astronomical rectangle, although this might belong to the first or third phase according to one's preferred theory.

In contrast to this open-minded approach came the assertion that 'it is an astronomical clock . . . its huge monolithic columns having been erected in two concentric rings so that the sun's disc can be framed exactly between two of the stones as it rises above the horizon at the winter solstice.' As sarsen pillars hide the midwinter sunrise from the centre of Stonehenge this idea has had little support.

Most improbable of all is the account of the stupidity of the Stonehenge builders. The incompetents who erected the last magnificent circle discovered they had blocked the ancient sight-lines with their massive columns. They overcame this oversight – literally – by drilling holes in the upper surfaces of lintel stones and setting sighting poles upright in them so that observers could stand on top of the stones and stare across the ring towards the poles and the midsummer sunrise. Balanced precariously on the immense pillars, the priests found they still could not see because they had unthinkingly erected the biggest of their trilithons in the way. So they pushed it over and, mumbling glumly in the dawn-lit wreckage, went back to their observations.

Even the most coldly analysed alignment presents problems. When the car park at Stonehenge was extended in 1966 three large and deep postholes were noticed about 250 metres north-west of the circle. Their positions are marked by white rings today. They had held tall posts and they aroused much enthusiasm. The late 'Peter' Newham, author of an excellent, highly regarded booklet on the astronomy of Stonehenge, wrote, 'these can be regarded as the most positive "astronomical" discovery yet made at Stonehenge . . . they align on sun and moon setting positions with an extreme accuracy.'

Accurate or not, there was a snag. The scientist who examined material from the holes commented that it was 'surprising that most of the charcoal should be pine'. Neolithic builders would surely have chosen sturdy oak for these high and exposed posts rather than pine. Oak was plentiful in their forests. At the nearby and contemporary sites of Woodhenge and Durrington Walls the rings and round houses were built of thick oak posts and it was oak that earlier people used for a mortuary house in the Fussells Lodge long barrow seven miles away.

The solution lies in the unpublished Carbon-14 dates for the Stonehenge postholes. One was for 6140 bc and the other for 7180 bc, long before Stonehenge, in the Middle Stone Age when the climate was beginning to warm and when wild ox and elk and deer grazed around the dense forests of . . . pine. If the posts near Stonehenge were Mesolithic, erected several thousands of years before the henge, then their extreme astronomical accuracy was entirely accidental. One nameless archaeologist suggested, not very seriously, that they must have been put up by an astronomer from outer space who had travelled to Earth in a Middle Stone Age spacecraft – a Star Carr!

It is tempting but dangerously wrong to transfer modern man back into the romance of prehistory, inserting his rational attitudes into the lifeless monuments of people whose values and beliefs were utterly different from ours, for it leads to misinterpretation like that of the car park postholes.

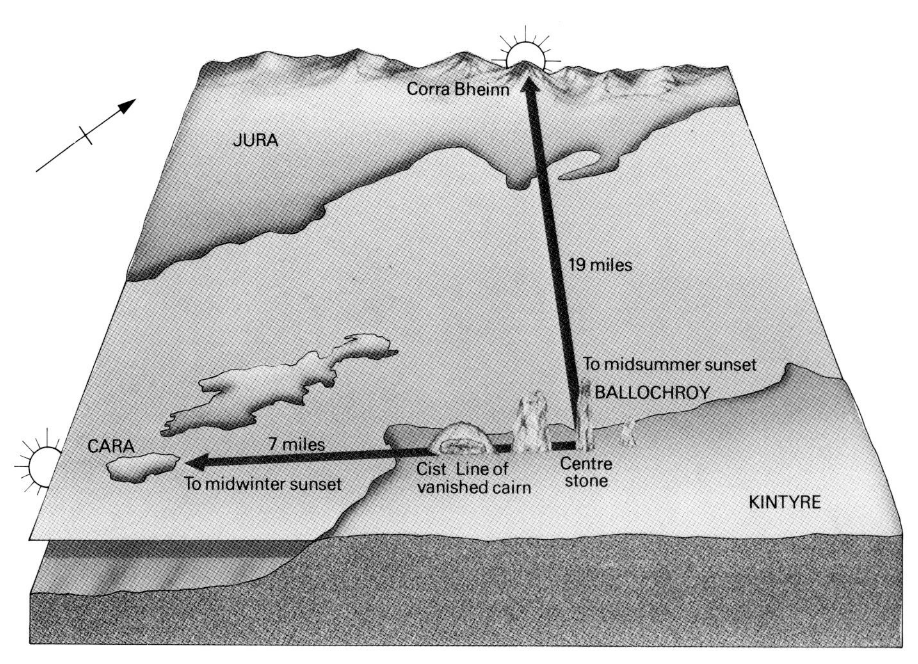

Left This drawing from William Stukeley's posthumous *Itinerarium Curiosum* II, of 1776, shows what Ballochroy originally looked like. The cairn obstructed any astronomical sight-line. *Above* The row of three stones at Ballochroy today, showing the sight-lines that have been suggested. If any such lines were intended, they can only have been symbolic ones.

That mistake shows how easy it is for anyone looking for astronomical alignments to be misled by the evidence unless every archaeological fact is considered. In Brittany Thom has suggested that an immense pillar, Le Grand Menhir Brisé, weighing over three hundred tons, was erected so that it would mark important positions of the moon. There are several objections. The places where the observers are supposed to have stood are not well marked. The pillar does not stand today but lies in four fragments disposed in such a way that the most probable explanation is that the stone broke while being raised and only its stump could be set upright.

What is not generally known is that the stone was to stand at the burial end of an enormous long barrow. Other Neolithic long mounds in the vicinity pointed either to east or south and had standing stones at the end where their burials lay. At one of them, Manio, five beautiful jadeite axes were set upright in the stonehole of the tall carved pillar. Inside the tomb was an axe-carving on a cist-slab. At Le Grand Menhir Brisé, as at Manio and Kerlescan and Mané er Hroek, where over a hundred axes were found, the builders needed a pillar to stand by the burials. When the stone broke, its stump still served this purpose. It had no astronomical significance but its original function is not obvious today because the long barrow has been obliterated by a car park. The stump, like so many other Breton pillars, was probably pushed over in the Christian period.

A second famous 'observatory' is the Ballochroy row of three stones on the Kintyre peninsula in Argyll. The central stone, at right angles to the row, is supposed to indicate with exceptional accuracy midsummer sunset over Corra Bheinn mountain on Jura nineteen miles away. A stone as little as two metres wide cannot define anything 'with exceptional accuracy', and it is ironically appropriate that in a recent book about archaeo-astronomy the author apologized that a photograph of Ballochroy had been 'taken from a point off the line of the central stone which is why it does not appear to be indicating the correct mountain top'.

The actual line of stones, being longer, is more promising. To its south-west it points to an exposed cist, and beyond that, seven miles away, to Cara island where the sun would have set at midwinter. What cannot be seen today is the huge cairn that once covered the cist and blocked off any view of the island where 'the midwinter setting Sun just grazed the end of Cara'. In his *Itinerarium Curiosum* II of 1776 William Stukeley included a sketch of Ballochroy 'on the roadside between Rivnahyrin [Rhunahaorine] and Clochau Cantyre [Clachan Kintyre]'. The three stones are there, beyond them is Karn Maur, the Great Cairn, and beyond that two smaller cairns and another standing stone. If this line ever was intended to point towards midwinter sunset, which is quite likely (as is the rough indication of midsummer sunset), then it was a symbolic line, joining the places of death with the sun.

If important settings like these are susceptible to criticism then the attempts of archaeo-astronomers to prove that stone circles were observatories are likely to be even less successful. Where people have endeavoured to do this, using precision instruments and objective recording, their results have been unconvincing, mainly because of the variety of heavenly bodies prehistoric people are supposed to have sighted upon. In any small region one would expect the communities to have looked towards the same object, whether the sun, moon or particular star, and to have used the same sort of sighting-device. Yet for five rings within a quarter of a mile of each other in Cumberland, Thom proposed sundry alignments, some good, some less exact, on sunsets and sunrises at various times of the year, moonsets and moonrises, on the settings of the stars Arcturus, Pollux and Deneb, and on the rising of Antares and Capella. The 'sight-lines', moreover, were not defined by one sort of foresight but by a mixture of outlying stones, circle-stones, unassociated standing stones and other circles.

Seven Cornish rings provided a similar diversity of lines towards sun, moon, Vega, Arcturus, Deneb, and Castor. It is not credible that groups in one area had such a range of targets with such varied foresights.

There are other objections. Stars were too dim for prehistoric men to have sighted upon, and what observations men did make were probably limited to the sun and moon. A society also would have found it difficult to decide where to build a stone circle if they wished it to contain more than one precise orientation that 'grazed' the side of a slope or was exactly defined by a mountain notch. In the hilly countryside of stone circles, as any field-walker knows, every step alters the angles of hillsides, bringing 'notches' into view, hiding others as one trudges downhill, so that trying to keep one alignment fixed in sight while searching for others – which the people would not know existed until they had seen them at midwinter or midsummer – would be akin to snatching at minnows in a reedy pond with a thimble.

Many astronomers, for example, have said that Stonehenge was deliberately built at the one latitude where maximum moonset and midsummer sunrise occur at right angles to each other. For this to be true people would have had to erect Stonehenge farther to the south, forty miles off the coast in the middle of the English Channel. The position of Stonehenge was decided, of course, by the existence of the many long barrows already standing on Salisbury Plain where Neolithic societies had been living for over a thousand years.

Astronomical overstatements about the precision of prehistoric people have confused the study of these societies, attributing to them techniques they would neither have recognized nor have been interested in.

To be acceptable, astronomical lines in stone circles must be defined by man-made foresights such as an outlying stone, a recumbent, or an entrance. Mountain ridges and notches cannot be accepted unless they are indicated by such features or a taller stone in the ring. Otherwise we can never be certain that an apparent alignment is not fortuitous. In Thom's sketch of the skyline at the Carles there are no fewer than sixty-two nicks in the horizon and prehistoric man may have looked towards any one of them. Euan MacKie has explained how cautious researchers should be, working 'on the assumption that any important lines planned by the circle builders were likely to be marked by some conspicuous aspects of the site's design', its axis or an outlying stone.

Even outlying stones cause doubts. The Heel Stone at Stonehenge was not in line with midsummer sunrise but several metres to the south of where the sun rose. People may have erected it there to allow the sun to rise above the dawn mists, but we cannot prove it. At Long Meg the outlier 'coincides with the winter solstice sunset, but Long Meg is too large and near to be used as an accurate foresight from the ring. Possibly the alignment was built into the structure to symbolically represent a principle that was important to the neolithic people of early Britain.' One would cheerfully agree with everything but the split infinitive in this statement by Ed Krupp, the American astronomer.

One of the most widely known of all outlying stones, the King Stone at the Rollright Stones, a weird pillar that crouches like a puff-adder outside the circle, is quite unastronomical. Sir Norman Lockyer wrote vaguely that it might have been aligned on a star. Thom suggested the rising of Capella in 1750 BC, but the star is too faint on the skyline and the date is too unlikely for this to be the right solution. The King Stone was more probably a marker visible from the lower slopes of the prehistoric trackway that passed the ring, announcing the whereabouts of the circle and the territory of its builders.

Nor can one always be sure that a standing stone some distance from a ring was an outlier of it. At the Merry Maidens in Cornwall Lockyer made two strenuous efforts to decode the circle. First he had a field wall broken down so that he could look towards the pair of standing stones, the Pipers, that were concealed from view. When the wall was demolished the stones were still miserably out of sight. Then he turned to another pillar, the Goon Rith or Red Downs, clearly to be seen at the west-south-west, 'I have not been able to find any astronomical use for this from the circle . . .' Lockyer wrote but, undeterred, he turned round and looked from the stone towards the circle, finding an alignment on the rising of the Pleiades in 1960 BC. This was almost sharp practice. It is one matter to look towards a thin pillar that defines an exact position on the horizon. It is improper to look towards as broad a target as a stone circle. With the stone standing 340 metres from the ring and with the Merry Maidens nearly 24 metres in diameter, this was no delicate line of Lockyer's but a beam almost four degrees wide. If the horizon had been only one mile away his target area would still have been 100 metres wide and he could have chosen any star that happened to rise there. Nor, of course, is there any proof that a stone as far away as the Goon Rith had any connection with the Merry Maidens.

Even so, outlying stones are among the best indicators of whether a stone circle had an alignment in it. Other features permit too great a latitude. One of the astronomers' favourite rings is the Carles near Keswick, because it provides a rich medley of stones and horizon features to align upon. A Mr Otley, as early as 1849, showed that the entrance was placed at True North, 'giving true solar bearings throughout the year'. A. L. Lewis, who believed that circle-builders looked upon hills as sacred places – as well they might – found two marvellous lines from the ring, one north-west towards Skiddaw mountain, the other north-east towards Blencathra, except that the lines were not quite accurate. 'Had the circle been put up in the exact position the good view would have been lost.' Lockyer thought the puzzling internal rectangle pointed to the rising of the Pleiades in 1650 BC, impossibly late in the Middle Bronze Age. And, just as he had done at the Merry Maidens, he looked from an outlier towards the ring and noted that this 'alignment' indicated May Day sunrise. This time his arc of vision was over twenty degrees wide. Morrow suggested a 1400 BC sight-line, the very time when the cold, drizzling climate was driving herdsmen off the hills. Anderson developed a solar fixation, discovering alignments towards the sunrise for 22 June, 1 May, 21 March, 6 November, 22 December, as well as 6 April sunrise over Great Mell Fell.

There are really only three feasible alignments at the Carles. The first and probably most important is shown by the northerly position of the entrance. It must be appreciated that no heavenly body rose or set there in prehistoric times. There was no Pole Star. The alignment was symbolic, perhaps obtained by taking a point midway between the risings and settings of the sun.

A second line is marked by a tall granite block which, unlike all the others, is set radially to the Carles' circumference at the south-east. From here to the corner of the rectangle and across the ring is the direction in which the midsummer sun would set, a time of awe for most prehistoric communities, and there seems to be a good reason for the alignment. But it is perplexing to find this dramatic line marked at its far end by a very low stone which is further diminished by the notchless Latrigg Fell looming behind it. In practical terms the alignment must be doubtful. If one reverses the sight-line, looking towards the high radial stone, there is an equally bland skyline where the sun rose in early February and November.

The third alignment at the Carles is towards a small outlier by the hedge a hundred metres to the west-south-west. This may have pointed to sunset in October and late February, but the stone is not big and is dwarfed by the Derwent Fells. It is also scarred by ploughmarks. It must have lain buried somewhere in the field where it had repeatedly damaged ploughs until a farmer had dragged it away to the hedge. There is a record of its lying there, used as a stepping-stone. It is only quite recently that it has been set upright. It has no validity as an astronomical outlier.

It would be tedious to examine a second 'astronomical' circle, Callanish, in the same detail, and the earlier work of investigators like Lockyer and Somerville can be ignored, although it is interesting to find John Tolund in his history of the Druids writing in 1726 that 'this Temple stands astronomically . . . I can prove it to have been dedicated principally to the Sun.'

Callanish is the remarkable Hebridean ring which encloses a passage-grave. An avenue approaches it from the north-north-east, and three rows of stones lead to it from east-north-east, south and west. Gerald Hawkins, author of *Stonehenge Decoded* and with a reputation for his work in archaeo-astronomy, wrote in the learned journal *Science* that the south 'row of stones . . . points to the rising, transit and setting of the moon . . . when it appears to come closest to the horizon', much as it did over the recumbent stones of Aberdeenshire. Hawkins added that 'midsummer moonset is over Mount Clisham, the highest point on Harris, and the avenue points to this mountain. Perhaps this alignment of the moon with the mountain was significant for the Callanish people.'

This was quite possible but it was unproveable. In his second book, *Beyond Stonehenge*, Hawkins wrote, 'my published calculations had been based on paper data, and a site inspection was called for.' So he visited Callanish. 'On the site I saw a complication . . . a low rocky outcrop obscured distant Mount Clisham', a sad end to his deduction. Only too often visits to the sites themselves contradict theories meticulously worked out in the study. Thom seems to have made this error when he wrote of the moon grazing the base and summit of Mount Clisham.

In 1978 a detailed plan of Callanish was published by the Geography Department of the University of Glasgow. 'The meaning and significance of the alignments and stone patterns is still the subject of argument. Some researchers attribute astronomical significance to these monuments and these theories are currently being examined.' One very detailed analysis by four university surveyors in 1975 of forty-six possible alignments in the rows and avenue at Callanish and between other rings in the immediate neighbourhood found that forty-five were unsatisfactory. 'We conclude that the one accurate astronomical indication at Callanish could easily have occurred by chance'. Another investigator, Gordon Moir, concluded that 'no feature of the main site at Callanish was designed with an astronomical use as its primary purpose.'

This does not mean that there were no alignments. There is plenty of evidence for approximate orientations on the sun or the moon among the stone circles of the British Isles. The recumbent stone circles prove that. It means simply that when one tries to refine such orientations into alignments finely set up for scientific observation the crudity of the stones and their closeness to each other defeats us. We are not sure if the stones are in their original positions. We do not know if stones are missing. And we can be deceived.

In the Lake District the delightful ring of Blakeley Raise lies so close to the unfenced road from Ennerdale Bridge that picnickers drive their cars into it. Shaggy cattle munch moodily between the stones. The ring is 'exactly twenty Megalithic Yards in diameter' and a line across it points precisely to where the maximum moon would have set, sliding down the shoulder of Screel Hill thirty-one miles away. This is strange. The stones of Blakeley Raise are set in concrete. They were put up by Dr Quine in 1925 and Miss Hodgson, a noted Cumbrian archaeologist and excavator, never believed that the reconstruction was correct. Its coincidental diameter and astronomical sight-line warn us of the dangers of other coincidences in these disturbed rings whose stones were so frequently interfered with by prehistoric people.

The circle that has caused more astronomical confusion than any other is Stonehenge. Quite unrepresentative of other stone circles, it has sometimes been taken as a starting point for a study of these rings, whereas it should be seen as an end – and a dead one. Nor was it the observatory beloved of so many archaeo-astronomers. It was for the dead.

Stonehenge: bones and batter-dashers

Because of the changes made to it, in architecture and in ritual, Stonehenge is a useful example of the convulsive history of stone circles. Its first structure may have been a timber hut in which corpses were left to rot. Later, incoming Grooved Ware people built a henge around it in which they buried their cremated dead. Then Beaker groups, who rejected cremation, started to put up a stone circle. But natives pulled it down and, instead, raised the gigantic sarsens that we know as Stonehenge today. Yet throughout these twists and turns the monument remained a temple in which sun, earth and death combined.

From the very beginning its associations with death were clear. Before it was built there were a dozen or more earthen long barrows nearby on Salisbury Plain, many of them having end-chambers of wood. Stone was scarce. Close to its future site was the small Amesbury mound in which a Neolithic family laid dried ancestral bones, leaving them there with some joints of ox and an entire goose. They may have carried the decaying skeletons from a neighbouring hut, the first structure on the site of Stonehenge, a charnel-house in which the few families left corpses to decompose before taking the bones to their respective long mounds. A round mortuary enclosure, its doorway facing the rising sun at midsummer, conveniently situated on the gentle downs, would have made an ideal ossuary.

We cannot be sure. There has been so much bad digging at the centre of Stonehenge from the time of James I onwards that although postholes have been discovered most of the evidence has been destroyed. So popular had Stonehenge become by the early eighteenth century that the enterprising Gaffer Hunt set up a liquor stall inside it. Unfortunately, he also dug a deep hole for a cellar under a fallen sarsen. About 1839 a Captain Beamish dug a hole 'about eight feet square and six feet deep in front of the altar-stone'. All he found was a lot of rabbit bones. Between Beamish, Hunt and others it is unlikely that recognizable traces of a central hut have survived.

Yet if it had existed it would explain the two definite astronomical alignments at Stonehenge. One, over the Heel Stone towards midsummer sunrise, is well known. The other, worked out by century-long sightings towards the shifting positions of moonrise, is not. These were recorded by rows of stakes long before the ditch and bank were constructed and it is improbable that observers sat shelterless year after year waiting to see the moon at its extreme. A hut is likely, planned so that midsummer sun and midwinter moon could shine through the doorway on the corpses much as the sun shone through the entrance of the later Woodhenge on the burial of the little girl there. The rough block of the Heel Stone and a row of smaller stones acted as outlying markers. The symbolism of this relationship between sun, moon and death is quite in keeping with the orientations of the long burial-mounds around Stonehenge. Four out of five have their burial ends facing either extreme moonrises or sunrises or towards the east where both sun and moon rise in the spring and autumn.

If there were a hut then the first enforced change to Stonehenge came when newcomers, Grooved Ware herdsmen, had a henge built round about 2800 BC, heaping the chalk into a high bank along the inner edge of a crudely quarried ditch. Respecting the sight-lines of this ancient sanctuary, they left a causeway at the north-east, its edges aligned on the outlying stones and emphasized by two entrance pillars of which only the fallen Slaughter Stone survives. But inside the henge they dug a wide ring of pits, called the Aubrey Holes after John Aubrey who was the first to notice these 'cavities' four thousand years after they had been filled in. These pits held cremations, a burial practice alien to the natives of Salisbury Plain.

There were fifty-six of the pits, and claims have been made that they were planned as a counting-device for the prediction of eclipses. The number is important. In comparable cemeteries at Dorchester, at Maxey and at Cairnpapple, where the pits are identical in their contents, their numbers have no astronomical significance and one must doubt the interpretation that has been placed on them at Stonehenge.

Stonehenge was a temple and a cemetery. Some of the Aubrey Holes immediately received burnt human bones. Others were backfilled and then redug for people to put in burnt soil, charred wood, cremated human bone – some neatly deposited, some scattered – with bone pins and flints, stone maceheads and the symbolic chalk axes, debris from pyres like that noticed in the recumbent stone circles of Scotland. There are, moreover, at least thirty other cremations from this period in Stonehenge, some at the south by the bank or in the ditch, others by the entrance. Some were buried years after the ditch was dug, showing that people had come here for centuries, laying their dead to rest in a place where they were expected to communicate with the spirits of the Other World.

Here also the people raised four stones in a rectangle that just fitted inside the henge. Its short sides pointed towards the midsummer sunrise, its long ones to the setting of the extreme moon. One might ask, though, why these stones, the Four Stations, were not arranged in a square, which would have been more symmetrical. The answer may be that the builders wanted also to record the time of May Day sunset, the 'Celtic' festival remarked on at Beltany, using the rectangle's west-north-west diagonal, although with an error of nearly a whole degree in the orientation.

The monument was not left alone. By 2200 BC, when Beaker people, who did not practise cremation, were dominant in Wessex, they began building two concentric rings of stones inside the henge, perhaps in imitation of the timber hut that had stood there. The funerary traditions of Stonehenge continued, explaining the recent discovery in the ditch of a burial of a young man accompanied by Beaker archery equipment.

Old ideas were abandoned. The diagonal sight-line across the henge was blocked by the stone circles. Ditches were dug around the Heel Stone and two of the Four Stations. The entrance was widened. And from it an earthen avenue was laid out along which people dragged magical stones transported from mountains far away in South Wales. These 'bluestones' came from the Preselis, which stood on the Wessex–Ireland trade-route that Beaker copper and gold prospectors would have known well. Over three thousand years later the achievement of moving these stones and Stonehenge's association with death still lingered in folk-memory. Early in the twelfth century AD Geoffrey of Monmouth recorded the legend that the magician Merlin was ordered 'to erect round the burial-ground the stones which he had brought from Ireland'. Even before Geoffrey this Ireland–Wessex link had been described in the *Mabinogion*, the collection of Celtic myths and legends. Branwen, daughter of King Llyr, travelled from Ireland to the Bristol Channel and ultimately to London, carrying the head of her brother with her. Ferrying four-ton bluestones may not have been much more difficult.

How such stones were linked with death is shown by the one that never reached Stonehenge. Bluestones are not natural to Wiltshire. Outside Stonehenge only one has been found anywhere there. It is supposed by archaeologists that the bluestones were canoed along the south coast of Wales to the Bristol Channel, up the Avon and then sledged a few miles to the headwaters of the river Wylye and, ultimately, floated almost all the way to Stonehenge. Near Heytesbury on the Wylye, high on the military danger zone of the Plain, is the long Bole's Barrow, excavated by William Cunnington in 1801. At its east end he found the bones of many skeletons. One seemed to have been beheaded. Near the bones was a large cist, on top of which were the skulls of several oxen. The rubbly walls of the burial chamber had collapsed and Cunnington had to get out quickly, 'for the large stones came rolling down so fast upon us that we were obliged to desist from exploring it further.' He took ten of the biggest stones for his garden, disposing them tidily around an ash tree on his lawn. One of them, he noted was 'the Blue hard stone also, ye same to some of the upright Stones in ye inner Circle at Stonehenge'.

It is possible that this bluestone, now in Salisbury Museum, had stood at the front of the long barrow, much like the Grand Menhir Brisé in Brittany. Other Wessex long barrows at Warminster and at Wor Barrow had standing stones at their entrances. It can be imagined how the addition of a 'foreign' bluestone would have enhanced the power of an ancient long barrow. At this time Beaker people were being buried under round barrows clustered in cemeteries around Stonehenge, perhaps after their bodies had been taken to the circle for funereal rites. One line of barrows to the east is known as the King Barrows. John Aubrey said 'there doe appeare five small barrowes . . . . At the ends of the Graves there were Stones, which the people of late (about 1640), have fetched away. For stones (except Flints) are exceeding scarce in these partes.'

The slow construction of the bluestone rings went on for a hundred years and then it was interrupted. Possibly the Beaker people were driven from Salisbury Plain after a rising by the natives. Whatever the cause, the stones were removed from the unfinished rings and in their place was set up a horseshoe of five mountainous trilithons. This was enclosed in a lintelled circle of vast stones, all of them sarsens from the Marlborough Downs to the north. What is of most interest about this structure is not the weight of the stupendous blocks, nor the method by which they were hauled by massed gangs over the twenty miles of uneven downland, but the manner in which they were shaped. There were pegs for the lintels, dowelled holes to fit them in, inset undersides, mortise-and-tenon joints, smoothed surfaces, all bashed out of intractable stone by people who were accustomed to building in wood but who had decided to make a ring of long-lasting sarsen. We have no need to search for the architects of Stonehenge in Brittany with its megalithic tombs or Mycenaean Greece with its stone walls and gateways. The builders were the inhabitants of Salisbury Plain, where there were no megalithic tombs and where there was a long tradition of woodworking. With the resurgence of native customs, now formalized in an Early Bronze Age heroic society of chieftains, warriors and bards, and herdsmen, it was predictable that such a grandiose project should be undertaken.

The old sight-lines were lost in the shadowed claustrophobia of the thick pillars. The axis changed slightly, adjusted roughly to 'the first-

Below Stonehenge, seen from the north, showing the perfectly horizontal tops of the lintels, shaped by men accustomed to building in wood.

gleam summer solstice sunrise . . . in 2045 BC'. But on that axis, just as one passed under the outer sarsen arches, there was a grave, already sadly disturbed when it was excavated, but lying there with Bronze Age pottery which showed its prehistoric origin. Sunrise and death were still joined together, as the carvings of axes, daggers and 'boats' at east, south and west of the ring remind us. Pieces of chipped stone in the barrows around Stonehenge tell the same story.

Some chieftain decided that the bluestones should be returned to the circle once some of them had been 'dressed' to shape. The chippings from them had a mystical quality. In the new pits where the bluestones were to stand outside the main sarsen ring people put small bits of bluestones at the bottoms of the holes, just as quartz and cremated bone had been placed in Scotland. When the observant Stukeley excavated a round barrow west of Stonehenge he noticed 'bits of red and blue marble, chippings of the stones of the temple', and nearly a hundred years later Hoare and Cunnington, reopening the same barrow, 'found a large piece of one of the blue stones of Stonehenge.' Other barrows in the vicinity also had bits of bluestone near their burials.

This belief that such chippings might absorb the powerful spirits of the dead need not surprise us when evidence of prehistoric man's obsession with his ancestors and with death survives everywhere on Salisbury Plain from the New Stone Age onwards. By the Bronze Age Stonehenge was surrounded by extensive lines of round barrows, some encircled by sacred banks that the dead could not cross, cemeteries of mounds in which powerful men lay buried, chieftains with their trappings of bronze and gold, jet, shale, amber, the aristocracy of Wessex laid to rest in a region of death with a temple of the dead at its heart.

If legends from the later Iron Age Celts are any guide it is likely that the funeral of a chief was both a time of mourning and also a time of festivity, with games in honour of the dead man: races, contests of skill and strength, sacrifices of animals, all centred around the solemn rites of death inside Stonehenge before the body was borne to its chalk-cut grave.

As late as 1500 BC, the time when a family was building the unpretentious rings of Sandy Road, Stonehenge four hundred miles to the south was still being altered. Some of the much-moved bluestones were reset in a circle around the five trilithons, while those that had been elegantly smoothed were arranged in a horseshoe inside the trilithons. The tallest of them was erected near the centre. A circle inside a circle, a horseshoe within a horseshoe, a central pillar. The interpretations are as many as the stones, but, fortunately, there are other facts to help us: the alignment of the sarsens; the graves on the axis; the carvings; and the graded heights of the trilithons.

Stonehenge had begun as a place where dead bodies were laid. It later became a place where families on the Plain met for their seasonal festivals, for trade, for marriages, for ceremonies of death and fertility. These traditions continued. But by the Early Bronze Age Stonehenge was a representation of power. Only the privileged entered its cramped, obscured precincts. It was they who conducted the ceremonies, and it was their funerals that were occasions of magnificence. No longer did men turn towards the midsummer sunrise, because dawn had given way to the Celtic night. It was the Great Trilithon that dominated one's vision, higher than any stone setting in the British Isles. It was aligned on the midwinter sunset. R. S. Newall, author of the official guide-book, explained how one of the bluestones, in its new position, emphasized this. 'The setting sun would have been immediately above it and framed by the stones of the great trilithon', blazing through its 'window' and reddening the top of the tall bluestone.

Perhaps this was why the trilithons were arranged in a horseshoe. Writers have speculated that such a setting symbolized the horns of a bull, itself a symbol of the sun and strength. A cult of the bull was widespread among other societies of the time, whether in Crete, in Greece or among the herdsmen of northern Europe. Ox-skulls have been found in British barrows, sometimes resting on the skeletons themselves. They have also been discovered at Stonehenge. Defending Inigo Jones's theories in 1655, John Webb remembered that 'the Sacrifices anciently offered at Stoneheng . . . were Bulls or Oxen, and several sorts of Beasts, as appears by the Heads of divers Kinds of them, not many Years since, there digged up.'

This refers to the 'excavations' of the Duke of Buckingham a few years before he was assassinated at Portsmouth. John Aubrey added that the Duke 'did cause the middle of Stonehenge to be digged; and there remains a kind of pitt or cavity still; it is about the bignesse of two sawe-pitts.' From it came 'Stagges-hornes, heads, and Bulls-hornes, and Charcoales'. In an interpolation which may refer either to a nearby barrow or to Stonehenge, he went on, 'There were also found Stagges-hornes a great many, Batter-dashers, heads of arrowes . . . bones rotten, but whether of Stagges or men they could not tell.' William Stukeley mentioned that Thomas Hayward, once the owner of Stonehenge, also 'found heads of oxen and other beasts bones, and nothing else.'

Heads of bulls, antlered deer-skulls, these may have been paraded here, or more probably deliberately buried by the stones as offerings in a temple that had been changed many times over the centuries. And today human cremated bone and animals' skulls still lie undisturbed there, although the skeleton has been taken from its grave facing the setting sun. Sunrise still casts long fingers of shadow across the stones of this temple and tomb. The carvings endure, inscrutable as death itself.

Lunacy, leys and legends

Folk-tales connecting girl dancers and stone circles are too many and too widespread in the British Isles to be accidental, and we may guess that dancing did take place inside the rings. Other legends of weddings and of the healing powers of the stones suggest memories of fertility rites and rituals of rebirth that the archaeological evidence also points to. In former times Stonehenge was sometimes called Chorea Gigantum, the Giants' Dance, and it was said that water poured over its stones would cure the sick. Such stories provide insights into otherwise forgotten meanings of the rings, and, used carefully, can be a useful means of learning more about our ancestors who left no written records of their beliefs. Folklore, however imperfect, preserves something of their world. It is quite different from what Leslie Grinsell has vigorously termed 'fake-lore', that hotch-potch of wishful thinking and, sometimes, of downright lies with which some writers today distort the past.

One quivers to read that Stonehenge is related to the Great Pyramid, the Somerset Zodiac and the island of Atlantis. This has nothing to do with archaeology or prehistory. If one reads such whimsy at all it should be with a chuckle and with uninterrupted disbelief.

Stone circles can be parachutes to paradises that never were. Among a collection of paperbacks about flying saucers, or gods from other worlds, or the occult, or ghostly Britain, or the romance of antiquity, many of the covers will have photographs of stone circles on them. Stonehenge appears most frequently, usually in dramatic silhouette, but Callanish and Brodgar too are popular, because their tall and thin stones also photograph well against the evening sky. Stone circles hint at mysteries beyond our understanding. So do many of these books.

It has been said, usually by themselves, that writers of escapist literature are entitled to their alternative interpretations because so few facts are known about the rings that almost any explanation can legitimately be offered for them. It is to be hoped that having got this far the reader will realize that this is untrue. A great deal is known about these prehistoric circles, and writers about them are as tied by the facts and by the ethics of scholarship as anyone else concerned with what has happened in the past. They should also weigh probability against improbability. Is it likely, for example, that priest-rulers from the Mediterranean had Stonehenge put up so that they could use it to predict eclipses to their own, awed people? 'Suppose they sent expeditions to England and Wales and Brittany to arrange for construction and observation. Then how did they keep in touch through the centuries? Were they capable of telepathy or teleportation, as Hindu sages were said to be? Probably no one will ever know.' (A. Landsburg, *In Search of Lost Civilisations*, pp. 109–10.)

One would think the architect of Stonehenge was more likely to be a Wessex chieftain than a flying fakir with a walletful of weather reports. But many writers believe that archaeology has provided too few answers too slowly for archaeological explanations to be acceptable. Of stone circles we are told: 'A few have received attention from archaeologists, most are little known outside their own region. To some people the rarely-visited circles appear to emanate powerful, almost tangible currents of energy.' (E. Pepper and J. Wilcock, *Magical and Mystical Sites*, p. 273.) The currents are probably rays of indignation from Aubrey, Borlase, Coles, Dymond, Keiller, Lewis, Lukis, Peter, Stukeley, Ward and other fieldworkers who tramped for miles to record the hundreds of rings in the British Isles.

But mystics believe the currents come from a power in the circle itself and can be detected by swinging a pendulum over the stones. 'There was some kind of force being extracted, and I couldn't tell whether it was coming out of me or out of the stone. Perhaps it was both . . . .' Mrs Smithett had a psychometric experience at the Rollright Stones as dusk came on. 'There is a definite change in the feeling of a stone circle after dusk. I don't like them after dark. The power seems quite different.' (F. Hitching, *Earth Magic*, p. 131.)

When Iris Campbell, another psychometrist (a person who divines the nature or spirit of an object by physical contact with it, or claims to be able to do so), visited the circle-henge of Mayburgh in 1944, she concluded: 'The site would seem to come in to a period approximately BC 15,000 . . . . One is very conscious of its period of decline and eventual break-up; what brought this about was due to a cleavage in the community that functioned here.' (J. and C. Bord, *Mysterious Britain*, p. 22.) As northern

Below A drawing by William Stukeley of the adjacent henges of Mayburgh and King Arthur's Round Table near Penrith, which he visited in 1725. From *Itinerarium Curiosum* II, published 1776.

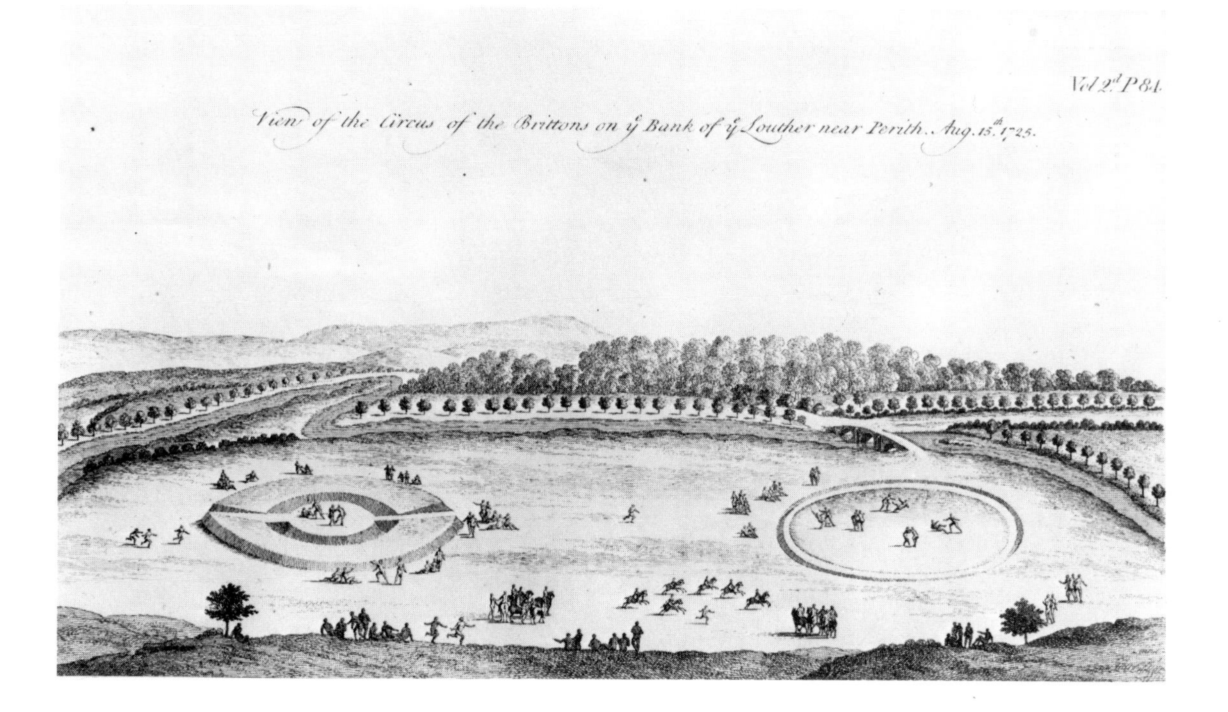

Britain was buried under the bitter snows of the Devensian Glaciation in 15,000 BC, with the countryside around Mayburgh covered in heavy layers of iron-hard ice, one can understand the decline in the community. It was too cold for a cleavage.

But if Iris Campbell was mistaken about the climate, it does not explain why other people have persisted in the von Däniken approach of making mysteries out of non-mysteries. John Wilcock wondered how the 'immense' circle of Callanish could have been constructed 'with nothing more than patience, rounded wooden staves and rawhide', and remembered: 'the legend of the priests of On who could raise huge stones by sound. Or the Chinese alchemist Liu An who was reputed to have discovered an anti-gravity liquid back in 200 BC. Or even the Buddhist jakatas which refer to a magical gem which can raise into the air any man who holds it in his mouth.' (J. Wilcock, *A Guide to Occult Britain*, p. 274.)

One would imagine from this that Callanish was composed of prodigious blocks, high as trees, thick as elephants. It is not. In this 'immense' ring, too small for table-tennis, the heaviest stone is the central pillar, tall it is true, but slender and tapering. It weighs less than six tons and could have been raised by fourteen adults with patience and rawhide without the benefits of On-gongs, levitating liquids and mouthfuls of rubies. What the rounded wooden staves were for is unclear.

They may have been for 'earth acupuncture'. Tom Graves, a dowser who once received a sensation like an electric shock when holding a pendulum over the destroyed Obelisk at Avebury, has described how stakes can be driven into the ground to heal the land and free it from its 'bad' energy. There is, apparently, no certainty as to whether these stakes should be left *in situ*. 'One dowser even said that the ground pushed out the stake when it was no longer needed. From my own practical work, it seems that both sides, as usual, are right. In one case at a stone circle, for example, I was "told" by my pendulum to remove some of the stakes after insertion, but to leave some of the others in place, pushed just below the surface. To my knowledge, they are still there now.' (T. Graves, *Needles of Stone*, p. 181.) It is to be hoped that no pots or bones were smashed, or charcoal contaminated by this vandalism.

The most lunatic of ideas about prehistoric monuments is that of ley-lines. These are fabrications of the twentieth century, invented by Alfred Watkins in the 1920s. He believed he could discern patterns of monuments reaching for miles across the countryside in precise, straight lines. To his undiscriminating eye it did not matter that the sites were unrelated to each other, some being for worship, some for warfare, others for herding cattle, nor that they were widely separated in time. A 'line' might consist of a prehistoric stone circle, a Roman temple, a Saxon church and a medieval castle. Having noticed that some of these 'alignments' passed by villages or farms with 'ley' in their names, he coined the term 'ley-line' and interpreted them as ancient trackways along which travellers and traders had passed.

There was a little sense in this because some pre-Roman sites were indeed built alongside tracks, although the trails themselves were anything but straight, following the natural meanders of hills, valleys and rivers. Watkins's leys, however, frequently shot across ravines or wallowed through the roughest falls of rivers, suggesting that prehistoric people were unbelievably stupid in their choice of routes. This problem has caused today's ley-liners to reinterpret the lines as a network of telepathic rays, of 'telluric' energy for the spiritual and physical re-energizing of the people. As one of their advocates remarked, 'This is extremely difficult to prove.'

In a spurious attempt to satisfy logic, the better ley-liners insist that on any acceptable line there should be at least four points within ten miles. The probability of finding four points is increased because all the following are admitted as valid markers: stone circles; standing stones; barrows and cairns, long and round; castles; mottes; moats; hill-forts; earthworks; churches; abbeys; droveways; crosses; ponds; other religious buildings; 'anything which is very old and traditionally sacred'.

Not surprisingly, archaeologists refuse to accept these fictitious and ludicrous lines. Ley-lines disprove themselves. From Stonehenge, in itself a compelling site to the ley-liner, a 'line' is supposed to extend six miles southwards to the earthwork of Old Sarum, then two miles further to Salisbury Cathedral, and three miles more to Clearbury Rings, a hill-fort of the Iron Age. The ley has been described as 'a remarkable alignment'. It is indeed. As a trackway it would have been a disaster, for within eleven miles it crossed four rivers, three times unnecessarily, slurped through a mile of primeval swamp and then waded across another river.

As a line it does not exist. Its south end misses Clearbury Rings by a full two hundred metres, even though Clearbury provided a wide target, and this must eliminate the hill-fort from the ley. Only three sites are left.

Stonehenge was built as an earthwork around 2800 BC and completed as a sarsen ring about 1500 BC, but Old Sarum was not begun for another thousand years, at a time when Stonehenge was falling into disuse. Over the following centuries of Roman dominance and Saxon invasion Old Sarum mouldered, its banks eroding beneath wind and rain. Then, with the Norman Conquest, a castle and an austere cathedral were built in its waterless interior, which soon became so congested with soldiers, clergy and civilians that there was continual bickering. So strong was the wind on the hilltop that the choir could not hear itself sing. Churchmen suffered agonizingly from rheumatism. A quarrel between Church and military caused the clergy to quit and build another cathedral elsewhere, thus producing the third point on the line.

As the shortest distance between Stonehenge and Old Sarum was necessarily a straight line, it was only with this third point that a ley-line could have been established, in Christian times, intentionally designed by a Christian bishop, Richard Poore. In 1220 the site for Salisbury Cathedral was chosen where three rivers met the Christchurch Avon on such marshy terrain that the church has since been known as the 'floating cathedral'.

That the chosen position for the end of the ley-line should be in the middle of a swamp might not matter to the really enthusiastic ley-liner. He would explain that the bishop had no choice because the position was already decided by the alignment between Stonehenge and Old Sarum.

If this is correct then it is strange that the site was not the first choice of Bishop Richard Poore. Originally he wanted the cathedral to be built on a drier site at Wilton, a good three miles west of the line. He only turned regretfully to the waters and reeds of Salisbury when the Abbess of Wilton refused him permission to build on her land. With more charity on her part the remarkable ley would have been dog-legged.

Statistically ley-lines are nonsense, and archaeologically they are appalling. As Kipling remarked,

There are nine and sixty ways of constructing tribal lays,
And – every – single – one – of – them – is – right.

When, therefore, we are told that from Arbor Low 'between 50 and 150 leys are said to emanate', we can dismiss this as one more example of the 'fake-lore' of which there is so much today. The people who put up the stone circles had no extraordinary or supernatural powers. They were men and women physically like us, with the same limitations of mind and body. Their beliefs were different because their lives were different. They had an acute and sensitive awareness of animals, plants, clouds and weather because these things were their intimacies, the framework of the world in which they lived. To protect their own frailties the people developed rituals to be elaborately acted out inside sacred rings. Nowadays, because two million nights have gone by, two hundred generations since the rings were built, what we know of these people and their rites must be thin and incomplete.

Yet stories that these circles were the remains of people turned into stone for dancing or playing on the Sabbath tell us not only the obvious truth that people used the rings but that probably it was a great number of people, not just a chosen few. There are no legends of petrified priests. Whether at the Hurlers where gamesters suffered or at the Rollright Stones where it was an army, the legends speak of a gathering of people. Very often these were girls punished for dancing, suggesting a memory of maidens and ceremonies of fertility.

A circle is a perfect dancing ground. Its spaciousness seems planned for that purpose, lines of people moving round and round to a background of rhythmic drumming and chanting whose patterns were determined by years of custom. It is useless to attempt a detailed reconstruction of anything as irrecoverable as this. The anthropologist Bernard Deacon described many of the dances he saw performed by the natives of the New Hebrides in the Pacific, some of whom were still erecting forms of stone circles in recent centuries. In one dance, the *Neleng*, the men decorated their heads with feathers, and five columns of body-painted dancers stood silently as two leaders began a slow approach, swinging their arms backwards and forwards to the accompaniment of 'a delightful chant'. They passed through the columns, circled them, and then circled the rows once more, this time imitating the flying of a hawk. Another man appeared on the dancing ground, pretending to aim a bow at them. Then all the men began dancing, slowly at first, but faster and faster until suddenly the archer flung out his arms and everyone fled.

Deacon made two comments. The first was that it appeared to 'be a sort of "play" in which birds and ghosts are the principal actors'. The other was about the women of the village.

> A circular fence is erected to one side of the dancing ground, enclosing an area in which the women stand during the *Neleng*. It is made as visibility-proof as possible, so that they cannot see through it. The reason given for this is that if the women were to see the dancers performing they would leave their husbands to follow these good-looking young men, being entranced by their splendid bodies.

It is dances of this type, designed as ceremonies to invoke the forces of nature, that we should visualize in the British stone circles, some of them performed at times of death and burial, others created to bring rain or ensure good weather. Of morality among these early societies we know almost nothing, although carvings on rocks in Scandinavia suggest that sexual attitudes were very different from our own, and that in some rites sexuality may have been an essential element. Slight hints of this may linger in the legends of weddings at Stanton Drew, or the Merry-Making of youths and girls at the Rollright Stones, or the betrothal of young couples at the Stones of Stenness in the Orkneys.

From Haltadans in Shetland to the Merry Maidens in Cornwall and to Athgreany in Ireland with its Pipers Stones, the legends of dancing and young girls in the rings are so many it would be foolish to ignore them. So would it be to overlook the constant association of the stones with water.

Many of the early circles were built by rivers or lakes. This may have been to provide easy access to the rings, but it may equally have been because water, the source of life, was necessary to some of the rites. Stonehenge's avenue led to, or from, the Avon. The avenues at Stanton Drew also were linked with a river. Stones at Rollright and Stenness were reported to go down to water at night, and water at Stonehenge, as the reader will remember, was believed to cure illness. Many of these legends also relate to children.

The past in the present

Dancing, water, children, healing, the stones, we are unable to put these into a complete and certain order today.

The sun may brighten this twilight. There are legends that the stones move when the sun has set, or turn round at dawn, and evidence is preserved in the stones themselves of orientations towards the sun or moon. Whether looking towards its rising over the Heel Stone or its setting at Long Meg, we can be sure that the movements of the sun were important to the circle-builders of western Britain. In the north-east it was the moon that people looked to. At the circle of Cothiemuir Wood the full moon at midsummer lifted a little above the horizon, then curved down towards the recumbent stone, shining beyond it on to the cist at the centre of the ring. The cist is ruined. Only the ponderous capstone remains, dragged out of place. Under it the pit is empty.

Stones like these, grass drooping over their edges, half-hidden between the tall standing stones, may tell us more about the people who used these rings than the circle-stones themselves. Where there has been a complete excavation very often charcoal has been found around these little grave-pits, and places where fires burned. Inside the cists or in hollows the bodies or burnt bones of children have been discovered, the young girl under the eastern stone of the Sanctuary, the cremation at Monzie by the north stone, the skull fragments at Loanhead of Daviot. At Castle Mahon the fiercely burnt ashes of a child lay near the pyre that had consumed it. Cremations of children were buried out of sight at the centre of the Druids' Circle. The split-open skull of the child at the heart of Woodhenge is as savage as the others.

Offering or sacrifice or both is perhaps not important. What matters is that these bones, little and pathetic, have been found in many rings linked by life and death to the sun or the moon. They had been dedicated by people who summoned ghosts of ancestors to the circles by rites of magical symbolism. To these spirits life was given so that life might be sustained, season by season, death by death, through the brief generations of that far-departed age.

It has always to be remembered that these things were not sterile and alone but were born of the environment in which the people lived, in a world where there were more fears than comforts. Even we are not immune from 'irrationalities'. When we touch wood or half-jokingly rebuke someone who says that it is bound to be a lovely day, we reveal our own persisting fear that there are forces that can be offended and provoked by our arrogance. If in the securities of our urban civilization we still perform little acts of avoidance or propitiation, it is even more understandable that prehistoric people should have held so desperately to their rituals of religion. Terrifying seas surged around them. The processions, the water, the sun, the moon, burials, children, the sacred enclosure, all these ensured some safety in the eddies of their existence.

In their lifetimes the people revered their ancestors, went to the circles where the powerful bones lay. Now they too are dead and it is we, descended from them, who visit the rings, seeking our own ancestors. We shall never see them, the painted bodies in the sunlight, darker figures against the moon, the dancers, the images of death. Yet the symbols and the dreads are constant through the centuries. The knowledge is the same. Youth is short and life must end. Death is always there.

Dancing girl of Syria, her hair caught up with a fillet:
Very subtle in swaying those quivering flanks of hers
In time to the castanet's rattle: half-drunk in the smoky tavern
She dances, lascivious, wanton, clashing the rhythm.

– Here's Death twitching my ear. 'Live', says he, 'for I'm coming.'
(Appendix Vergiliana, *Copa Surisca.*)

Below Ardblair, near Blairgowrie, in Perthshire. Here, the dust of the dead and modern petrol fumes are commingled.

Visiting the circles

For anyone wishing to see a stone circle the choice is a wide one and easily made, because rings in good condition exist in all the highland regions of the British Isles wherever prehistoric man could farm. The reader is warned, however, that Ordnance Survey maps are indispensable for locating the sites. Not only do they give clear indications of where megalithic rings are and which roads lead to them, but they are also helpfully selective. Only about one-third of the sites are shown and these, for most people, are the best. Many of the stone circles still stand. Others have been destroyed, however. Strichen in Aberdeenshire was demolished in 1965 and the stones lie tumbled in the thick pasture grass of a field in which there is nothing to recognize as a circle. At other despoiled rings sometimes just one stone remains for cattle to rub against. Ruins like this are disappointing to visit, particularly if they are far from the road.

For a double safeguard the reader should refer to the guide-books in the reading list. The descriptions in them explain exactly what exists today and what has been found from excavation. Many of them also indicate whether the site is owned by the State or is in the care of the National Trust. The majority of our ancient monuments are still on private property, and permission to go to them must be obtained from the landowner, who frequently lives conveniently at a nearby farm. I have met with nothing but courtesy from farmers on whose land circles lie, a helpfulness mixed with curiosity about their strange stones, although it is a politeness that would soon vanish if gates were left open or crops trampled through. It may be frustrating to be forced to stare across a wheat field at an inaccessible ring, but it is better merely to stare than to crash through someone else's livelihood.

It is pleasantly surprising to find that many of the famous stone circles require only a short walk, this probably being the reason why they are so well known. In Cornwall the Merry Maidens, with a well-defined eastern entrance, is in a field right against the road. So are the Rollright Stones in Oxfordshire, the circle on one side of the lane, its distorted outlying stone on the other, the pillars of an old burial-place a wide field away in the distance. Even the spectacular Callanish, seemingly remote and unreachable in the Outer Hebrides, is a mere path's length from the road.

Of all the rings maybe the simplest of all to visit, though somewhat hazardous, is Ardblair near Blairgowrie in Perthshire. The road runs straight between the stones and continues straight for half a mile in either direction so that any attempt to plan the circle is akin to measuring the starting-grid during a Grand Prix race. About 1856 the road was widened and the stones, several of them fallen, were set upright in beds of concrete. Today this typical six-stone ring of central Scotland with its massive south-west block can be seen without even leaving the car, so that, in the evocative words of Fred Coles, who surveyed so many Scottish circles seventy years ago, 'the very dust of human interments of three thousand years ago is, in these days, almost commingled with the road metal dust raised by motors and other means of twentieth century locomotion.'

There are many rings in Britain that are as easy of access as these, and their quietness more than compensates for the ropes and railings around Stonehenge and Avebury, where millions of tourist feet have worn hollows into the central areas and the banks.

Even more rewarding to the resolute are the rings that lie miles out into the moors, where only the slow, mournful piping of a curlew is louder than the wind brushing through the grass and heather. Threestone Burn at Ilderton, far out on a hill-slope in the Cheviots; or Borrowston Rigg, far from the road across the swirling Earnscleugh Water and up the precipitous edge of Dabshead Hill, its low stones set in a vast egg-shaped ring obscure in the stillness of the landscape; these rings, and the wreckage of the Machrie Moor stones on Arran or the Druids' Circle alongside a deserted trackway on a headland high above Conway Bay, these are the circles that most of all have kept something of their prehistoric past, if only because there is nothing modern to divert the mind from their austerity.

Maps and compass and weatherproof clothing are essential. I have been soaked just going to the stones at Lundin Links, on a golf-course, and I have been lost in a sudden mist of cloud that came down on Whiteholm Rigg so that even although only a couple of hundred metres from the car I could see nothing more than a hand's length from me and had to compel my mind to trust my compass.

Maps, moreover, should be up to date. Once, in 1968, I walked three miles, and a thoroughly unpleasant walk through reeds and across the De Lank river and through a settlement of horse-flies, across Bodmin Moor from the Trippet Stones to Stannon, only to find that my 1946 one-inch map did not show the 1950 road that led to a quarry next to the circle.

Even maps cannot help the unobservant. Field-walking and planning with students in south-west Scotland, I took them in search of the little ring at Drannandow, a few miles north of Newton Stewart. After a good stroll across the gentle countryside, we came to the crest of a slight hill near to where the ring should have been. I took careful bearings on a ruined cottage, a hilltop, took back-bearings on the route we had followed, but could see the circle nowhere. It was one of the kinder girls who pointed out that we were actually standing in the middle of it.

Every circle is unique. Sometimes they are concealed in trees or in bushes, hard to see, more difficult to plan. Sometimes one can reach them only to be frustrated by the unclimbable wall of a deer park, as we were at Kiltierney in Ireland. Occasionally there are distractions of a safari of hens clucking between the stones, or a herd of inquisitive cows – or a bull – or the landscape itself, like the brooding, grey-clouded mountains of the Preselis that dominate the Gors Fawr ring in south-west Wales. I once encountered a mouldering fleece, rigid and immovable, draped over one of the pillars of Ninestone Rigg and found it almost impossible to concentrate on measurements with the lank, unwashed hairs twitching in the breeze near my head.

Yet Guidebest in a tree-shaded hollow by the Latheronwheel river far to the north in Scotland, or Altarnun where wild ponies graze on a Cornish moor, these are rings whose very loneliness gives pleasure. Even the mile of scratching gorse that separates Boscawen-Un from the road is unimportant when one sees the beauty of this circle with its monumental centre stone and its lichen-mottled granite pillars. This is true also of Cauldside Burn. The walk is long, there is a reedy swamp to be avoided, there is a steep hillside, but then there is the circle, half-swallowed in the rising peat, there is a cairn alongside it with an opened cist near its top where the burnt bones of some Bronze Age person once rested, and beyond, towards the hillside, there is a standing stone, a circular ring-cairn, its central space where bodies were lain overgrown and desolate, and beyond that, inconspicuous among the wilderness of natural boulders, one of the finest decorated stones in prehistoric Scotland, a perfect spiral carved on its flat surface. This combination of magical art, burial-place and stone circle leads the mind into congenial and perhaps unprofitable conjectures about the associations between these monuments, how old they were, whether of the same period, what their uses were, where the people lived who had built them.

Fifty sites to visit

In this selective gazetteer the name of the stone circle and its grid reference are followed by simple directions for finding the ring. In brackets after this are given the shape of the ring and its diameter, or diameters if it is not circular, in metres.

In the plans standing stones appear as black areas, and fallen stones as outlines; stippling indicates an earthwork. In every case the top of the page represents due north.

Below Carles, Castlerigg.

THE SCOTTISH ISLANDS

THE RING OF BRODGAR *Orkney Mainland*
CALLANISH *Lewis Outer Hebrides*
CNOC FILLIBHIR *Lewis Outer Hebrides*
GARYNAHINE *Lewis Outer Hebrides*
STENNESS *Orkney Mainland*

Although both are remote from the great areas of population in prehistoric Britain, the islands of the Outer Hebrides and the Orkneys are each quite different in terms of their megalithic monuments. On Orkney Mainland and the islands to its north there are many chambered tombs, built more than five thousand years ago by Neolithic farmers, some from the Scottish mainland, some from Ireland, who buried scores of bodies in these passage-graves. Undoubtedly in early prehistoric times there were many people living in these distant but attractive lands. And this large population explains why there are also two great circle-henges here, the Ring of Brodgar and the Stones of Stenness, two adjacent banked rings big enough to accommodate large assemblies of people as they participated in their communal ceremonies.

In the Hebrides only the western coasts with their fertile sandy soils tempted man to settle. There are few chambered tombs on the island of Harris and Lewis and perhaps no more than half a dozen small stone circles. Were it not for the sudden marvel of the monuments around Loch Roag on Lewis – ellipses, flattened circles, concentric rings and avenues – few seekers of megalithic rings would ever visit here. But the stone circles at Callanish, Cnoc Fillibhir and Garynahine are as siren-like as those at Brodgar and Stenness. They are certainly different but their call is as sweet – and as irresistible.

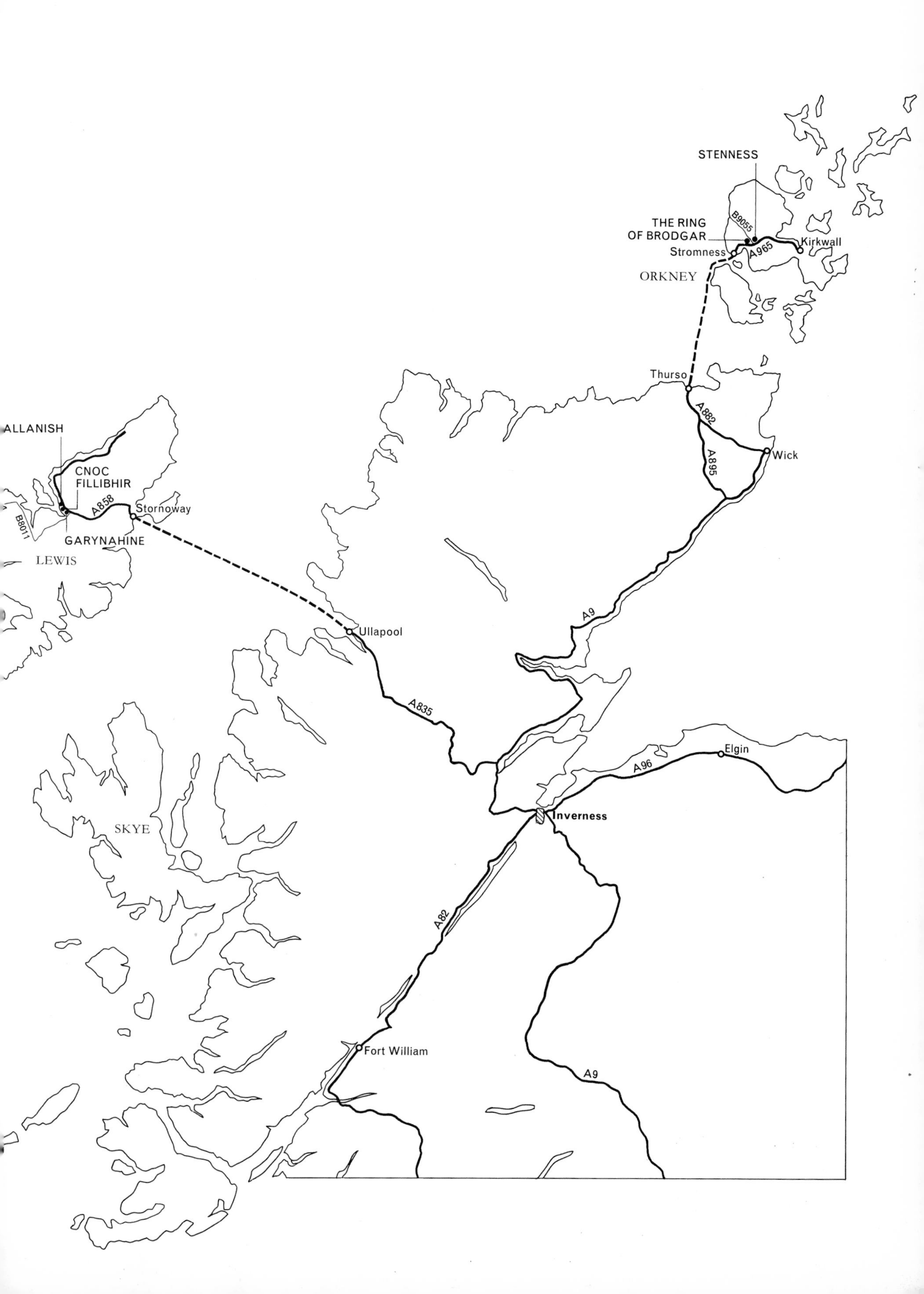

STENNESS
THE RING
OF BRODGAR
B9055
Stromness
A965
Kirkwall
ORKNEY
Thurso
A882
Wick
A895
ALLANISH
CNOC
FILLIBHIR
A858
Stornoway
B8011
GARYNAHINE
LEWIS
A9
Ullapool
A835
Elgin
A96
Inverness
SKYE
A82
Fort William
A9

The Ring of Brodgar

Orkney Mainland: HY 294133. **10 miles W of Kirkwall, 4 miles NNE of Stromness, to W of the B9055. In State care. Signposted. (Circular, 103.6 metres.)**

This gigantic circle-henge, its slender columns rising blackly on a neck of land between the lochs of Stenness and Harray, is one of the most beautiful stone circles in Great Britain. Although it has been partly demolished, the height of the stones and the graceful western arc of the circle give a vivid impression of the original strength and authority of this ring.

Its site was on an east-facing slope, perhaps because no level area could be found for one of the biggest rings in the British Isles. A vast circular ditch was battered and hacked out of the sandstone bedrock, a ditch wider than a street and deeper than a vault, the smashed bits of rock being heaped into an outer bank that today has disappeared. We do not know how

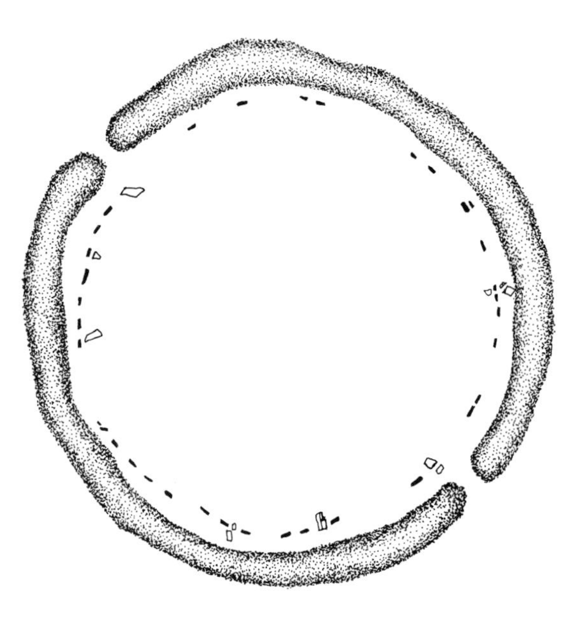

Opposite The Ring of Brodgar.
Below Brodgar from the south. There is a causeway across the rock-cut ditch on the right.

many people were involved in this fanatical quarrying, but Renfrew has calculated that at least eighty thousand man-hours of work were demanded by it, three months continuous digging for a hundred labourers.

Two causeways were left across the ditch at north-west and south-east, and across them some sixty long, thin slabs were dragged and put up in a perfect circle around the central area. Hardly a mile to the north is a quarry by Bookan farm and it may be from that vicinity that the stones came. The local flagstone splits naturally into elegant and tapering planks of stone ideal for the columns of a stone circle. Thom has pointed out that the ring was laid out on an almost exact north-south axis, not uncommon among these great open rings.

There is no known date for Brodgar, although rough stone axes and deliberately broken shaft-hole battle-axes of the Early Bronze Age have been found in its neighbourhood. If the adjacent circle-henge of Stenness is earlier than Brodgar then the latter may have been built around 2500 BC, when the population on Orkney was increasing.

On a low platform 150 metres to the east-south-east, is a pillar, the Comet Stone. Any astronomical significance it may have had remains unclear.

Opposite The Comet Stone outside Brodgar.
Below Prison bars for the spirits of the dead.
Over A frost-split slab at the end of one stone arc of the Ring of Brodgar.

Callanish

Lewis, Outer Hebrides: NB 213330. 13 miles W of Stornoway on a minor road S of Callanish village. In State care. Signposted. (Flattened circle, 13.1 × 11.3 metres.)

With some justification the Standing Stones of Callanish has been called the Stonehenge of the North. The dramatic design of its tall pillars and rows and avenues has exercised the imaginations of antiquarians ever since the circle was first mentioned by John Morison three hundred years ago:

> In severall places there are great stones standing up straight in ranks, some two or three foot thick and 10, 12 and 15 foot high; It is left by traditione that these were a sort of men converted into stones by ane Inchanter . . . it cannot but be admired how they could be caried there.

The site is also known as Tursachen, the place of mourning or of pilgrimage. Until well into the nineteenth century couples would go to the stones to make their marital vows.

It can be assumed that Callanish belongs to the Bronze Age. On North Uist to the south there are many Neolithic chambered tombs, built not on the sandy soils near the coast but on the uplands that provided good grazing. There are few of these passage-graves on Harris or Lewis and even these few are concentrated in the hills of the east. There must

have been extensive forest on the western lowlands. At Northton, only thirty miles south of Callanish, a Neolithic community around 3300 BC had to clear away trees before they could establish a settlement. When this was abandoned a thousand years later as the sea-level rose, the woodlands regenerated. Callanish, so near the coast, must have been erected at a time when the climate was mild and when crops and cattle could be raised on the rich open soils of the machair.

Bronze Age people, probably no more than a score or so altogether, hauled long slabs to the sloping ridge that had been chosen for Callanish. All were of the easily split Lewissean gneiss

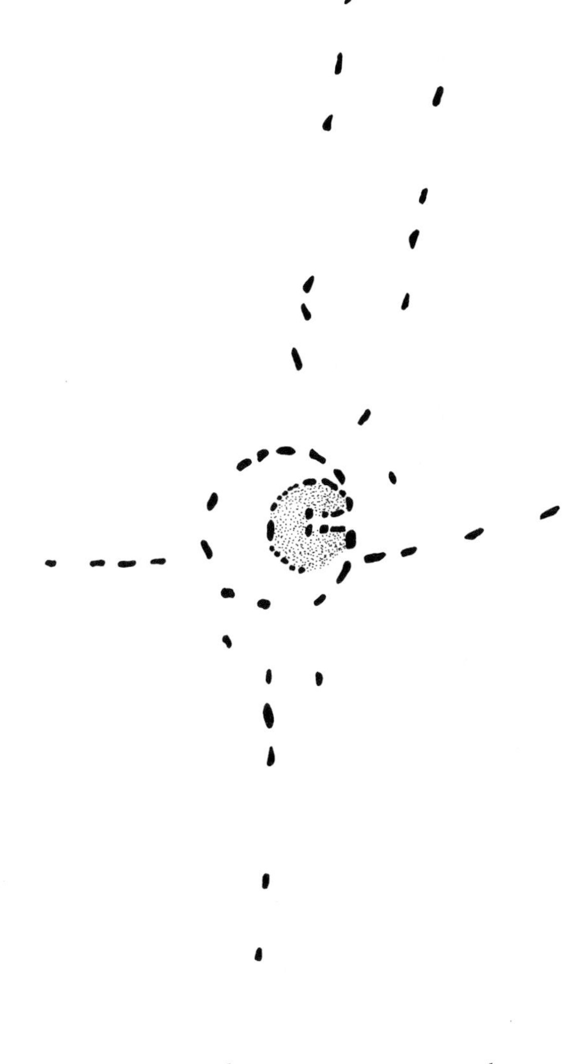

'You are not wood, you are not stones, but men.' William Shakespeare.

that was plentiful here, and the tallest was erected at what was to be the centre of the circle. Around it thirteen pillars, almost as tall, were set up and a low stony bank was heaped round their bases. From the ring extended lines of pillars. A double row or avenue stretched downhill north-north-eastwards towards a tiny bay. There were three single rows, one pointing directly westwards towards a nearby sharp fall in the ground, another east-north-eastwards, and a third going to the south where the ground rose to a sudden rocky outcrop that obscured the skyline behind it.

It is an impressive complex that becomes more understandable if the project is regarded as uncompleted. It is probable that the circle was meant to be concentric with four avenues leading to it from east, north, south and west, much as the despoiled Broomend of Crichie in Aberdeenshire (NJ 779196) had avenues on either side of it. Whatever the explanation, the work was interrupted.

Squashed inside the ring is a minute chambered tomb, its roof gone, its eastward passage robbed of its roof, its side-slabbed chamber open to the sky. As later peat accumulated it absorbed the tomb and the bottoms of the stones and only a hump-like dome showed where the grave lay. But it is clear that this little mound was deliberately built inside the ring by people of another cult who had taken over the site. They may have been the intrusive group who interrupted the work. We know little about them. An excavation in 1857 found only fragments of bone in a 'black unctuous matter' in the tomb, probably a mixture of peat and animal remains and charcoal. Callanish keeps its secrets.

The tallest stone was raised at the centre of the circle.

Above Callanish. The stones straggle proudly along their ridge, stark against the western sky. *Opposite* The eastern line of pillars.

Over The Standing Stones of Callanish. 'It cannot but be admired how they could be caried there.' John Morison.

Opposite Beside Loch Roag, the stone circle of Cnoc Fillibhir, seen from the west.

Above The northern avenue at Callanish, with the west row to the right.

Cnoc Fillibhir

Lewis, Outer Hebrides: NB 225325. **12½ miles W of Stornoway, 1 mile SE of Callanish village. A short walk W of the A858. (Outer ring, elliptical, 17.4 × 14.1 metres; inner ring, elliptical, about 9.6 × 6.6 metres.)**

Closely grouped around the inner shores of Loch Roag, one of the few good bays on the western coast of Lewis, are several stone circles, as well as standing stones and the remnants of other indefinite structures. Not only do the great stones of Callanish itself rise here, high and clear on their ridge, but there are less well-known rings whose varied architecture testifies to the medley of beliefs that must have prevailed in this small fertile area. Cnoc Fillibhir is one of these circles.

It was built on a low ridge from which Callanish is visible to the north-west, and like Callanish it was built of slim pillars of gneiss that now lean outwards, their coarse surfaces whitened by countless storms and blizzards. There are two concentric rings here, the outer perhaps of thirteen stones like Callanish, although only eight now stand, and an inner ellipse where four stones survive of an original eight. The stones are firmly held in packings of small boulders, the pillars of the inner ring being somewhat taller than those of the outer, as is customary in concentric rings. The presence of such a double circle of thirteen stones so close to Callanish lends support to the idea that people intended to construct a

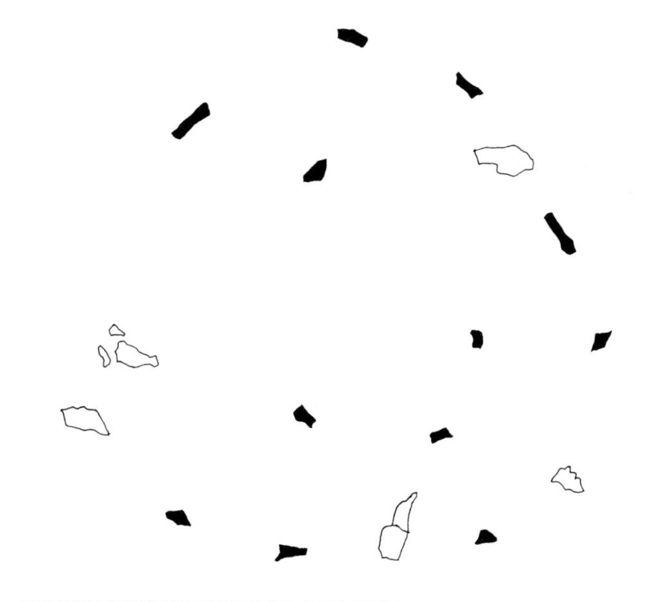

concentric circle at Callanish also but that the project was never completed.

Less than a quarter of a mile west of Cnoc Fillibhir and down near the coast are the attractive stones of the Loch Roag circle (NB 222325), a plain ring on a low ridge. It is an ellipse 21.6 × 18.2 metres in size, by far the biggest ring in the district. Placed as it was on a broad tract of fertile land it may also have been the earliest.

Below left Looking east, three stones of the inner ring framed between the foreground pillars.
Below right The south-west stones, pillars of gneiss formed millions of years ago.

Garynahine

Lewis, Outer Hebrides: NB 230303. **12 miles W of Stornoway, 2 miles SSE of Callanish village, to W of the B8011. (Elliptical, 12.9 × 9.2 metres.)**

The stones of this small but imposing ring are outlined conspicuously on a ridge above the peat-cuttings that border the road to its east. From the circle the pillars of Callanish can be seen two miles away to the north. All the rings are inter-visible here, although whether this was true in what may have been a wooded prehistoric landscape is uncertain.

Garynahine is a plain ring of broad and scarred slabs of gneiss. None of its stones weighs more than about two tons, light enough to have been dragged here and erected by the ten young adults of a twenty-strong family, and it was probably for such a group that the ring was intended, a shrine and temple at the edge of their territory. The other rings here – Callanish, Cnoc Fillibhir and Loch Roag – are hardly bigger, and the entire Bronze Age population of the district may have been no more than a hundred people.

Near the centre of Garynahine is a diminutive stone. Around it people had made 'a rather dilapidated cairn' which has been dug into without known result.

The ellipses, flattened circles, concentric rings, avenues and centre stones of the rings

around Loch Roag are astonishing in their variety. The only comparable region is the Lake District, with complexes such as Lacra (SD 151812) and Moor Divock (NY 490227). These little Bronze Age rings belong to the same period as the Loch Roag circles, as does the concentration of rings with centre stones in south-west Scotland (see Glenquickan). It is possible that people travelled northwards along the Atlantic seaways in search of land, finding it on the quiet shores of the Hebrides where the differences in their ritual architecture were finally melded within the baroque design of Callanish.

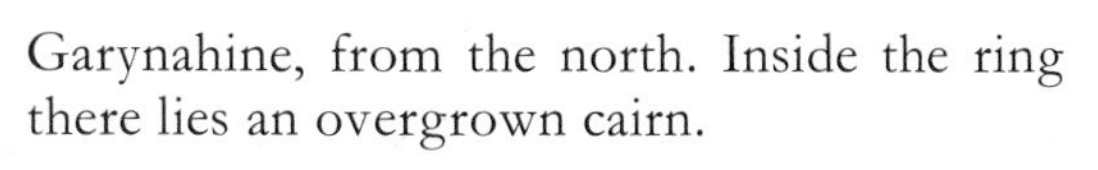

Garynahine, from the north. Inside the ring there lies an overgrown cairn.

Stenness

Orkney Mainland: HY 306125. **9 miles W of Kirkwall, 4 miles NE of Stromness on the B9055. In State care. Signposted. (Circular, 31.1 metres.)**

A mile south-east of the Ring of Brodgar across a narrow isthmus between the lochs of Harray and Stenness are the remains of the circle-henge known as the Standing Stones of Stenness. Ruined, many of its stones removed, its bank weathered and its ditch half-filled with earth, this ring still gives a sense of prehistory.

This is partly because of the magnificent monuments around it. Hardly half a mile east is Maes Howe, without doubt one of the finest passage-graves in Europe with its superb corbelled roof, its side-cells and its later Viking runes. Its long, bent passage admits the direct light of the sun only at the midwinter setting. A mile and a half to the west is Unstan chambered tomb where the bones of Neolithic people were discovered. Six miles away is Wideford, another passage-grave perched on a hill, and rather nearer is Cuween. Inside were the skulls of five human beings and twenty-four dogs. It was people related to these tomb-builders who erected the tall stones of Stenness.

Stenness was a place of assembly. Standing as it does at the spot where the land contracts between the lochs, it may have been constructed at the very edge of a territory as a sanctuary where both natives and strangers could meet in safety for trade and ritual. Such a function would explain the presence of the Watch Stone, a towering monolith nearly six metres high standing to the north-west of the ring where the isthmus begins, as if telling travellers that this land had been claimed.

The building of the circle-henge was demanding. Tons of solid rock were hacked out to make the ditch, and with the use only of

antler picks, stones and a few wooden levers this must have taken months to accomplish. It has been calculated that had fifty people laboured here day-long it would have taken them six months to make the ditch and bank alone. Then twelve long sandstone slabs had to be manhandled on sledges – if there were wood enough for such luxuries – across the mossy, weedy landscape of drab grasses from their quarry and across the single entrance at the north-west, to be put up in a perfect circle on the central plateau.

We know when this work was done. Two radio-carbon 'dates' averaged about 2960 BC, late in the Neolithic but when many of the chambered tombs were still in use and when people were living in the famous village of Skara Brae only six miles away. It may have been such communities with their grooved ware pottery who were the celebrants at

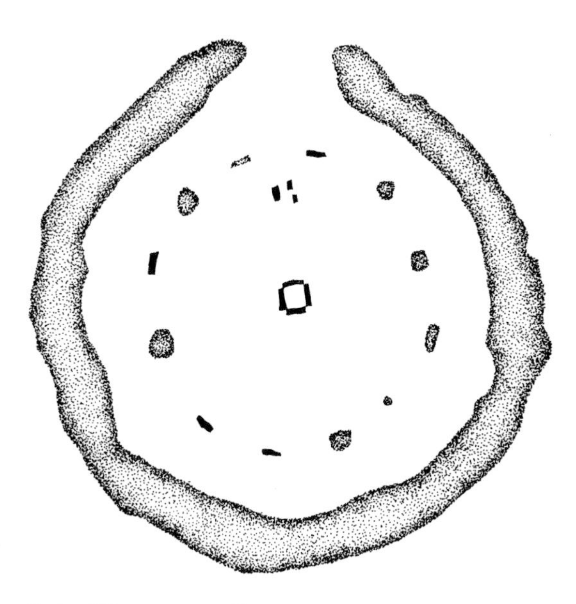

Below The two smaller stones may be remains of a Cove like that at Cairnpapple.

Stenness, for a grooved ware bowl was found in the ditch near the entrance here.

Just inside this entrance the remains of a little mortuary house of timber were discovered. From it a cobbled path led to a rectangular 'hearth' lined with slabs, very like the setting inside Balbirnie, Fife. In it seaweed had burnt. Beyond it were pits filled with rich earth mixed with seeds of fruit and grain. One might guess at rites of homeopathic magic, the deposits of food representing the harvests needed by the people and communicated to the forces of the Other World through the spirits of the dead whose bodies had lain inside the wooden charnel-house.

Once a perforated stone slab stood just to the north of Stenness. This Stone of Odin as it was called was destroyed in 1814, but it had stood above the height of a man on a little rise in front of the loch of Harray. Its head-sized perforation was about half-way up the stone and courting couples would make their vows by holding hands through it. Legends of fertility were attached to this pillar as to holed stones elsewhere in the British Isles.

Opposite Two circle stones and, behind them, the loch of Stenness. The ring may have been built as a sanctuary for both ritual and trade.
Below Looking north-east from the Standing Stones across the loch towards the Ring of Brodgar, a mile away.

Opposite Garynahine. The small ring was probably erected by a single family group.

Above Stenness. These Orcadian sandstone flags may have been quarried from the ditch itself.

NORTH-EASTERN SCOTLAND

BALQUHAIN *Aberdeenshire (Grampian)*
BERRYBRAE *Aberdeenshire (Grampian)*
CLAVA CAIRNS *Inverness-shire (Highland)*
CORRIMONY *Inverness-shire (Highland)*
CULLERLIE *Aberdeenshire (Grampian)*
LOANHEAD OF DAVIOT *Aberdeenshire (Grampian)*
OLD KEIG *Aberdeenshire (Grampian)*
SUNHONEY *Aberdeenshire (Grampian)*

There is probably a denser concentration of stone circles in this region than anywhere else in the British Isles, one splendid cluster to be found at the head of Loch Ness, the other more numerous group in the foothills between the mountains and the coasts of the north-east. Although separated by seventy miles or more of prehistoric forests, the rings in the two areas must have been related and of all the British stone circles they are the most informative about the beliefs of their builders.

Around Inverness on the sandy soils of the valleys are the Clava cairns, a mixture of chambered passage-graves and ring-cairns, both with circles graded in height towards the south-west around them. Cupmarks and quartz accompanied the burials in these monuments.

Far to the east in the foothills of the Grampians are the famous recumbent stone circles of Aberdeenshire and Kincardine, their stones also graded in height, and also surrounding ring-cairns in which cremated bones were placed. Like the Clava cairns these rings have cupmarks and quartz, but they also have the anomaly of the recumbent stone between their two tallest pillars, an architectural feature seemingly derived from Irish traditions.

Here, too, are much smaller and plainer rings, sometimes late Four-Posters, sometimes diminutive ovals, sometimes striking rings of standing stones with a huddle of cairns at the centre. Circles like Cullerlie survive as memorials of megalithic building that continued well into the Bronze Age, the diminished versions of the recumbent stone circles of earlier centuries.

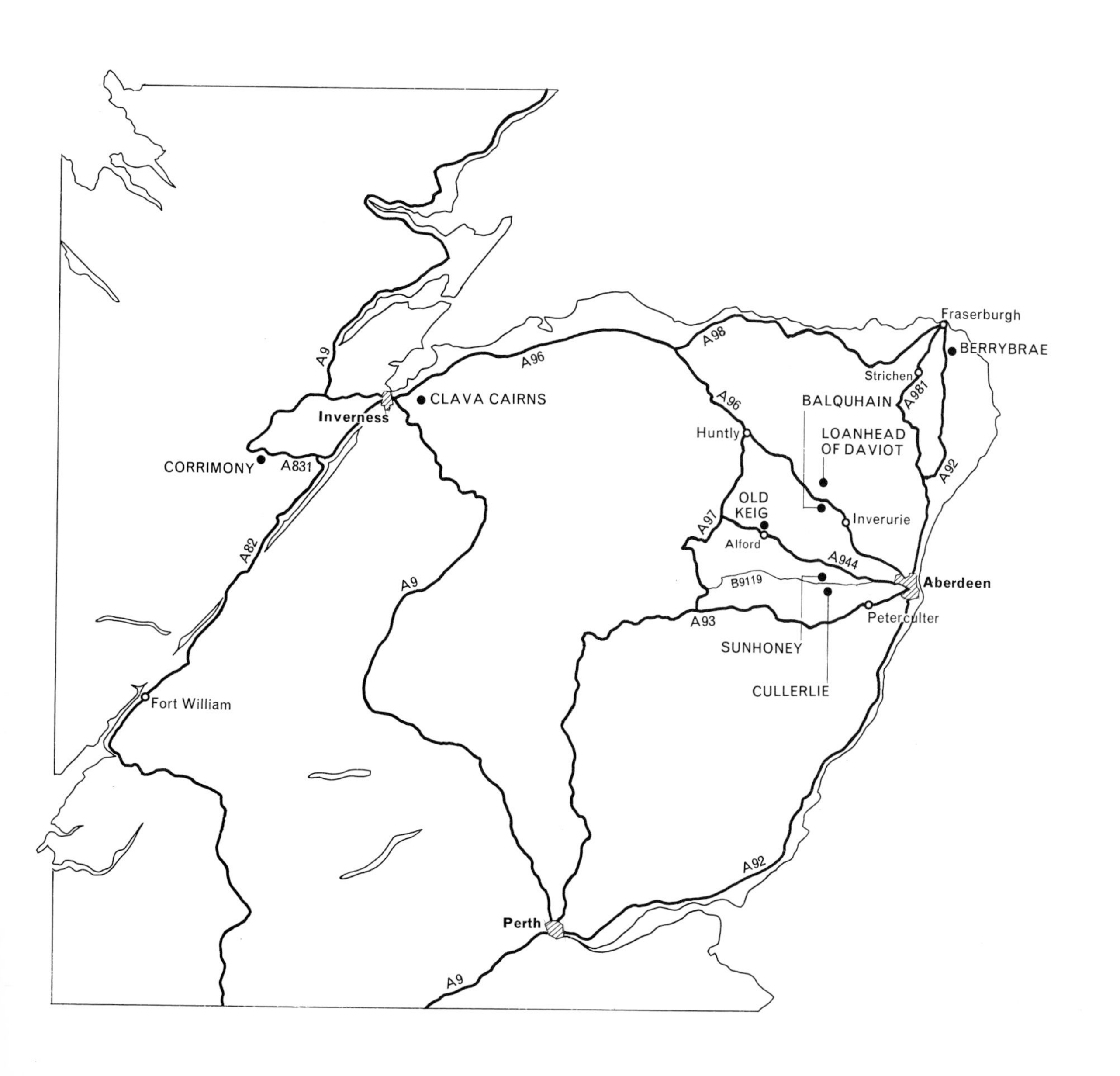
Fraserburgh
BERRYBRAE
Strichen
A98
A96
A981
BALQUHAIN
CLAVA CAIRNS
Inverness
Huntly
LOANHEAD
OF DAVIOT
A9
CORRIMONY
A831
A92
OLD
KEIG
Inverurie
A97
Alford
A82
A944
A9
B9119
Aberdeen
A93
Peterculter
SUNHONEY
CULLERLIE
Fort William
A92
Perth
A9

Balquhain

Aberdeenshire (Grampian): NJ 735241. **3 miles NW of Inverurie, on S side of a gentle hill midway between the old Balquhain castle and Inveramsay. A ¼ mile walk uphill through fields from the A96. On private land. (Circular, about 20.4 metres.)**

The situation of this ruined but charming ring at the edge of a hill-terrace is typical of recumbent stone circles. Once Balquhain had ten standing stones, but two have now fallen and four of the smallest at the north have been removed. The recumbent lies at the south-south-west of the ring, supported by a thick block beneath it upon which it was levered into a horizontal position. Its west flanker still stands but the eastern one has fallen outwards towards the tallest of all the stones, the outlier, a shapely pillar of white quartz which must have stood brilliantly at the edge of the terrace, perhaps as a territorial marker.

The three remaining standing stones of the ring decline from the flankers. A limited excavation in 1900 discovered 'a rough pavement of boulders' deep under the turf with some large, rugged stones outside them, probably the remains of a ring-cairn which may survive relatively undamaged despite the ploughing of the site.

There are several cupmarked stones, as always concentrated in the vicinity of the recumbent. The tumbled east flanker has four carvings on its upper surface in a little group.

The recumbent may have a cupmark on its top but this could be no more than a hole drilled for gunpowder in the nineteenth century. It is the stone next to the west flanker that is richest. On its outer face there are at least twenty-five cupmarks, a diffused spread of them near its tip and a tight horizontal line of six near its base, with another line extending vertically from them. All attempts to 'decipher' them, if indeed they have any recoverable message, have so far failed entirely.

Opposite Balquhain. The recumbent stone leans inwards behind its fallen east flanker.
Below The west stone. Its cupmarks have been interpreted as symbols of the moon.

Above Balquhain, '. . . a dismal cirque of Druid stones, upon a forlorn moor'. John Keats.

Opposite The quartz outlier, now ravaged by ice and creeping lichen.

Berrybrae

Aberdeenshire (Grampian): NK 028572. **6 miles SSE of Fraserburgh, 5 miles ENE of Strichen, on a minor road near Newark farm. (Elliptical, 13.0 × 10.7 metres.)**

This reconstructed recumbent stone circle stands in a field at the corner of two country lanes, its stones shaded by a ring of trees planted around it in the last century inside a little wall. From it the sea is visible and within a few miles are two other well-preserved rings, Aikey Brae (NJ 959471) on the private Parkhouse Hill, and Loudon Wood (NJ 962497) on boggy Forestry Commission property.

This region had fertile patches of soil and the rings were erected near them. Berrybrae was put on a slight rise and its site was levelled by the digging out of a wide platform before the stones, all local and granitic, were hauled to the ring. The effect of this levelling can still be seen at the south where the natural slope falls away sharply.

The remains of the ring-cairn with its three cremations have been covered over. Around 1750 BC Food-Vessel people came here and vandalized the little ring. They smashed the tops of the smaller stones whose stumps now poke unevenly from the drystone wall that stutters from stone to stone around the ring in the continuous barrier that these people preferred. The stones for the wall came from the despoiled ring-cairn that was almost completely removed.

In the inner face of this wall at the north-west the people deposited a neat pile of freshly broken urn sherds, and at the west by the recently re-erected pillar they laid a beaker under a plank of wood. It was a rite very similar to that enacted at Balbirnie in Fife. It was the

charcoal from this piece of timber that provided the two radio-carbon dates of 1500 ± 80 bc and 1360 ± 90 bc, averaging 1430 bc or about 1750 BC.

How long the circle had been standing before this interference is uncertain, but it was probably a rather late recumbent stone circle. Unlike the majority of these rings the Berrybrae recumbent was not aligned on the maximum but the minimum midsummer full moon, being placed at 232° from the north. Both Loudon Wood (192°) and Aikey Brae (184°) are much closer to the south.

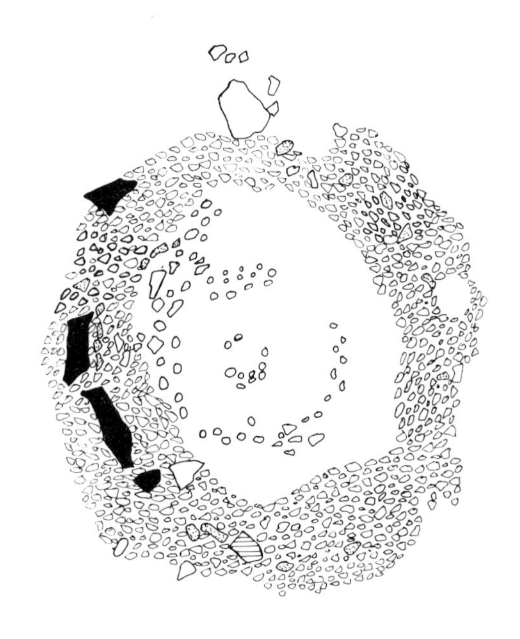

Opposite From the north, 1975. The upright ranging-poles show the positions of the missing stones. Note the fallen stone in the right foreground. *Below* From the east, 1976. The fallen stone, re-erected, stands on the right.

Clava Cairns

Inverness-shire (Highland): NH 757444. 5½ miles E of Inverness, ½ mile SE of Culloden battlefield, on a minor road between Clava Lodge and Balnuaran farm. In State care. Signposted. (SW ring, circular, 31.8 metres; centre ring, circular, 31.6 metres; NE ring, egg-shaped, 31.6 × 29.7 metres.)

Around the headwaters of the Ness, now channelled by the Caledonian canal, and farther to the east in the valley of the Spey, is a remarkable collection of prehistoric cairns, the Clava passage-graves and ring-cairns of Inverness-shire. To their north in Sutherland and Caithness were quite different burial-mounds, the long Orkney–Cromarty chambered tombs put up by other people. To their south was the desolate chasm of the Loch Ness valley, its austere slopes littered with grey, dead boulders. To the east were forests and more mountains. But around modern Inverness the land was pleasant, the soils were good, the rivers flowed quietly for the people's cattle. As early as 3700 BC a family of Neolithic farmers built a strong wooden cabin here, and perhaps a thousand years later other people constructed a ring-cairn exactly over the overgrown spot where it had stood. How the location was known is one of archaeology's mysteries. The Raigmore ring-cairn can still be seen on a modern housing estate on the eastern outskirts of Inverness (NH 687456).

Within the Clava group, so-called from the most visitable of these cairns at Balnuaran of Clava, there are two types of cairn. First are the

passage-graves, high round mounds with stone-lined passages that led from the south-west sector to a central and circular roofed cell where the dead were laid. Secondly, there are ring-cairns, round and low with uninterrupted banks enclosing a central circular space with no roof. Both types have weighty kerbs that rise in height towards the south-west, and most of them have stone circles around them, the stones again increasing in height towards the south-west section of the ring. As in many other regions of the British Isles, there are clues that their builders were numerate. Many of the Clava rings have twelve stones whatever the length of their circumference, which suggests that twelve was a preferred number. For the interested visitor a cautious remark should be made. There is no proof that any one of these monuments was constructed in a single operation. The stone circle may be contemporary with or earlier or later than the cairn. As very often, and particularly with the ring-cairns, the ring is of a different shape from the cairn – elliptical, flattened or simply irregular – it seems likely that it was put up at a different time, probably later.

Many of the Clava cairns are ruined, standing on arable land where their stones have been used for walls, drains and farmhouses, but one excellently preserved group still exists at the Balnuaran of Clava complex downhill from Culloden battlefield, in the customary low-lying position. It is an unusual group because in it two passage-graves flank a ring-cairn, whereas most Clava cairns stand alone, but this makes it all the more rewarding to visit.

The first cairn to be seen is the south-west passage-grave, its sullen grey cobbles rising from a wide circular platform of stones and earth upon which the cairn was constructed. Outside the cairn there were originally eleven thin sandstone slabs and a round boulder which has now been built into the wall of the road. Two stones are missing. Heavy kerb-stones surround the cairn, becoming higher, wider and thicker as they approach the en-

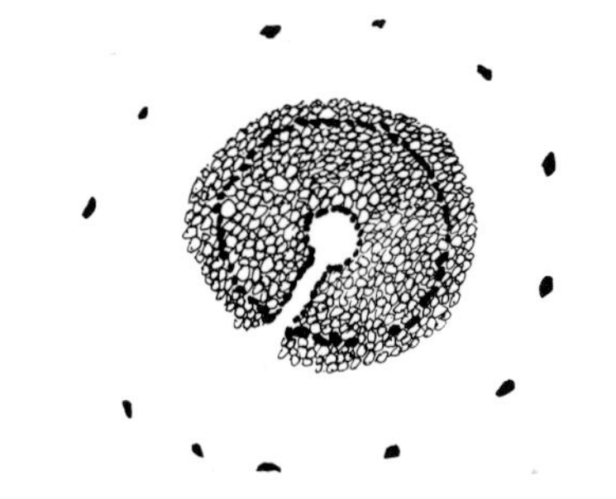

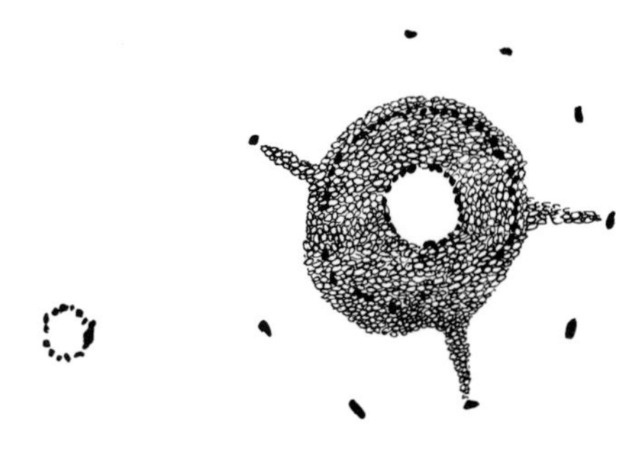

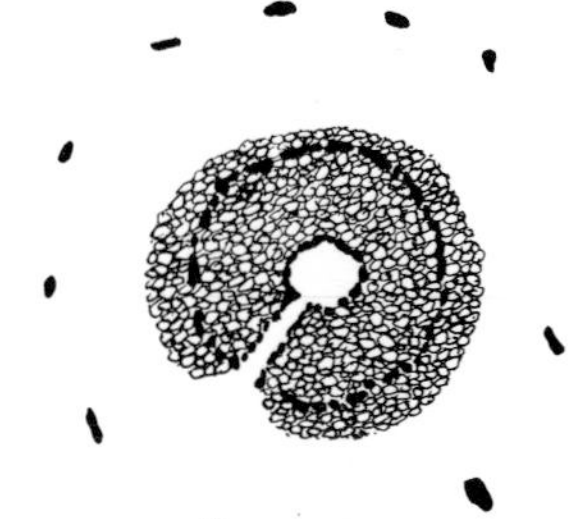

Opposite Clava. The roof of the passage-grave has collapsed, exposing the chamber.

trance. The circle-stones also are graded. The entrance, at the south-west, leads down a long passage to the chamber whose roof has collapsed but in which the carefully erected side-slabs for the wall are well displayed. Unfortunately, the cairn was 'excavated' in 1828 and many of its contents are lost, but it is thought that two coarse pots with cremated bone in them were found here, some of the burnt bone lying on the gravel floor of the chamber. There are two cupmarked stones. One at the west of the chamber has twelve markings, and the western circle stone has three cupmarks on its inner face. Thom suggested that observers sitting in the chamber might have looked towards the setting sun at midwinter, its rays shining down the passage.

To the north-north-east of this cairn is the ring-cairn, much lower because its central area was never roofed. Its circle of stones also was graded in height towards the south-south-west, where the tallest stone is now a mere broken stump. Within the ring, bordered by heavy boulder-kerbs, is a mass of cairn-stones across which one must walk to reach the oval central space lined with flat slabs. It is now open to ground level but before its excavation in 1857 stones lay in it. It had already been rifled and 'some form of cist or stone setting had been destroyed. The central area was blackened by charcoal, and there was a sparse scatter of cremated human bone.' Causeways of packed cobbles lead from the cairn out to three circle-stones at east, south

and north-west, but their purpose is unexplained. Two eastern kerbs have cupmarks.

North-east of the ring-cairn is the second passage-grave, its roof fallen like its partner's. Again the cairn stands on a platform, has a stone circle graded in height, has big kerbstones, a south-west passage and a central chamber. The inner wall of this is still quite high and curves slightly inwards but not enough ever to have had a beehive roof. It was probably topped with a wide flat slab. A 'few bones' were discovered in the chamber. The western stone of the chamber is cupmarked and there is a clutter of cupmarks on the kerbstone at the north of the cairn. It is remarkable how these decorated stones tend to be in cardinal positions despite the south-western locations of the entrances. It is also noticeable that very few bodies, either as skeletons or as cremations, have been found in the Clava cairns, which may have been shrines, not tombs.

Just west of the ring-cairn is a little ring of boulders. Excavation in 1953 of its central area showed that there had been a shallow grave from which the body had disappeared, dissolved by the acid soil. A scatter of white quartz pebbles lay at its western end and the eastern boulder had some cupmarks and some cup-and-rings marks on it.

Opposite Circle stone, platform and the heavily kerbed north-east passage-grave.
Below The midwinter setting sun once shone down this passage on to the bones of the dead.

Corrimony

Inverness-shire (Highland): NH 383303. 19 miles WSW of Inverness, to N of a minor road off the A831. In State care. Signposted. (Stone ring, circular, 21.3 metres; platform, ovoid, 18.9 × 17.4 metres; cairn, flattened, 15.2 × 13.7 metres.)

Corrimony passage-grave, probably the best preserved of all the Clava cairns, stands far to the west of the main group in the extensive flood-plain that stretches on either side of the river Enrick. The site was a good one for prehistoric man, with productive soils and an abundance of building-stones from the banks of the river only a short distance to the north.

The family group that raised this cairn first built a level platform of coarse stones and earth, roughly oval in outline, and on it they laid out a ring of large boulders with another ring just outside it, flattened at the north-west, of slabs set on edge. These were to be the kerbstones of the cairn. A gap was left at the south-west where two splayed hefty stones were set up as portals for the entrance. It may have been at this stage that much broken quartz was scattered around the entrance, sanctifying it. Many fragments were subsequently found underneath the cairn. From the two entrance stones a low and narrow passage was constructed of heavy uprights surmounted by crude drystone walling to maintain a horizontal line for the roof, which was made of flattish lintels. A rounded stone was set firmly in the floor halfway along this passage.

The chamber is small. Two people standing side by side with outstretched arms could touch both sides. For its walls fifteen blocks were arranged in a poor circle, supporting drystone walling that corbelled inwards to make the beginnings of a dome; but the workmanship was never good enough for this to be successful and the chamber was roofed with a table-sized flat slab which has now been dragged to one side on top of the cairn, leaving a cavity down which one can stare into the central area. There are numerous cupmarks on this slab. Their clean-cut lines show that they have not been long exposed to the weather and they must have lain on the underside of the stone, facing downwards into the obscurity of the chamber where dead bodies lay.

Outside the platform of the cairn is a ring of standing stones. These were set up in a fairly good circle. Strangely, at the east there was never a stone, just an irregular layer of cobbles. Bearing in mind the cardinally marked positions in other stone circles and the positions of the cupmarked stones at the Balnuaran of Clava 'cemetery', this would seem to be a deliberate orientation on the part of the builders.

The 1952 excavation found little. The floor of the chamber was laid with water-worn stones beneath which there was a layer of yellow sand. At its centre were flat slabs with charcoal around them. No body or bones were discovered, but in the sand was a stain, the last traces of a body that had decomposed here.

Around it were signs 'that fresh sand had been strewn over the area at intervals and consolidated by trampling'.

This evidence of activity in the chamber with people moving around the central burial suggests that ceremonies took place here that were not necessarily funerary. The fact that there was only one body also argues against Corrimony having been a tomb. It was more probably a family shrine, hallowed by the deposition of a corpse, in which rites involving the sun and death were acted out.

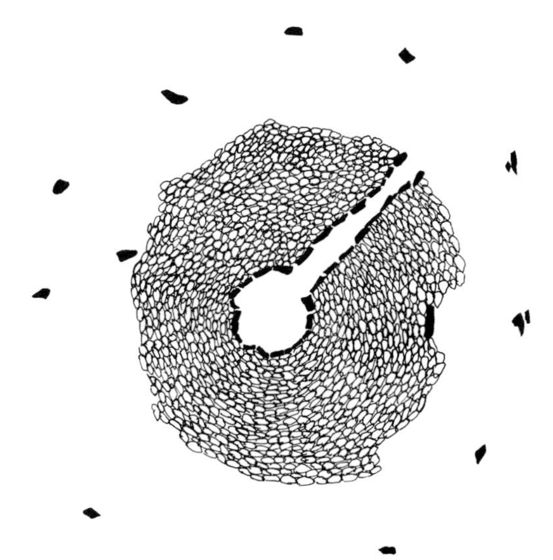

Below Down this low, dark passage the dead were carried to the chamber beneath, where torches burned.

Cullerlie

Aberdeenshire (Grampian): NJ 785043. **9 miles W of Aberdeen, 4 miles WNW of Peterculter, on a minor road from Garlogie to Peterculter. In State care. Signposted. (Circular, 10.1 metres.)**

This ring, in a district of swamps and waterlogged land, was built on a skilfully chosen patch of gravel, probably the only dry spot in a boggy landscape. Peat formed over the site during the Iron Age and the lower parts of the circle-stones show decided indentations where the acidic waters have eaten into them over the past three thousand years or more. Today the visitor can see the stones and the cairns, which have been reconstructed. There is an explanatory sign by the circle.

Prehistoric people levelled the site, which is much more even than the surrounding beds of gravel. Then eight squat boulders of coarse-grained pinkish granite were brought here. Their tops were bashed into rough pyramids, as were their bases, which then acted as wedges that drove deeply into the yielding gravel. This shaping made it easier for a few men and women to raise these stones, the heaviest and tallest of which weighed three or four tons.

Inside the ring eight tiny circles were constructed, the largest at the centre having two rings of deeply set kerbstones in it. The seven smaller rings surrounded it. A surprising fact about these rings, built by Bronze Age peasants, is that all but one of them, at the south-south-west, have eleven stones. The central ring has concentric settings of eleven stones each. This must have been intentional even though its significance escapes us, and the correspondence between the eight circle-stones and the eight inner rings also is unlikely to be coincidental.

When the circle and these little rings were completed, a ceremony of dedication took place. Bundles of dry willow branches from the riversides were carried into the centre of the ring and fires were lit that left reddened patches all over the floor up to the very edge of the circle. Such burning certainly took place after the stones were standing, for several of the boulders had patches of grey or pink near their bases, caused by the scorching, and a wind blowing in from the north spread ash around

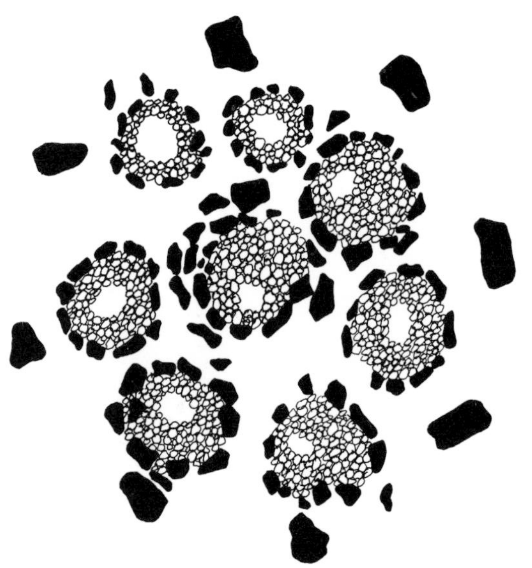

the bottoms of the smaller stones at the south. Many of the inner rings also were burnt.

Later these inner rings were used for further rituals that involved fire and human bone. Fragments of skulls and limb-bones mixed with oak charcoal were placed in the central ring, which was then filled with stones, turning it into a cairn. In other rings there were badly built cists aligned east-west, holding a few splinters of limbs amongst oak charcoal from pyres that must have burnt elsewhere. In the ring at the north-east, much disturbed by later people, little parcels of bone lay amongst the charcoal. The ring at the west, just north of the one with only nine kerbstones, had a paved floor on which there was a capstone. Beneath it was a pit in which a fierce fire of hazelwood had blazed. Fifteen bits of arm-bone and leg-bone lay in the charcoal. North of it the smallest of the rings also had a pit whose contents were embedded in a layer of oak charcoal.

Despite the complexity of the ceremonies, the stone circle at Cullerlie did not last long. In the layer of earth which slowly accumulated over the interior with the passing of the centuries there were many stones. 'They obviously represented cairn-stones which had been either thrown out or had fallen in the course of time.' Cullerlie, like so many other rings, may have been wrecked in antiquity.

Opposite Under the cairns the soil had been reddened by the burning of willow branches.

Loanhead of Daviot

Aberdeenshire (Grampian): NJ 747288. **5 miles NNW of Inverurie, ½ mile NW of Daviot, E of a minor road. In State care. Signposted. (Circular, 20.5 metres.)**

About 1820, by order of the minister there, a 'Druidical temple' was removed from Daviot churchyard. Either because it did not offend his Christian sensibilities or because he had no jurisidiction over it, the minister did nothing about the other ring which stood on Loanhead farm only half a mile away.

Loanhead of Daviot is at the north-east corner of a hilly rectangle about ten miles long by five deep between the rivers Urie and Don. In this rectangle at least fifteen recumbent stone circles were erected on the low grassy slopes that fringe the Grampians. Only five miles south is the attractive Easter Aquorthies ring, its recumbent supported by two heavy stones (NJ 732208). To the east the land sloped down to forests and to the west the landscape was commanded by the sharp prow of Mither Tap, clearly visible from Loanhead of Daviot until the present trees were planted.

Although no radio-carbon dates are yet available for these central Aberdonian rings, the discovery of Neolithic pottery in some stoneholes at Loanhead suggests that this was an early ring put up before Beaker people entered this part of Scotland around 2400 BC.

It is easy to visualize a few families around 2500 BC staking territories of four to six square miles in this congenial countryside and combining to build each other's ritual centres. If no more than six groups first settled here there would have been a population of some two hundred people, half of them adults and quite adequate to shift the ponderous stones of their respective circles.

Before any stones were brought here the hillslope where they were to stand was levelled, rubble laid down and soil spread to make an even surface where the ground demanded it. Then ten stones of local granite were laid alongside the holes that had been prepared for them, the lowest pillars opposite the place where the recumbent was to rest. This point was already fixed, just to the west of south (196°), where the full midsummer moon would have begun to sink in the night sky, passing behind the silhouetted flankers before disappearing in the southern mountains.

The recumbent, whose base had probably been battered to a shallow point, was manoeuvred into a slight pit and its end levered up and down until its top was exactly horizontal and packing-stones could be jammed under its sloping ends. The flankers, also in shallow sockets, were propped against the recumbent and the other roughly shaped circle-stones put up, workers heaving their bases down ramps into the stoneholes and hauling the pillars upright from inside the ring. Five small cupmarks were carved in a vertical line on the inner face of the stone next to the east flanker, the pillar that stood directly in line with the midwinter sunrise.

Once the circle was completed a funeral pyre of willow branches was lit at the centre of the ring, burning hotly on the bare earth until the soil was reddened and hard-baked. When the ashes had cooled the burnt bones were raked out. One piece of bone, one sherd of pottery and one lump of charcoal were set in a little pit just to the east of the pyre. Everything else was removed and the people laid an irregular crescent of loose stones around the place where the fire had burnt, rather like a horseshoe with its open end facing the recumbent stone.

At the foot of each circle-stone a little cairn was built with a fair-sized stone at its

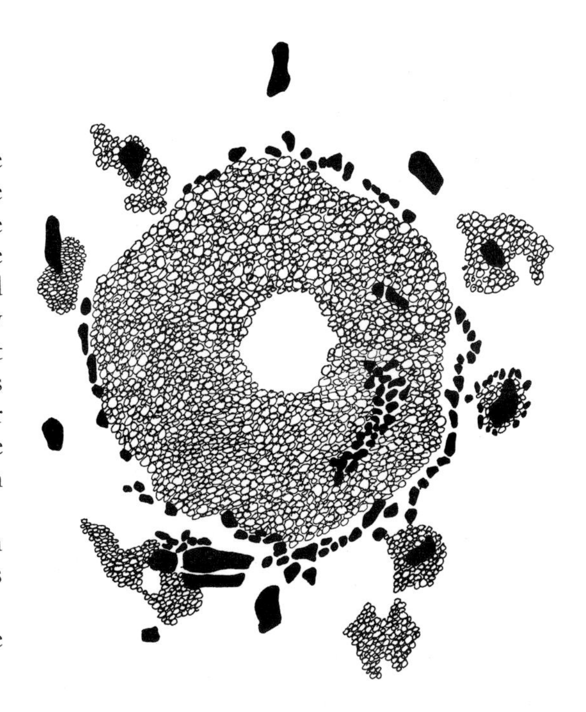

Below From the west. Beyond the ring are the remains of an enclosed cremation cemetery.

centre. In these cairns excavators in 1932 found bits of pots that had been intentionally broken, presumably as offerings, but never any human bone. Going clockwise around the ring from the west flanker, the first stone had three small sherds in its cairn; the next several bits of bucket-shaped urn; the next was disturbed by modern quarrying; stone 4 had a single sherd; stones 5, 6 and 7 several bits of pottery; and by stone 8 a little cist had been added in the Early Bronze Age, and a tiny pygmy cup put in it.

Such deposits were obviously important to the circle-builders and they were carefully concealed. Yet the truly important part of the monument was the ring-cairn that was now constructed inside the circle of stones, a ring of blockish kerbstones graded in size towards the recumbent and with stones heaped inside them making a knee-high cairn with a well-defined oval space at its heart. Here the people scraped out a deep pit through the earth where the pyre had flamed. Ten smaller pits were dug into this space but none of them contained bone. Instead, the whole central area was found to be covered with a hard, compacted layer under which there was a thick black layer of charcoal with some five pounds of adult burnt bone in it, the remains of human forearms and arms, thighs, femurs, vertebrae, but also containing 'some 50 pieces of skull bones of children, perhaps from 2 to 4 years of age'.

This ring with its solar and lunar orientations, its cupmarks, its broken pottery and its cremated human bone was not destroyed in antiquity. Instead, in later centuries, a Food-Vessel community built their own cemetery alongside the circle, an oval rubble bank with two entrances surrounding a series of pits in which food-vessels and urns with their human bones were buried. It can still be seen today, lying unimpressively by the stone circle in which the recumbent stone has split, fractured by the cold of hundreds of Scottish winters.

The ring-cairn, recumbent stone and flankers of Loanhead. 'Antiquities are history defaced.' Francis Bacon.

Old Keig

Aberdeenshire (Grampian): NJ 593195. **11 miles W of Inverurie, 2½ miles NNE of Alford. Private. Ask permission at Old Keig farmhouse. (Circular, about 25.6 metres.)**

As long ago as 15 June 1692, the Reverend James Garden of Aberdeen wrote to 'his honoured friend, Master John Aubrey', mentioning 'that some persons who are yet alive, declare, that many years since, they did see ashes of some burnt matter digged out of the bottome of a little Circle (sett about with stones standing close together) in the center of one of those monuments which is set standing near the Church of Keig . . .', almost certainly the recumbent stone circle that was re-excavated by the prehistorian Gordon Childe in 1931 at Old Keig. From it came flat-rimmed ware and some beaker pottery which may have been made around 2200 BC. A mile to the east of this ring is the tree-hidden Cothiemuir Wood ring (NJ 617198).

Old Keig is best approached from the north, walking downhill through an avenue of trees to the circle, which is now in a melancholy state. Stones lie where the excavation left them, kerbs of the ring-cairn are overgrown and the site is miserably neglected.

Excavation showed that, after the turf had been stripped off, a pyre of hazel with some birch, willow, alder and oak branches collected from the edges of the forest by the riverside had burnt in the interior of the circle of stones. Through this reddened patch a great pit had been dug and even after the seventeenth-

century depredations it still had charcoal, sherds of pottery and human bone in it.

The recumbent stone is astounding. This incredible monster of sillimanite gneiss is not local but may have been dragged, all fifty tons of it, from the Don valley somewhere between Kemnay and Tillifourie several miles to the south-east. Nor was that all. One can still see how its base was fashioned to a gradual point and on this it was tilted up and down in its pit until it was perfectly horizontal. The packing-stones that supported it are still there. Even in wreckage this circle reminds us of the compulsions that drove people to such efforts.

Opposite A stone horizon for the setting moon.
Below The enormous recumbent stone.

Sunhoney

Aberdeenshire (Grampian): NJ 716058. 13 miles W of Aberdeen, just N of the B9119. Private. Ask permission at Sunhoney farm. (Circular, 25.3 metres.)

Placed at the crest of a hill from which it is conspicuous from all directions, Sunhoney is a wonderful ring to visit, for it is largely unspoilt and has an air of peace about it. One must approach from the farm across land that is often deeply muddy in wet weather and sturdy footwear is recommended.

The ring is now enclosed in a low, mouldering wall whose inner edge is lined with trees that dapple the circle in shifting brindles of sunlight and shade. Eleven stones of red granite stand here, the lowest opposite the close-grained granite of the recumbent that has fallen outwards so that its keeled base is open to view. A wide stony bank curves between the circle-stones, some of which have today been re-erected.

Opposite Sunhoney's cupmarked recumbent.
Below The flankers and fallen recumbent from the south, with the lowest stones behind.
Over Loanhead of Daviot.

It was only in the central ring-cairn, however, that cremations were discovered. Here the stones of the inner circle were reddened by fire and here there were deposits of burnt bones and charcoal, the usual relics of the type of rites that took place here. The 'beautiful smooth and flat' recumbent was aligned, like those of several other rings near Sunhoney, towards the minimum full midsummer moon at 230°. It has a whole series of cupmarks on its upper face. Unless the stone has been turned around these markings would have faced inwards, for it surely was the straight outer edge that once formed the top of this recumbent. That it has fallen is suggested by the heavy supporting block that now lies near but separate from it. There are twenty-eight well-formed cupmarks on this stone in frustrating patterns that defy present interpretation. People have claimed that the constellation of Ursa Major is depicted among its designs, but this theory does not bear scrutiny.

A mile west of Sunhoney is the circle at Midmar Kirk. In 1787 a kirk was built alongside it. In 1914 a burial-ground was laid out near the church and the circle was de-turfed. Despite protests that no stone was moved, the ring looks suspiciously rearranged.

Opposite Morning sunlight on the Clava Cairns. *Below* Sunhoney from the east, a largely unspoilt site.

Above Sunhoney. Sunlit stones stand now like the dead fingers of time.

Opposite Sunhoney's flankers and recumbent stone, viewed from outside the ring.

CENTRAL AND WESTERN SCOTLAND

BALBIRNIE *Fife*
CROFT MORAIG *Perthshire (Tayside)*
LUNDIN FARM *Perthshire (Tayside)*
TEMPLE WOOD *Argyll (Strathclyde)*

From Edinburgh northwards through Fife there are very few megalithic monuments. This is mainly because of the forests that spread in these lowlands in prehistoric times. Where men settled they built in wood and it is interesting that in three recent excavations of stone circles in central parts of Scotland the stones were discovered to have been preceded by a ring of posts. Timber circles were found at Balfarg, at Moncrieffe (NO 133193) and at Croft Moraig, reminding us that what we see on the surface may not be the structure prehistoric people saw.

At the edges of this great blanket of trees over south-east Scotland people travelled cautiously, seeking good land. Many of them settled on the fertile land of Fife and at least two stone circles were erected there, one the circle-henge of Balfarg, the other the smaller and much-changed Balbirnie.

It was in Perthshire, however, that there was the greatest variety of rings. Here along the passes that led to Loch Tay and ultimately to north-east Scotland traders and travellers moved, exchanging gifts with the natives, resting for a winter, departing, and the effect of this flux and disturbance can be seen not only in the 'local' rings of six or eight stones or the peculiar rectangles known as Four-Posters but also in the 'foreign' larger open circles – Coilleachur near Aberfeldy (NN 845466), Inverarnon at the farther end of Loch Tay (NN 316185), and Croft Moraig with its sequence of changes.

Over in the far west, in Argyll, stone circles were almost non-existent. Perhaps there were too few people, perhaps there were other cults. Just one or two miserable rings of stones are scattered amongst the hills. Otherwise, only in the Kilmartin valley with its chambered tomb, its cairns and standing stones was there a megalithic ring, the remote and unusual Temple Wood for which so many astronomical claims have been made.

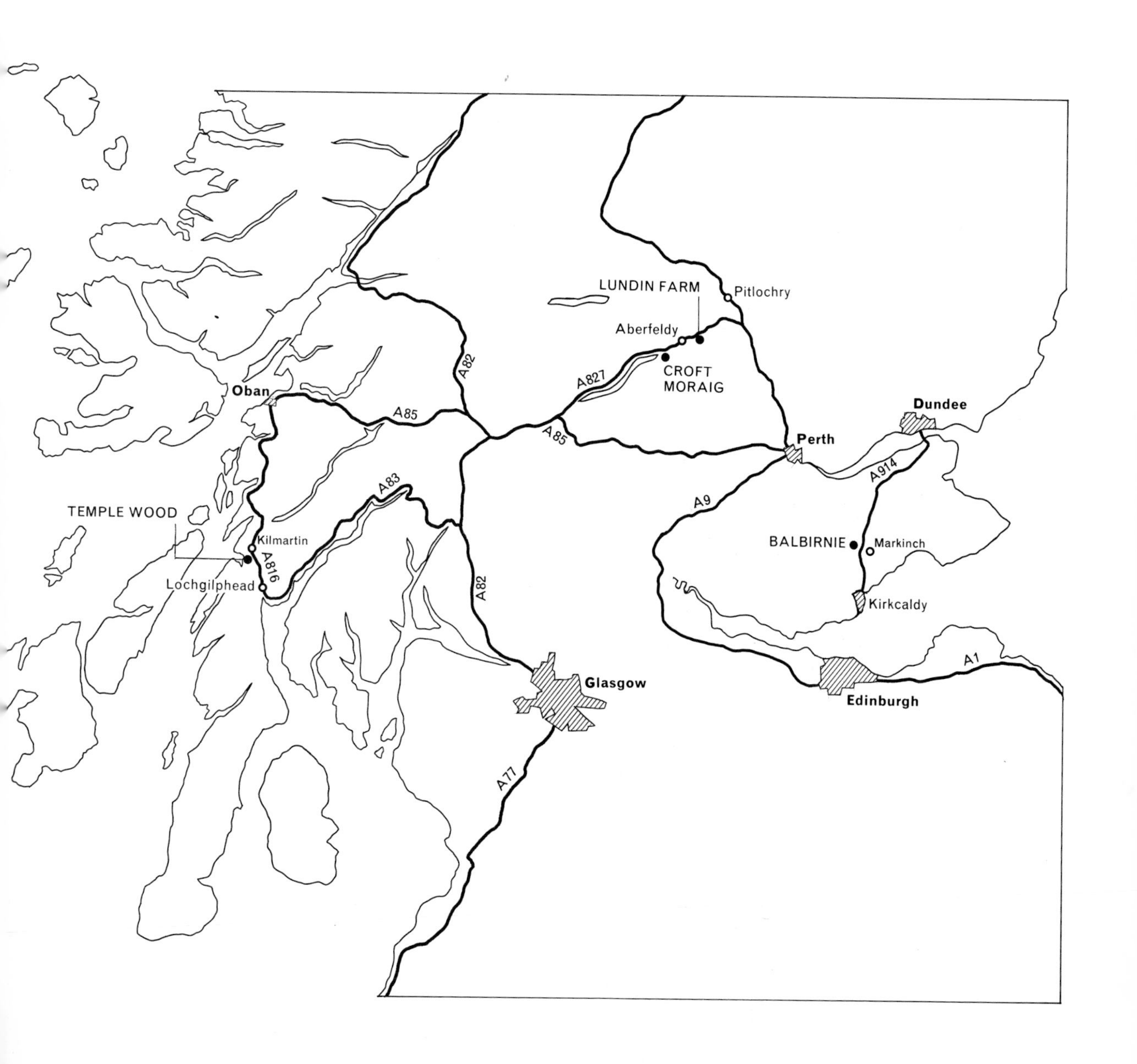
LUNDIN FARM
Pitlochry
Aberfeldy
CROFT
MORAIG
A827
A82
A85
Oban
A85
Dundee
Perth
A914
A9
TEMPLE WOOD
A83
BALBIRNIE
Markinch
Kilmartin
A816
Lochgilphead
A82
Kirkcaldy
A1
Glasgow
Edinburgh
A77

Balbirnie

Fife: NO 285030. 6 miles N of Kirkcaldy, 1 mile NW of Markinch. Private. Ask at Balbirnie Lodge. (Elliptical, 15 × 14.0 metres.)

Balbirnie is a beautiful ring to visit because its recent excavation and reconstruction have restored it to a good condition, and it is possible to see the stones of the circle, the mysterious rectangular setting at its centre, and the cupmarked cists without the usual distraction of grass waving and drooping over the interior. What cannot be perceived is the complicated history of the circle. Like many other rings in the central regions of Scotland, Balbirnie was altered several times. It has also been moved. Because of modern road widening the ring now stands one hundred and twenty-five metres south-east of its proper position.

Only three hundred metres to the west are the mutilated bank and ditch of the enormous circle-henge of Balfarg (NO 281032), perhaps dug out and built by Grooved Ware people around 2700 BC. A causeway was left at the north-west. On the central plateau, nearly sixty metres across, the people put up a massive ring of timbers whose posts increased in width and height towards the south-west where two colossal trunks towered into the sky. A palisade may have hidden the ring from the outside world. This impressive timber circle, however, was later replaced by a ring of ten or eleven stones.

The relationship between Balfarg and this circle is not known, although it is possible that the small ring performed a function rather similar to that of the Sanctuary near Avebury, as a charnel-house where dead bodies were exposed until the flesh had rotted from them, leaving the dry skeletal bones to be taken to the circle-henge for the final ceremonies of mourning, burial and feasting.

At Balbirnie, on a gentle terrace not far from the Firth of Forth, the excavations of 1970–71 revealed that the first monument on the site had been a ring of stones, none especially large and all of the local sandstone, arranged in an ellipse with its long axis laid out towards the south-west. The stones may have been graded in height towards the south. Before erecting the stones the people put cremated bone in the holes of all four eastern stones as though to add power to them. A couple of pieces of grooved ware in the north-east stonehole suggest that this ring may have been built around 2100 BC.

At the centre a square was constructed, edged with thin slabs and about three metres across. Delicate flecks of cremated bone lay there. Other stones may also have stood here, some of them decorated with cupmarkings which have been interpreted as solar symbols of death. If such stones were here then they were broken and removed from the setting when Balbirnie was taken over around 2000 BC, by another group who dug out pits for two stone-lined cists to the south-east of the square, using the decorated stones for their side-slabs. Cremations were laid in the cists but the cemetery was soon disturbed when a Food-Vessel community came to the ring.

These people preferred complete enclosures to circles of spaced standing stones, and they constructed a stony bank between the pillars. Then they removed one cist, built two more to receive the burnt bodies of women and children, one with a bone bead, another with a pot and a flint knife. A beaker was placed between two planks inside the ring and a cairn was heaped over the whole interior. Into this cairn even later people inserted sherds of deliberately broken urns and many cremations. Today the cairn has been removed, but the cists survive to show the alterations prehistoric people made to Balbirnie's little stone circle.

Opposite A re-erected stone at Balbirnie.

Croft Moraig

Perthshire (Tayside): NN 797472. 4 miles WSW of Aberfeldy, to S of the A827 and 2 miles E of Loch Tay. In State care. Signposted. (Outer circle, 12.2 metres; inner oval, 7.6 × 6.1 metres.)

'The public road between Aberfeldy and Kenmore passes so close to the Stones that the most unobservant pedestrian or rider – always excepting the begoggled motorist – cannot but see the green mound bristling with great grey Stones; secondly because the drivers of the coaches plying on this road jog along a trifle more deliberately past the mound, and the magical words, "Yon's the Druid Stones" cause all eyes to turn for one brief moment to the left.' The fine field archaeologist Fred Coles wrote that in 1909 and his words remain true. Croft Moraig is a magical place.

It stands at the head of the Tay valley, which for centuries had been a thoroughfare between south-west and north-east Scotland. Irish pottery and stone axes discovered as far north as Aberdeenshire demonstrate the journeyings that must have occurred along the lovely waters of Loch Tay year by year. Chambered tombs and the great Neolithic mound of Pitnacree nine miles north-east of Croft Moraig show how early this busy region had been occupied. During the Bronze Age families cleared tracts of land on the wooded hillsides and raised their own stone circles, ellipses of six or eight stones or the small and intriguing

Four-Posters, rectangles of four tall pillars that are common in this part of Scotland.

Croft Moraig must belong to quite an early phase of prehistory, built at some time late in the Neolithic but still being altered in the Bronze Age as other people came into the region, taking over land and changing customs. Its history of alteration shows how much we still have to learn about early prehistoric societies. Balbirnie and Balfarg in Fife, Berrybrae in Aberdeenshire, Moncrieffe and Croft Moraig in Perthshire – all have been excavated in the past twenty years and instead of being the

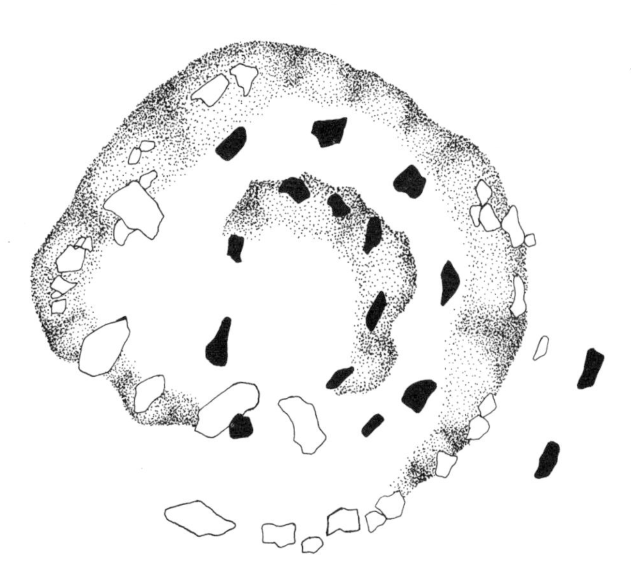

Below Croft Moraig. Ruined as they are, the stones keep their heavy, desolate splendour.

simple ring of stones that was expected every one has revealed evidence of change, even destruction, suggesting that hostility and antagonism were more prevalent between prehistoric people than archaeologists had previously thought.

The earliest structure at Croft Moraig was a horseshoe-shaped setting of fourteen posts with its open end to the south-west, an arrangement reminiscent of the horseshoe of trilithons at Stonehenge though in reverse. Short parallel rows of three posts approached this timber setting from the east, maybe the remnants of a porch leading to a small wooden hut whose purpose is unclear. Possibly it was the dwelling-place of a priest, a witch-doctor, a shaman, the holy man of the community. At its centre was a flat natural boulder near which there was the charcoal-strewn place where a hearth had burnt.

The building was important enough to have been repaired, as the re-cut postholes show, but eventually it was dismantled. The site was levelled with stones and earth. Eight unshaped boulders were dragged to the platform and set up in a small oval graded in height towards the south-west. Near the top of the low stone at the north-east are some cupmarks and it is interesting to find that from the centre of the oval this stone was roughly in line with the midsummer rising sun.

Around this oval a bank of heavy stones and earth, some eighteen metres in diameter, was carefully constructed, and it is still to be seen in places today. There may have been two entrances through this bank, at north-east and south-west, but stone-robbing in the nineteenth century has destroyed a large section at the north. In the gap at the south-south-west, the people laid a long and irregular stone with twenty-three cupmarks on its upper surface. This supine stone, for which the inspiration may well have come from even more magnificently decorated stones outside the entrances of the Irish passage-graves of Knowth and New Grange, must also be related to the recumbent stone circles of north-east Scotland,

'Remnants of history that have casually escaped the shipwreck of time.' Francis Bacon.

not many miles away, where the recumbent is often cupmarked. Such an association makes the discovery of dense concentrations of white quartz inside Croft Moraig's oval all the more significant. If such quartz really did symbolize the moon and death, then the cupmarked, prostrate stone there in line with the midsummer full moon tells us something of the beliefs of its builders. Pieces of coarse local pottery and some finer ware suggest that this second phase at Croft Moraig may have begun as early as 2500 BC.

Perhaps many years later, this oval was enclosed in a circle of twelve heavy stones with two more set up outside at the east as portals very like the entrances of some Lake District rings. The inner oval was overshadowed by these great blocks of schist and epidiorite, which were set up in very shallow sockets and with few packing-stones around their bases. The two outliers were even bigger, huge, smooth-faced monsters dominating the entrance through which the equinoctial sun would have shone. Outside each of these stones was a deep pit in which the excavation of 1965 found no burial, or pot or tool. The soil however, was so acid in the locality of Croft Moraig that any body would have dissolved in it, and it is likely that these holes were graves dug by Beaker people who came to the stone circle some time after it was built. Beaker burials at the foot of standing stones are well known in other parts of Britain.

Five hundred years may have passed between the first timber lodge and the final stone circle here, five centuries during which beliefs changed, new people came to the area, sometimes peacefully, sometimes as enemies who acquired land and ritual centre by force. The 'great grey Stones' of Croft Moraig witnessed these changes.

Croft Moraig. The inner and outer settings of the later circles, on their platform.

Lundin Farm

Perthshire (Tayside): NN 882505. **1¾ miles NE of Aberfeldy. To S of the Grandtully–Aberfeldy road by the private road to Lundin farm. (Rectangular 4.0 × 3.4 metres.)**

This site, which should not be confused with the tall stones of Lundin Links on a golf-course in Fife (NO 404026), is a good example of the group of 'circles' known as Four-Posters.

The 'family' rings around Tayside have distinctive characteristics and each group occupied fairly well-defined regions. The rings suggest that their builders were numerate, for the monuments in each group are composed of specific numbers of stones. They also enclose burials, although these, in some cases, were possibly added by later people. Around the western and northern shores of Loch Tay are several ovals made up of six stones, probably erected in opposing pairs. Farther to east and south and in the low-lying neighbourhood of Perth are rather larger rings of eight low stones. Along Strathtay and at the entry to the Glenshee pass that climbed northwards over the mountains to Braemar and north-east Scotland were Four-Posters.

These strange rectangular 'rings' can also be found in Aberdeenshire where this four-stone tradition may have started. They have many features in common with the recumbent stone circles. Their stones are graded in height, often towards the south-west, they stand on hillsides, some have cupmarks on them, and almost invariably they have a central deposit of cremated bone. If they did originate in north-east Scotland, however, they are to be found over a wide area. In the restless centuries of the Bronze Age people moved over great distances. Four-Posters can be found in Northumberland, on the island of Arran, in Wales, and there is another in south-west Ireland where Lettergorman stands in County Cork (W 263455). They are most numerous in Perthshire.

The four stones of Lundin Farm stand proudly on a natural mound of moraine gravel from which there is a marvellous view westwards towards Ben Lawers. The stones of quartziferous schist are all local. At some time early in the Bronze Age a small band of people stripped the turf from this mound, hollowed out its top, and dug a U-shaped ditch around the hollow. In the hollow they dug a tapering pit which was the focus of their ceremonies. At its bottom they placed some organic material, tipped some gravel, earth and quartz over it and then dropped slivers of partly burnt bone and three human teeth on the upper layer. The contents of this pit would seem to be offerings, mainly of rich loamy earth that intimated the needs of the people for good harvests and plentiful food. The cremated bone was small in quantity and cannot be considered a proper burial. Nor can another little deposit by the pit.

Broken pottery, damaged flints, cremated bone were scattered all about the hollow, 'killed' objects that could enter the Other World of the dead. The pit was filled and earth was scattered all over the top of the mound, hiding everything under a skin of soil. It was

only then, when the site had been consecrated, that the four stones were erected, the tallest at the north-east, reversing the usual grading.

The Four-Poster can be regarded, therefore, as a framework surrounding an area of magical importance where the spirits of the dead were placed in contact with the forces of nature in the earth. Sealing these things from the profane world, a small cairn was piled over the central area, covering the hollow and its ditch.

(Finds from the 1962 excavation of Lundin Farm, including sherds of a very early beaker, are now in the National Museum of Antiquities of Scotland, Queen Street, Edinburgh. Open weekdays and Sunday afternoons.)

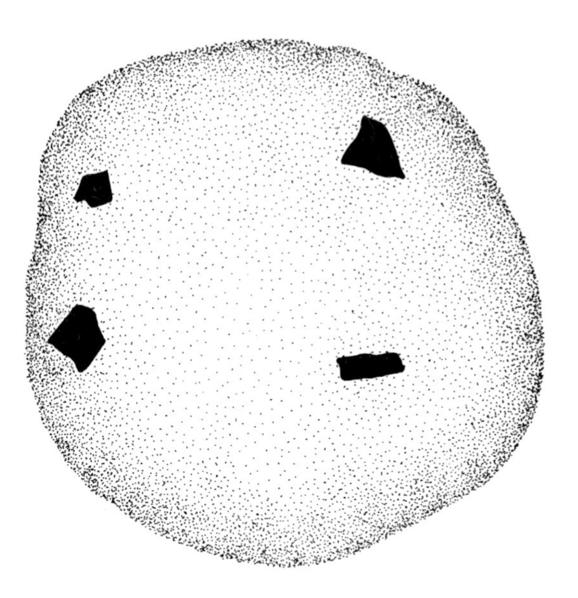

Below Lundin Farm. A typical Four-Poster, it stands lonely in the winter landscape.

Temple Wood

Argyll (Strathclyde): NR 826979. **$6\frac{1}{2}$ miles NNW of Lochgilphead, 1 mile SSW of Kilmartin on a minor road W of the Kilmartin Burn. (Circular, 13.4 metres.)**

For anyone wishing to see a selection of Bronze Age monuments concentrated in a small and easily walked area the Kilmartin valley will be attractive. Here, within a few miles of each other, are cairns, standing stones, cupmarked boulders, a henge and a stone circle. For good measure there is also a late Iron Age hill-fort with Pictish carving at Dun Dunadd (NM 837936).

This was a populated region from the Late Neolithic onwards and the reason is clear. To avoid the dangerous western seas voyagers travelled the waters to the east of the Kintyre peninsula, past Arran, until they reached the head of Loch Fyne, where a short portage brought them to Loch Crinan, from which they could take their boats northwards between the islands. More and more people passed this way, trading or seeking land, during the Bronze Age and some must have lingered in the fertile triangle of well-watered land in the Kilmartin valley to the north-east of this overland route between the lochs.

Standing stones would have told them that people already lived here. The chambered tomb of Nether Largie South, just across the lane from Temple Wood stone circle, shows that even in the Late Neolithic there were settlers here, and a beaker found inside the tomb suggests that Beaker people may have taken over the district around 2200 BC.

It is possible to descend into the interior of Nether Largie North cairn to see the decorated covering slab of the cist with its carvings of axes, cupmarks and Irish halberd that once faced downwards over the corpse that rested there. Other profusely carved rocks can be found to the south at Achnabreck and Cairnbaan. Tall standing stones with tiny ones set around them and with pairs of stones to their north or south rise from the flat meadows by Kilmartin and at Ballymeanoch where their eastern faces are pocked with cupmarks. Here also is a henge, its bank worn down, its two entrances weathered. A cairn that was added to it contained a beaker dated to about 1900 BC.

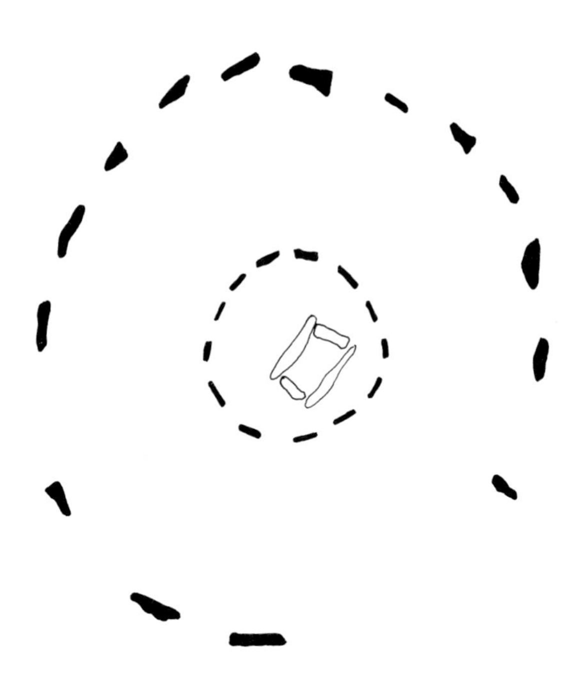

Here, under the mountain slopes of this megalithic valley, is the little stone circle of Temple Wood, miles away from any other ring, its stones light and easily moved and quite unlike the high pillars of the standing stones a field or two away. The ring rests uneasily at the foot of the western hills like an intruder unsure of its place here.

It was first properly excavated in 1929 when it was discovered that there had been twenty stones in the ring, all local and of a colour like early morning mist. Within the past few years carvings have been noticed on two of them, in particular a superb double spiral leading to a much poorer one on the side of the northern pillar. The interior of the circle was covered in a layer of cobbles. At the centre, beneath this, was a cist, its capstone long since removed. Recent meticulous excavations have found traces of a cremation in it. Its side-slab had been set up on an east-west axis conforming with the shadow of the midwinter setting sun. About this cist was a round setting of thin slabs which although continuous had two little stones jutting from them like a false entrance. A second cist, lidless but with relics of a cremation, also lay inside this ring. So did an

Opposite The small stone circle of Temple Wood, the notched western skyline behind.
Over Glenquickan, from the east.

odd little 'box' of stones with a further deposit of burnt bone.

People eventually covered the cists and the box with a cairn. Near it two other cairns were raised, one over a cremation in a pit, the second empty but with a floor of stones.

Between the circle-stones there remained two courses of drystone walling, well made, of shaped stones, and this attempt to convert a circle of standing stones into an unbroken bank suggests that Temple Wood, like Balbirnie and Berrybrae, had been modified by latecomers to the ring who had little respect for the original stone circle.

Opposite The central setting at Torhousekie.
Below Temple Wood. The carved northern stone.

THE SCOTTISH BORDERS

CAIRNPAPPLE HILL *West Lothian (Lothian)*
GIRDLE STANES *Dumfriesshire (Dumfries and Galloway)*
GLENQUICKAN *Kirkcudbright (Dumfries and Galloway)*
LOUPIN' STANES *Dumfriesshire (Dumfries and Galloway)*
TORHOUSEKIE *Wigtownshire (Dumfries and Galloway)*

There was a great difference between the south-east and south-west borders of Scotland in prehistoric times. The wooded hills and valleys of the south-east were unattractive regions, difficult to travel and more difficult to settle in, and it remained an area largely unoccupied well into Bronze Age times when the growing population forced people on to the uninhabited uplands. In consequence there are only a few stone circles here and these are generally tiny and late rings like the tumbled Harestanes in Peebles-shire (NT 124443). The exceptions are Newbridge and Cairnpapple, both large and near Edinburgh on an important north-south route.

The south-west of Scotland had a more involved history. The coastline here was much more travelled, with traders and incomers from the Lake District, from Wales and from Ireland constantly voyaging along its waters. Neolithic chambered tombs, denuded of their long mounds, slump along its low hills and sandy tracts of good farming land, and Bronze Age barrows and cairns are scattered on the higher ground inland. Valleys and hill-ridges provided access to the central parts of Scotland, and from the New Stone Age onwards people trudged along these trackways, speaking warily to strangers in the lingua franca of simple words and signs.

Dozens of traditions and customs mingled along this south-western coast. Beliefs from England, Ireland, central Scotland were known and accepted, intermixed, and produced a medley of stone circle styles. Here there are recumbent stones, centre stones, concentric rings, tall south-west stones, huge open rings like the Twelve Apostles outside Dumfries (NX947794) and Whitcastles (NY 224881). Even though many of these rings are ruined this is still a rewarding region for anyone wishing to see a variety of stone circles within a few miles of each other.

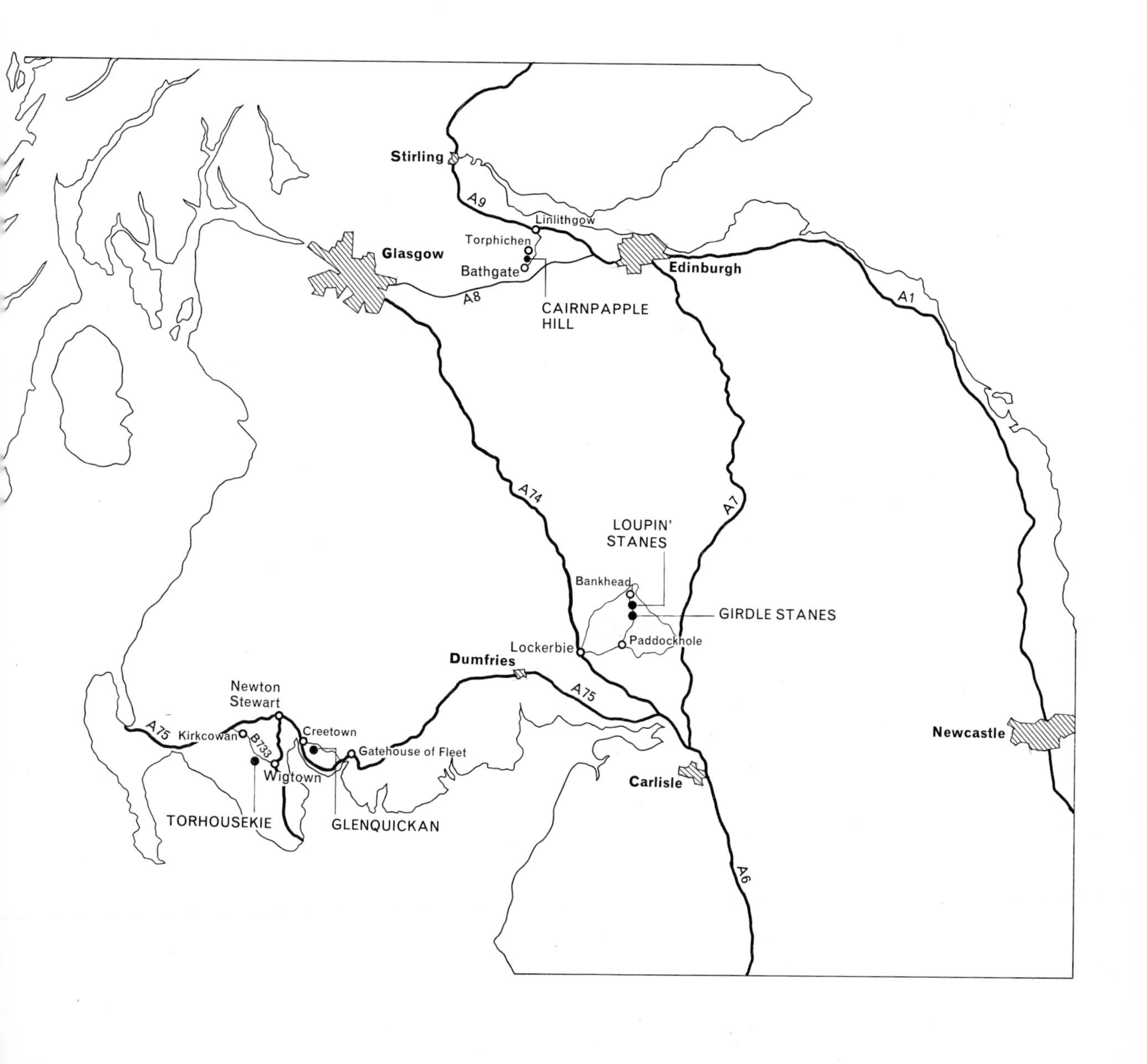

Stirling
A9
Linlithgow
Torphichen
Glasgow
Bathgate
Edinburgh
A8
CAIRNPAPPLE
HILL
A1
A74
A7
LOUPIN'
STANES
Bankhead
GIRDLE STANES
Paddockhole
Lockerbie
Dumfries
Newton
Stewart
A75
A75
Kirkcowan
B733
Creetown
Gatehouse of Fleet
Wigtown
Newcastle
Carlisle
TORHOUSEKIE
GLENQUICKAN
A6

Cairnpapple Hill

West Lothian (Lothian): NS 987717. 15 miles W of Edinburgh, $1\frac{1}{4}$ miles ESE of Torphichen. On a minor road from Bathgate to Linlithgow. In State care. Signposted. A small admission charge. Leaflets and photographs on sale. (Egg-shaped, 35.1 × 28.0 metres.)

This much-modified site from which every stone has been removed stands on a lofty hill of basalt from which the North Sea to the east and the island of Arran to the west are visible on clear days. Even with no stone circle to be seen Cairnpapple is well worth visiting , for it is a fine example of the alterations and destruction done to these monuments in antiquity. It is also possible to climb down into the later round barrow and see the place where first Beaker people and then Food-Vessel groups buried their dead.

On this hill during Neolithic times a small community dug out a rectangular setting of pits very similar to the famous Aubrey Holes of Stonehenge and, like them, backfilled and then opened again for burnt human bones to be put in them. These were not complete cremations but little pockets of bone that must surely have been offerings. Broken stone axes from the Lake District and from North Wales were discovered at ground level here during the excavations of 1947–8.

Around this religious centre great forests of oak and hazel darkened the landscape, but the site itself must have been kept free of trees and must have retained its tradition of being a holy place, because years later people from the south raised a circle-henge here. This structure was so like Arbor Low in the Peak District and Avebury in Wiltshire that there must have been contacts between those areas and Scotland in the years around 2500 BC. Work-gangs hacked a deep, oval ditch into the bedrock and heaped up a bank outside it in layers of turf and stone and boulders. Causeways for entrances were left at north and south. To the central area the people dragged twenty-four heavy boulders. Although these have gone their filled-in holes show how big they must have been. In plan the ring was egg-shaped, not conforming to the elegant outline of the ditch and bank. Two extra stones were erected within the ring near the entrances as though to emphasize them. Three more stones were set up at the centre of the ring, two side-slabs and a massively broad back stone, as much as five metres wide, to make a Cove very like those at Arbor Low, Avebury and Stanton Drew, where remains of these box-like structures can still be seen. At Cairnpapple it faced west-south-west.

Near it and alongside some circle-stones were patches of burnt soil, and some large pits were dug by the Cove. In these scraps of cremated bone were found, suggesting that here too funerary ceremonies had taken place, dead bodies being brought to the ring at auspicious times of the year. Cairnpapple must have been an impressive site to which scores of native people came for such ceremonies.

It did not last. Around 2100 BC Beaker people pulled down two of the Cove stones,

buried a man in an oval setting of small stones by the remaining slab and heaped a small cairn over the grave. This too was changed. Food-Vessel people, who seem often to have taken over and smashed stone circles, came to the circle-henge. On the central plateau they constructed two cists for burials, hauled down the stones of the circle and used them as kerbs for an even larger cairn which they piled over the Beaker mound. During the Middle Bronze Age the cairn was enlarged still further for more burials. As late as the Iron Age more graves were dug to the east of the cairn.

The remains of all these phases can still be seen. The bank and ditch survive, the stone-holes are reconstructed, and a ladder descends into the womb of the cairn where the dead were laid in this desecrated stone circle four thousand years ago.

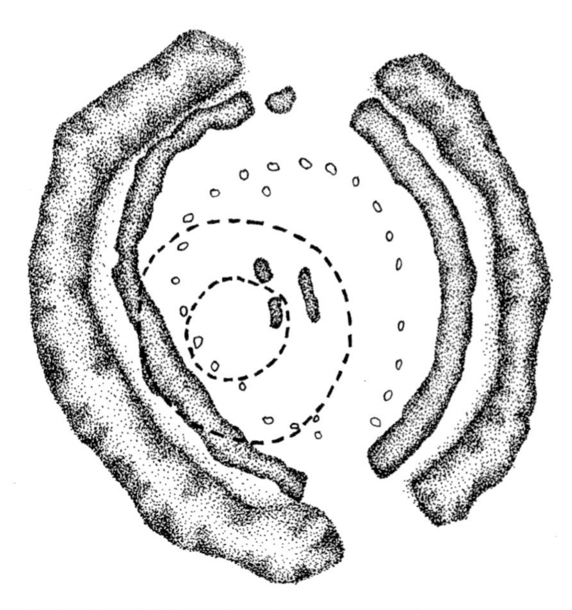

Below Food-Vessel kerbstones stand outside the Beaker cairn, now reinforced with a concrete dome. Photograph: Crown Copyright.

Girdle Stanes

Dumfriesshire (Dumfries and Galloway): NY 254961. 11 miles NE of Lockerbie, just S of Bankhead on a minor road to Castle O'er and Paddockhole. On private land, downhill from the road, by the river in trees. (Circular, about 40 metres.)

The Girdle Stanes is a large ring, a circle-henge with all the characteristics of the Lake District sites and probably influenced by a knowledge of those splendid rings.

It was built on a fairly level stretch of land alongside the river White Esk, with towering hills all around it. Since it was erected the river has changed course and carried away the western arc. There may have been as many as forty stones here originally, substantial granite blocks mottled with green lichen, leaning or fallen on the weathered crest of a wide grassy bank. The tallest stone now is at the north. At the east, beneath the trees, two stones stand just outside the circumference to form an apparent entrance like those at Long Meg and Swinside. Like many other great Neolithic stone circles the Girdle Stanes occupies a low-lying position near water.

Over a hundred metres to the north-north-east, on a ridge, are two fallen outlying stones, neither of them large. These may be the final

stones of an irregular line that is said to have meandered northwards to another ring, the Loupin' Stanes (NY 257966), a third of a mile away. In 1911 the outliers were examined to see if they were correctly placed to have been astronomical forsesights from the Girdle Stanes. One was thought to have been aligned on the rising of Capella in 1360 BC, which would have been about a thousand years after the Girdle Stanes was built. The position of the other stone was doubtful and no worthwhile analysis could be made of it. As with so many other outliers, the insignificance of these stones argues against such interpretations.

The embanked stones lean together under the trees. In the background is the entrance.

Glenquickan

Kirkcudbright (Dumfries and Galloway): NX 509582. **6 miles W of Gatehouse of Fleet, 1¾ miles E of Creetown on S side of the old military way, the Corse of Slakes road. On private land. (Flattened circle, 16.8 × 14.6 metres.)**

On the hilly wilderness of moors between Wigtown Bay and the Water of Fleet there are dozens of prehistoric monuments, from the chambered tombs of Cairnholy in the south by Kirkdale Burn to cairns, standing stones and circles like High Auchenlarie (NX 539534) and Cauldside Burn (NX 529571).

In this mélange of megalithic and sub-megalithic sites there is the wonderment of Glenquickan, an unimpressive ring in itself but possessing one of the most spectacular centre stones in the British Isles. Even from a short distance the circle-stones are unobtrusive in the wiry grass, twenty-eight rough and water-worn slabs with their longer faces along the circumference. About a metre away from the true centre rises a huge cylinder of granite, man-high, a metre thick, and some four tons in weight. There are other rings with centre stones in this district, Claughreid (NX 517560) and Lairdmannoch (NX 662614) among them, all ruined, but showing how popular this particular cult was in south-west Scotland.

The whole interior of Glenquickan is littered with cobbles like the floor of a cairn and this may give a clue to the significance of the

centre stone. Where such rings have been excavated very often burials have been discovered at the base of these great stones which may be 'ancestor' pillars, supposedly the habitation of the spirits of the dead. Such embodiments of death would be regarded as highly potent and would need a protective barrier of stones around them.

A second ring once existed in the field to the north-west of Glenquickan but it has now been destroyed.

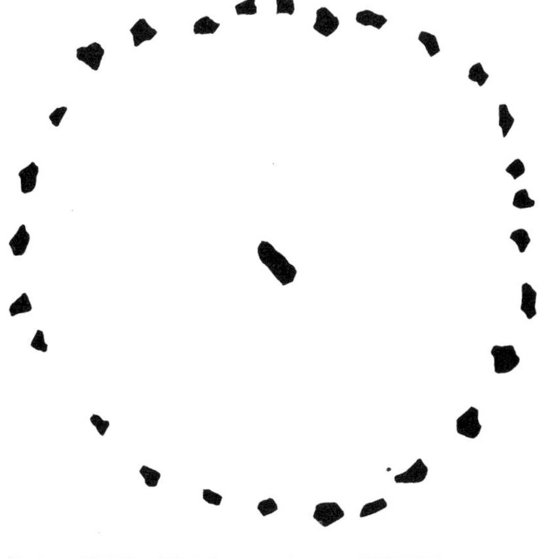

Below left The most perfect centre-stone circle in the British Isles.
Below right The builders of the ring may have seen it as the home of ancestral spirits.

Loupin' Stanes

Dumfriesshire (Dumfries and Galloway): NY 257966. 11 miles NE of Lockerbie and ⅓ mile N of the Girdle Stanes. On private land. (Flattened circle, 13.4 × 10.9 metres.)

Among the most bizarre of the eccentric circles of south-west Scotland are the misshapen tiny rings with two very large stones in their south-western quadrant. There are hardly any other rings like these elsewhere and it must be assumed that these are very local variants, distantly related to the recumbent stone circles of north-east Scotland, with their tall flankers.

Ninestone Rigg in Roxburgh (NY 518973) and perhaps Burgh Hill also (NT 470062) belong to this tradition but the most accessible and rewarding site is at the Loupin' Stanes, five hundred metres north of the Girdle Stanes circle-henge, which must have been several centuries old when this second ring was built.

The stones stand on an artificial platform up to half a metre high and almost perfectly horizontal. This levelling, which is also a feature of some recumbent stone circles, suggests that the builders were concerned with some astronomical alignment. On the platform they erected twelve stones, ten of them low, but placing two radically taller pillars at the west-south-west. Because these stones seem to provide an unequivocal sight-line, we made a careful plan of the ring and checked the compass-bearings. The alignment across the ring faces 246° between the pillars and looks towards an elevated skyline which has no remarkable notch into which the setting sun

might sink. Nor was the alignment related to any important setting of the sun or moon but, instead, appeared to indicate sunset in early November or late January, rather odd times of the year for early pastoralists to choose.

Alexander Thom also was unable to find any significance for these stones, although he did think there might have been a solar alignment to the Loupin' Stanes from a collapsed ring just to its east-south-east. This turf-creeping circle, about 22.8 × 18.6 metres in size, can still be made out in the pasture field.

Opposite Loupin' Stanes from the west. The ruins of a second ring lie tumbled in the background.
Below The two bulky stones at the south-west.

Torhousekie

Wigtownshire (Dumfries and Galloway): NX 383565. 6 miles SSW of Newton Stewart, 3 miles W of Wigtown on S side of the B733 from Wigtown to Kirkcowan. In State care. Signposted. (Flattened circle, 21.4 × 20.0 metres.)

Well to the west of the smaller rings on Cambret Moor, this circle stands on the sandy Machars near a source of copper a few miles to the north-west. Its position on a slight terrace was made level by the construction of a raised platform of earth and small stones. On this nineteen granite stones were erected, graded in height from the lowest, half a metre high, at the west-north-west, up to the tallest, a metre high, at the east-south-east, where there is a flattened arc to the ring. The smaller stones are closer together and also thinner, the lowest slab-like stone being opposite the bulkiest boulder.

Inside the ring are three other stones in a line, the two outer being fat, rounded boulders, one fallen forwards. Between these is a smaller stone, making a setting which mirrors the arrangement of the flankers and the recumbent in the circles of north-east Scotland. These three stones stand at the base of a D-shaped rubble bank with a hollowed interior and this is presumably a grown-over ring-cairn in which cremated human bones were buried.

With its platform, its graded stones, its flankers and ring-cairn Torhousekie contains all the features of a recumbent stone circle, and it is

probable that it was constructed by people who had seen some of the great rings in Aberdeenshire. Only the orientation is different. Whereas the majority of recumbent stones were placed in the south-west sector of the ring, Torhousekie has its recumbent pointing towards the east-south-east. This, however, is little different from some of the later recumbent stone circles in Kincardine where the recumbent was not only placed in the south-east quadrant but often was situated well inside the circle as is the Torhousekie boulder.

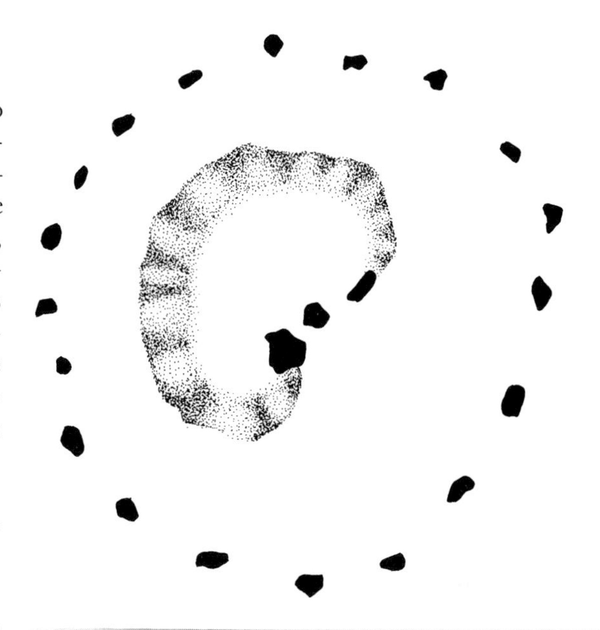

Below left Torhousekie from the east, with the recumbent and its flankers near the centre.
Below right A three-stone row east of the circle.

WALES

CERRIG DUON *Powys (Brecknockshire)*
DRUIDS' CIRCLE *Gwynedd (Caernarvonshire)*
GORS FAWR *Dyfed (Pembrokeshire)*

The stone circles of Wales are in many ways quite different from those of England, being the products of small and isolated communities whose contacts with other regions were rare and slight. In coastal areas, visited by traders and where sea or gentle river valley provided easy travelling, the stone circles do resemble those of neighbouring areas, even though they are usually smaller. But inland, among the narrow passes between the mountains or on the high moors far away from other people, families put up rings no bigger than would be needed by a few men and women and whose stones could easily be manhandled into place. Many of these tiny rings have characteristics probably derived from the greater circles of more populous areas but here transformed into strange forms as though their meaning had not been properly understood. There are avenues of stones so low that the grass hides them, and which pass to one side of the ring instead of joining with it. There are outlying stones as bulky as a solid telephone kiosk. In each region of Wales there are small groups of rings, each area different and remote from the next, and every circle surprising.

It is, for example, only recently that the ring at Walton in Powys (SO 245607) has been recognised as a Four-Poster. Quite why a 'Scottish' circle should be built far away in central Wales is one of the mysteries that make these Welsh rings so interesting, and so well worth visiting.

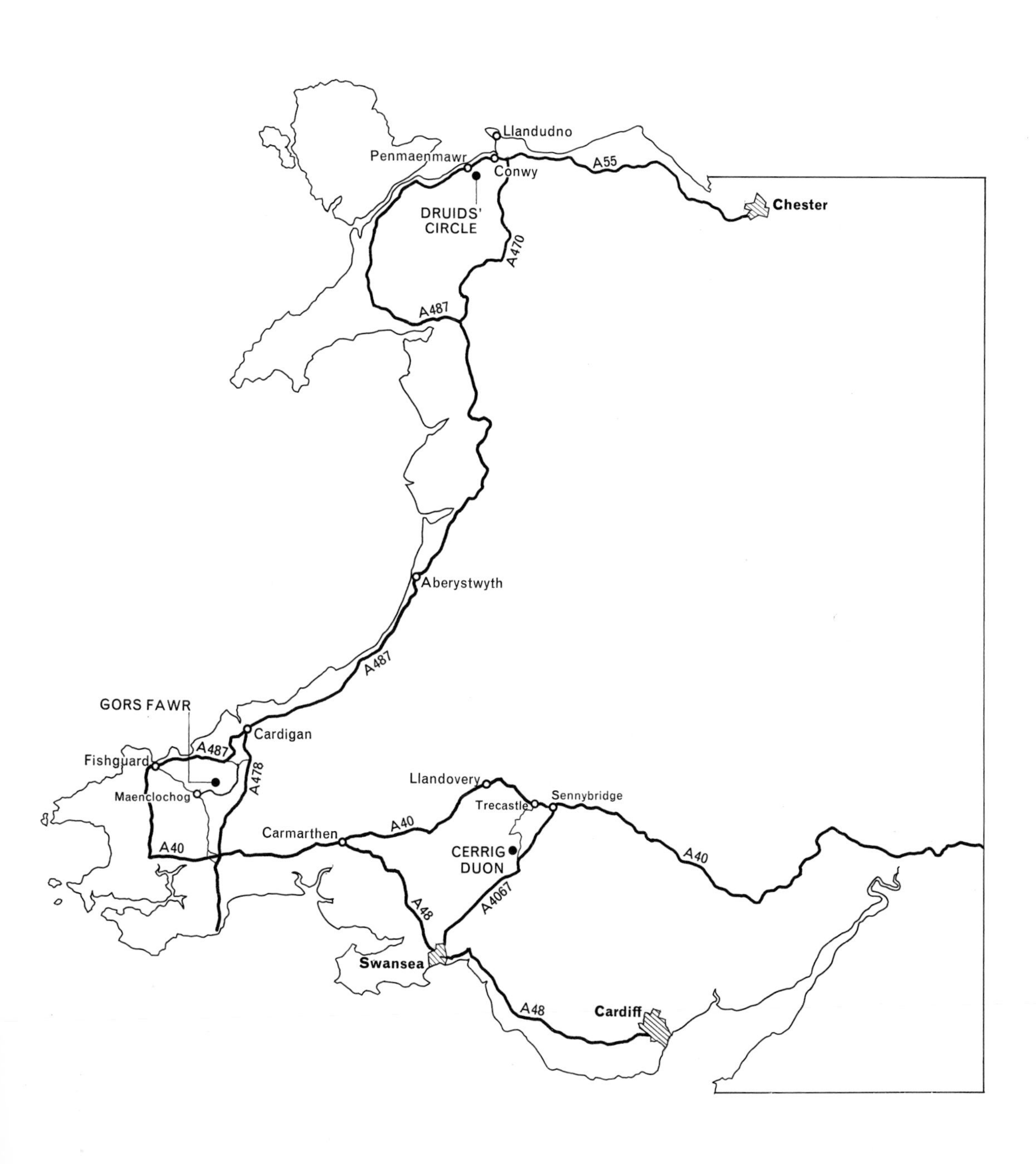
Llandudno
Penmaenmawr
Conwy
A55
Chester
DRUIDS'
CIRCLE
A470
A487
Aberystwyth
A487
GORS FAWR
Cardigan
A487
Fishguard
A478
Maenclochog
A40
Carmarthen
A40
Llandovery
Trecastle
Sennybridge
CERRIG
DUON
A40
A48
A4067
Swansea
A48
Cardiff

Cerrig Duon

Powys (Brecknockshire): SN 852206. **10 miles SSE of Llandovery and 7 miles SW of Sennybridge, to W of a minor road S from Trecastle. (Egg-shaped, 18.2 × 16.8 metres.)**
A simple description of Cerrig Duon, sometimes known as Maen Mawr, as a stone circle with an outlier and an avenue of stones would seem to place it in the same class of megalithic complex as Avebury and Stanton Drew. This would be far from true. Although the architecture of the Welsh ring may owe something to those enormous circles, a child could step over its stones and could pick up any one of the avenue stones without strain.

Cerrig Duon's inconspicuous ring lies at the head of a low hill with one gigantic block, Maen Mawr, the Big Stone, outside it to the north-north-west. Two tiny stones peep from the ground beyond it. The circle-stones are so small that only Maen Mawr can be seen from the road lower down to the east and it is this outlier that a visitor should look for. It is so heavy that forty or fifty men and women would have been needed to lift it upright, three or four families who lived further down the valley where there was water and good farming soil. The circle may have been erected at the very edge of their land. There is also a short tapering avenue rising from the roadside stream.

It is unlikely that the heavy-set Maen Mawr could have been used for refined astronomy, but it is ideal as a directional marker. A distant

standing stone (SN 855215) is set like a playing card with its thin side pointing towards Cerrig Duon half a mile to the south. From this stone only Maen Mawr can be made out and it may be from this direction that strangers and traders approached Cerrig Duon's lonely ring.

Opposite Cerrig Duon from the north. Maen Mawr, the Big Stone, with the tiny circle-stones behind it.
Below A cumbersome sandstone block, Maen Mawr is an improbable astronomical foresight.

Druids' Circle

Gwynedd (Caernarvonshire): SH 722746. **On Penmaenmawr headland 4 miles WSW of Conwy. A steep walk from the minor road at Capelulo or from the end of the track at SH 744747 beyond Plas Tirion. (Elliptical, 25.7 × 24.5 metres.)**

There are only a few stone circles around the North Welsh coasts, most of them plain rings that seem to have been the centres of small groups of people. This coastline was much travelled in prehistoric times. To the north-west were the Lake District 'factories' of stone axes whose products were traded as far as southern England. To the west was Ireland, from which copper and gold articles were sent out across England during the Bronze Age. In North Wales itself were other axe-factories, henges near Bangor, and chambered tombs that testified to Neolithic occupation on fertile patches of land in Snowdonia and on Anglesey, hardly a prehistoric day's journey from the Druids' Circle.

This well-known ring stands high above the sea on a wind-blown stretch of moorland, and from the tussocks of reedy grass to its south one can look past the ring and out across the waters of Conway Bay to the mass of Great Orme's Head. From the south, then, the circle can be seen, but from the north-east it is even more spectacular for its stones stab out of the skyline of a buckled ridge. It is clear that its position was chosen to be conspicuous, and for a simple reason. It was built right against a prehistoric trackway along which traders passed, stepping quietly past this ring whose stones dominate the view.

There is a whole line of monuments in the vicinity. The Graig Lwyd axe-factory is only half a mile away. East of the Druids' Circle is a five-stone ring (SH 725747) very like the little recumbent stone settings of south-west Ireland (see Kealkil). A dense concentration of white quartz pebbles was found in it. To the west is a ring-cairn (SH 721745), dated to about 1780 BC, in which charcoal and burnt patches of ground were noticed near the cremated bones of a young woman.

But it is the Druids' Circle that is the focus of the group. In 1695 Edward Lhwyd described the ring as 'the most remarkable monument in all Snowdon . . . a circular entrenchment . . . on the outside whereof, there are certain rude pillar-stones pitcht on end; of which 12 are now standing, some 2 yards, others 5 foot high'. It is little different today. Thirty or so granite stones, all local and fairly large but not carefully chosen for their heights, are unevenly spaced around a worn-down bank of earth and stones, the entrance marked by taller stones at the west-south-west. The interior is level.

Excavations by W. Griffiths in 1958 revealed that the centre contained a crude scatter of stones laid down to conceal several cremations. One almost at the exact centre of the ring lay in a tiny, diamond-shaped cist whose long sides pointed towards the entrance. In it, beneath a food-vessel urn, were the cremated bones of a child about eleven years old. The burnt bones of another child of the same age were found in another cist nearby. A bronze knife had been

placed with it. Yet another cremation near the middle of the circle had been buried in a pit from which a shallow trench led to a wide hole lined with whetstones, perhaps the equivalents of those chalk axes thought to be solar symbols that have been discovered in some southern English ceremonial centres. More cremated bone lay over these sandstone tools.

In appearance the Druids' Circle is like the Westmorland ring Gamelands (NY 640082), where the stones also stood in a low bank, a similarity not unexpected in the years around 2100 BC when people and ideas were moving along the ever-busier trade-routes of the north. Of all the British stone rings the Druids' Circle appears the most ominous, with its seeming, stark evidence of sacrifice. The children's bones and buried whetstones surely proclaim that they were dedications, offerings of death for the sake of the living.

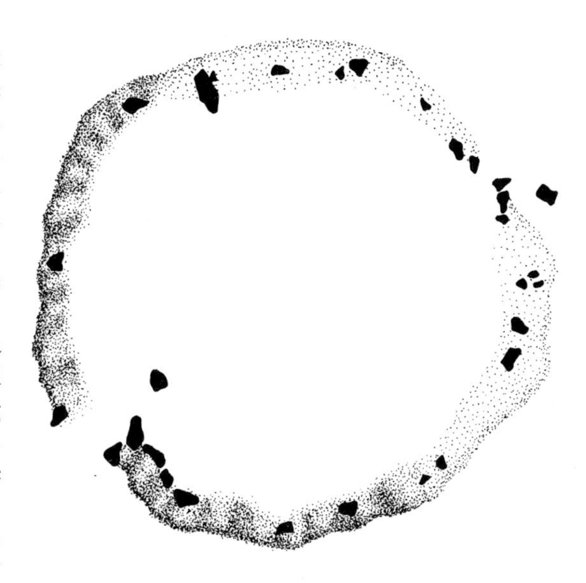

Below One of the stones is reputed to bend over towards anyone who swears near it.

Gors Fawr

***Dyfed (Pembrokeshire): SN 134294.* 10 miles S of Cardigan and 3¼ miles ENE of Maenclochog. Just to the W of a minor road from which it can be seen. (Circular, 22.3 metres.)**

This circle of igneous boulders stands on common land in full view of the dark Preseli mountains that rise to its north. Stone battle-axes were manufactured there at the very end of the New Stone Age, and it may have been past Gors Fawr and past the circle-henge of Meini-gwyr (SN 142266) to its south that the bluestones were dragged on the first stage of their journey to Stonehenge. Beaker people certainly visited this region. There are several ruined chambered tombs nearby and some earthworks which may be the remains of henges.

At Gors Fawr, the Great Wasteland, people erected sixteen weathered stones in a perfect circle, but were careful not to make their tops level. Instead, the heights rise towards the south with the same kind of deliberate grading that can be seen in the remarkably similar Fernworthy (SX 655841) a hundred miles away across the Bristol Channel on Dartmoor. There the stones rise towards the north, and it is interesting to find how often the cardinal points of north, south, east or west are stressed by taller stones in the stone circles along the western coasts of Britain. At Gors Fawr and Fernworthy it is possible that the architecture was influenced by people voyaging around the coastlines of the Severn Estuary in search of

copper ores during the early years of the Bronze Age.

Over a hundred metres to the north-east of Gors Fawr are two large standing stones on an axis east-north-east / west-south-west of each other and at a tangent to the ring. Their relationship to the circle is unclear, and the various astronomical suggestions which have been made are unconvincing.

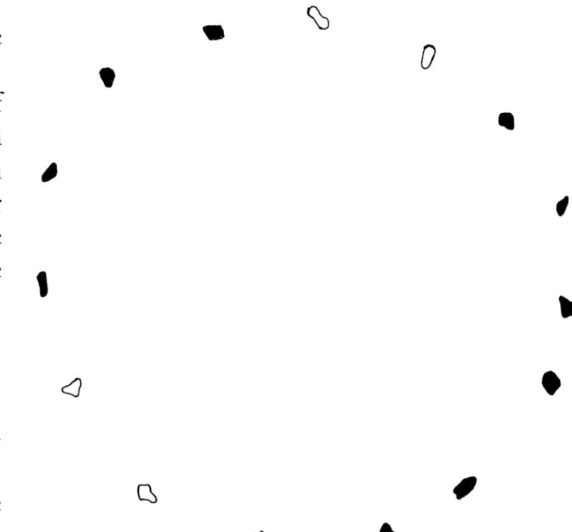

Opposite Gors Fawr from the south. The mist-covered Preselis loom across the landscape.
Below The weathered outlying stones to the north of the circle.

IRELAND

BALLYNOE *County Down*
BEAGHMORE *County Tyrone*
CASTLERUDDERY *County Wicklow*
DROMBEG *County Cork*
KEALKIL *County Cork*
THE LIOS *County Limerick*
LISSYVIGGEEN *County Kerry*
NEW GRANGE *County Meath*

The stone circles of Ireland vary in every region. It would seem that despite the prospecting and exploitation of natural resources that had gone on since earliest times, first the searching for stone that would make good Neolithic axes, and then the locating of the copper ores and gold that Irish smiths sought for their products during the Bronze Age, every area of Ireland kept very much to its own customs. There is some overlapping of ideas but it is slight.

In the south-west in Cork and Kerry there is a multitude of recumbent stone circles, quite spacious rings like Drombeg near the coast and much smaller sites inland in the hills, where the stones of Kealkil enclose a space hardly big enough for four or five sheep to graze in. The burials and recumbent stones of these sites distinguish them from the earthen-banked circles farther north in Limerick. The great central space of the Lios has far more in common with the henges of the Atlantic coasts, and this is also true of Castleruddery, far to the east, on the very fringe of the thin line of true open circles around the Wicklow mountains and along the coast northwards.

Whether New Grange, beyond the mountains, was once a huge plain ring of stones into which the magnificent passage-grave was introduced is still unclear, but it seems certain that Ballynoe in County Down was once free of its present central cairn. Along this eastern coast of Ireland there are other examples of open rings that were surely related to the megalithic circles of the Late Neolithic in England.

The circles of Northern Ireland are different. Among the hills of Ulster the majority of the rings are small, of many stones, and with cairns slumping at their centres, built when the ageing megalithic tradition was fading out of prehistory. Rings like Beaghmore, even though they are small and low and late, are as distinctive as any in the British Isles. They are also just as enigmatic.

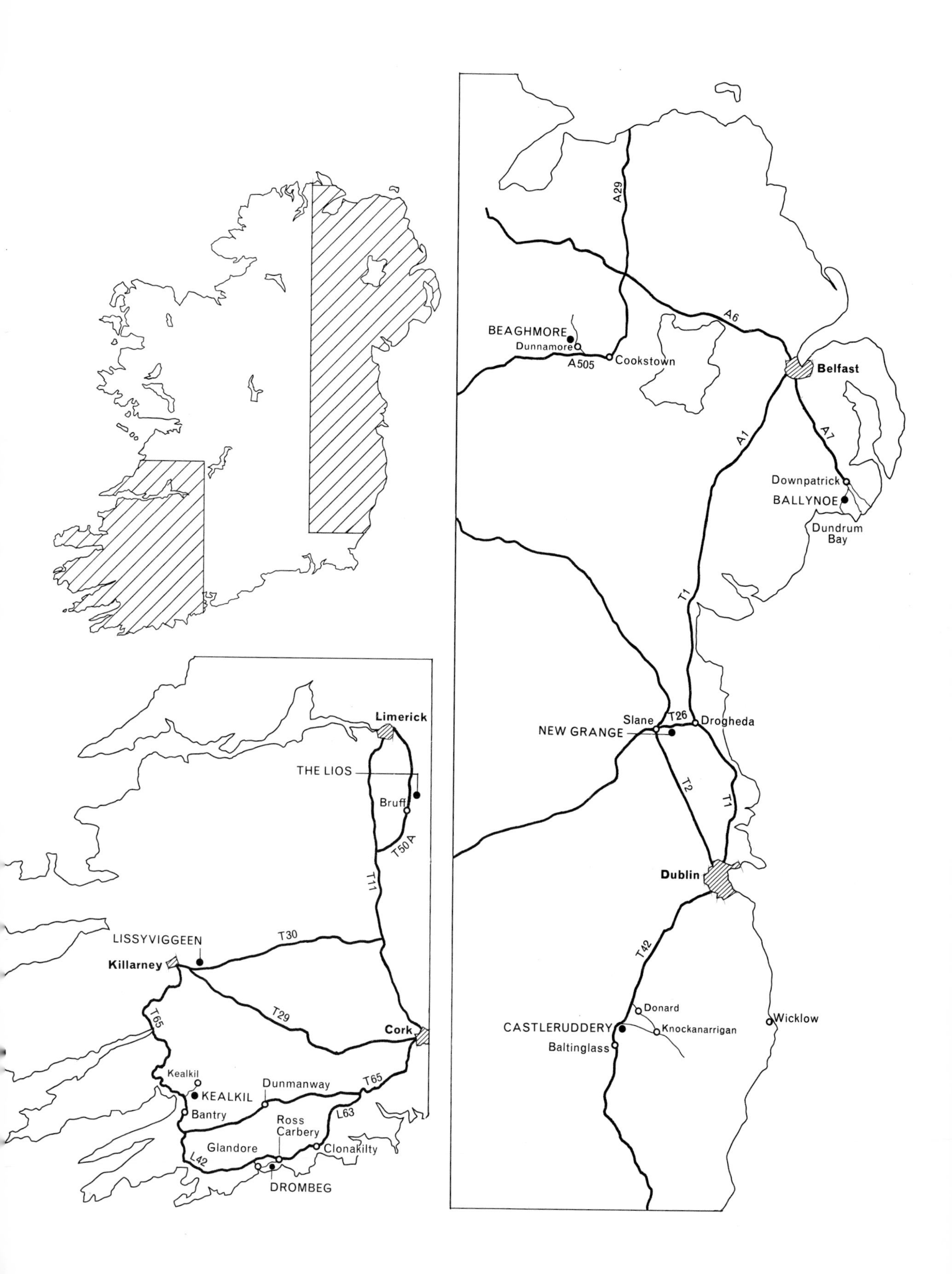

BEAGHMORE
Dunnamore
A505
Cookstown
A29
A6
Belfast
A1
A7
Downpatrick
BALLYNOE
Dundrum
Bay
T1
Slane
T26
Drogheda
NEW GRANGE
T2
T1
Dublin
T42
Donard
CASTLERUDDERY
Knockanarrigan
Baltinglass
Wicklow
Limerick
THE LIOS
Bruff
T50 A
T11
LISSYVIGGEEN
T30
Killarney
T29
Cork
T65
Kealkil
KEALKIL
Dunmanway
T65
Bantry
L63
Ross
Carbery
Glandore
Clonakilty
L42
DROMBEG

Ballynoe

County Down: J 481404. 2½ miles S of Downpatrick, 2 miles N of Dundrum Bay, in a field off a minor road. (Circular, 33.5 metres.)

Ballynoe is probably the finest open stone circle in the whole of Ireland, a huge ring of boulders built on low ground with the land falling away to the south-west where the Mourne mountains rise darkly in the distance. Not far to the south is the rock-strewn beach of Dundrum Bay, ideal for people setting out across the waters of the Irish Sea, and among the sandhills whose grassy hummocks line this shore dozens of places have been unearthed where New Stone Age people lived for a while, burning fires, shaping flint tools, eating from coarse pots that they decorated with cockle-shell impressions. It was in this region of Neolithic activity that the stone circle of Ballynoe was erected.

Like other great Neolithic rings it was put up on low land near water, the Minerstown river passing just to its east. The circle also is unique inasmuch as there is direct proof of its antiquity. One small sherd of Carrowkeel ware was found in it, flaky, crumbly, with large grits in its body, and patterned by pressing the end of a bird-bone into the clay before firing, made by some woman in the Late Neolithic period nearly five thousand years ago.

It was the scattered families of this time that built Ballynoe as a communal temple and place of assembly. There is a remarkable resemblance between it and the Cumbrian ring of Swinside across the sea, and as a natural sea-route would have been from Dundrum Bay to the Duddo Sands near Swinside it is likely that these two splendid circles were in some way related.

Over fifty large boulders were brought to Ballynoe. There are many glacial erratics of Ordovician grit in the locality and it was these that the builders put up in a circle, the stones set closely together as in the other great open rings of the English Lake District. There is no sign of shaping on these irregular boulders but two even more ponderous blocks do rise above the others at north and south in the cardinal positions noted in other open rings. At the west-north-west are two external uprights some three metres outside the circumference and two long strides apart from each other, forming a portalled entrance like those of Swinside and Long Meg and Her Daughters in Cumberland.

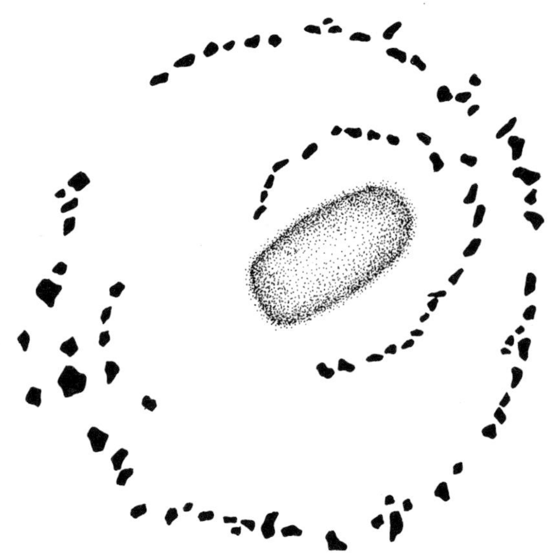

Outside the ring are unobtrusive outlying stones, two in line at the north, two at the south, another at the south-west and others at the north-west. These seem too low to have been used astronomically by an observer from the ring. It may be that the directions of the midsummer and midwinter sunsets were marked by some of them, acting not as foresights for precise observations but as crude calendrical pillars.

Inside the stone circle is a Bronze Age mound which the 1937–8 excavations proved to contain cists. As in so many rings, later people deliberately buried their dead in this ancient holy place. Here they constructed several large cists east–west of each other in the eastern half of the circle and placed cremations in them. Around these cists they arranged an oval of heavy kerbstones and inside it laid smoothed, egg-shaped stones known as baetyls and possibly with some sexual significance. A low cairn was piled over the cists and this, in turn, was covered with an oval mound of earth. A crescent of standing stones was raised to the west of this multiple-cist barrow, roughly in line with the original entrance.

Opposite Entrance stones at Ballynoe, often called the most magnificent open stone circle in all Ireland.

The visitor therefore will not see Ballynoe in its original state with an open central space for the ceremonies of its builders. Yet even with the intrusion of the Bronze Age cairn the stone circle remains impressive and grand.

Opposite Gors Fawr. A single standing stone rises proudly against the rain.
Below Ballynoe, looking to the south-west. The later grass-covered cairn can be seen inside the huge Neolithic circle.

Beaghmore

County Tyrone: H 685842. $8\frac{1}{2}$ miles WNW of Cookstown and W of minor road from Dunnamore to Broughderg Bridge. In State care. (Irregular rings. Eastern pair: A – 11.9 × 9.6 metres; B – 10.0 × 9.8 metres; centre pair: C – 17.1 × 15.9 metres, D – 16.8 × 16.2 metres; northern ring: E – 19.5 × 16.8 metres; south-western pair: F – 8.5 metres, G – 9.8 metres.)

Dotted on the hillsides of the Sperrin mountains of northern Ireland are countless rings whose circumferences are studded with stones hardly bigger than a football and almost as easily lifted. Such rings are in no sense megalithic. Many of them lie on southern slopes, sheltered from the winds and drizzle of this region, and often they are in pairs,

especially in County Tyrone where there are groups of three or four rings very close together as though put up in succession over a hundred years or more. Sometimes they were laid out near older chambered tombs, suggesting that even though customs had changed there had been small family territories in this area for many centuries.

The architecture of these rings is mixed. There are some concentrics in the south, there are plain rings and rings with short rows by them and, towards the east coast, even rows of three stones with no stone circle at all. There are rings with centre stones. Yet there is one feature that is common to most of them. They are either very close to a cairn or have a cairn inside them, once again affirming the strong connection between stone circles and burial. The seven rings of Beaghmore are no different. Here there are paired circles with long rows of small stones and shorter rows of tall stones, and with cairns in which cists, pottery and cremations have been found.

These sites were discovered during the cutting of peat which had grown over the complex and the rings were partly excavated between 1945 and 1949. The tips of other stones can still be seen untouched on the other side of the road.

The circles had been built on a terrace of sandy soil overlooking the river valley to the north-west. As one walks in from the east faint traces of a Neolithic field wall can be seen running north-south before one comes to the first pair of rings on the right, known as A and B. Two long splayed stone rows and two shorter rows of taller stones converge on a low cairn that lies between them. The circles yielded no finds but the cairn had a polished stone axe from Antrim in it.

A second field wall lies between A, B and the next pair, C, D, two grossly irregular rings with two rows leading to a cairn touching the north of D. It held an empty cist but inside C there were the remains of pits, hearths, charcoal, flints and shouldered Neolithic pottery, all of which looks like the remnants of an early New Stone Age ritual centre known to archaeologists as a Goodland site where offerings of fertile soil and broken objects were given to the forces of nature. Ring C seems to have been intentionally built on top of this sacred area.

Beyond C, D lies the buckled ring E, built around a cairn from which a row extended. It is the strangest of all these strange settings. There was a cremation in the cist and bits of fungus, moss and twigs with a stone laid on them. Broken skull fragments were spread on this stone. Inside ring E there are needles of upright stones in a wild confusion and no one could ever have danced here.

To its south is another cairn covering a pit with some oak wood in it, and then there is the last pair of rings, F, G, lying on either side of a row of little stones that passes between them to a cairn with a bank and outer ditch around it.

It is likely that the Beaghmore rings are later than the cairns they surround. Two radiocarbon 'dates' from F, G's row and cairn averaged about 1930 BC. Peat from the ditch was dated to 950 BC. The stone circles probably were built quite early in the thousand years between these dates, successive family monuments of the Middle Bronze Age, part cemetery, part temple, erected at a time when peat was already inexorably beginning to destroy by its encroachment the good land on which these farmers lived.

Opposite Circle E, with a cairn and rings F and G behind it to the north.

Castleruddery

County Wicklow: S 92.94. 4¾ miles NE of Baltinglass, 2½ miles SSW of Donard, on S side of a minor road from Coolmoney Camp to Knockanarrigan. Circular bank, 29.3 metres.)

Neglected, knee-high in grass and surrounded by round-crowned hawthorns whose May blossom speckles the bank, it is difficult to appreciate how important Castleruddery must have been early in the Bronze Age when Beaker copper prospectors and the Wicklow mountain goldminers passed by its brilliant entrance.

It is not properly a stone circle but a henge, with a stone-lined interior. It was constructed on the summit of a hill just east of the valley into which the Little Slaney flows. Six miles north is the lovely Athgreany stone circle (N 930032) and only two miles to the south is the Boleycarrigeen ring, its stones embedded in a low earthen bank.

There is a bank also at Castleruddery, five paces wide, hip-high, but with no ditch, and the soil and turf that composed it must have been scraped from the land around. One or two small stones can just be seen like kerbstones along its outer edge but its interior is lined with boulders of all sizes, some rough and rounded, others fallen blocks. There are at least twenty-nine stones and the fragments of others lie haphazardly in the grass. Most spectacular of all is the entrance, planned to be at the exact east. Two enormous stones flanked it, portals of white quartz so heavy that a hundred people

would have been needed to drag them uphill. Other tumbled stones lead like an avenue from the east towards this dazzling entrance.

No excavation has been recorded at Castleruddery but there are other ditchless henges in Ireland at the Lios and near New Grange in County Meath, and across the sea at the Welsh Ysbyty-Cynfyn (SN 752791), and at Mayburgh in Westmorland (NY 519284), all large amphitheatres where people met for their rituals. Interestingly, Mayburgh also had an eastern stone-lined entrance with stones leading to it.

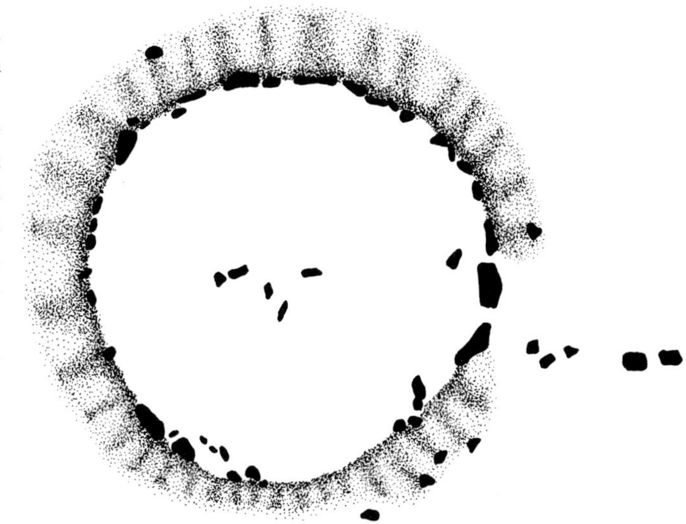

Opposite Two of the huge stones that line the interior of this neglected earthwork.
Below A majestic block amid the long grass.

Drombeg

County Cork: W 247352. 10 miles WSW of Clonakilty and 3 miles W of Ross Carbery. On S side of the road from Ross Carbery to Glandore. (Circular, 9.1 metres.)

Below The portal-stones at the entrance to the recumbent stone circle of Drombeg. The earth between these taller stones had been trampled by many feet.

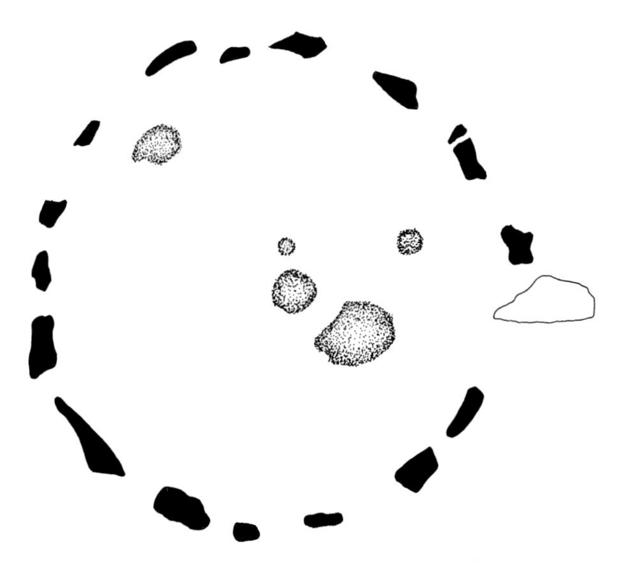

Five hundred miles of land and sea away from north-east Scotland is the only other concentration of recumbent stone circles in the British Isles, some eighty rings along the undulating coastline of south-west Ireland and farther inland in the Boggeragh mountains. A casual visitor would hardly notice the similarity between the circles here and the Scottish megalithic giants. The Irish rings are only half the size and their recumbent stones are not block-like monsters but thin slabs like elongated paving-stones. Nor do they have flanking stones. Instead, the tallest pillars stand on the other side of the ring, forming entrances. Some of these portal-stones were set at right angles to the circumference, as at Bohonagh (W 308368) and Maulatanvally (W 263443), in a way which emphasizes the opposed entrance even more. No ring-cairn was built inside the Irish circles but they were sometimes placed alongside the rings and, despite their differences, each architectural feature of the Scottish rings is found in the Irish, modified, displaced, but present. It is probable that at some time during the Early Bronze Age settlers came to this region, perhaps after a generation or two of migration from Scotland, and eventually began to build monuments in imitation of rings that they may have only heard described. The recumbent, its orientation, the graded stones, the nearby ring-cairn, central cremations, all these occur in the Irish recumbent stone circles. Even quartz fragments have been discovered in some.

Drombeg, also known as the Druid's Altar, is perhaps the best to visit because of its 1957 excavation. The family that was to erect its stones first levelled the terrace where it was to stand, filling in hollows with broken rock, laying down small stones to raise the western side until the floor was horizontal. To this platform they brought seventeen slabs, mostly sandstone from nearby, and having scribed out a circle they dug a shallow socket for each stone, shaping the holes for individual pillars, calculating the depth to achieve the graded heights that were obligatory, the dressed tops of the neighbouring stones sloping up to the recumbent. The excavator thought that the smallest stone was so obviously phallic in outline that it must have been chosen for its symbolism, especially as it was placed against the high 'female' lozenge of the east portal.

The recumbent is not gigantic but it does have a beautifully flat upper edge bearing a cupmark surrounded by the pecked outline of an axe. There is another cupmark near it.

It is possible to reconstruct the ceremonies here, held probably as the midwinter sun was setting behind the recumbent. Somewhere nearby a pyre had blazed, burning the bones of a young adolescent. From the ashes the people raked smouldering charcoal and bone which they packed into a freshly broken pot wrapped round with thick cloth. They carried this vessel and its contents to a pit near the circle's centre, pressing it firmly down and putting other sherds by it. They piled soil over this deposit and added a pinch of charcoal before filling the pit to its brim with soil. Into a smaller pit immediately to the north they packed darker, richer earth. The associations seem clear.

Needing fertile land and good harvests the people turned to the forces of the earth, supplicating them in a ring designed by the shape of its pillars to act as a centre of fecundity at the deadest time of the year. To give it strength they offered the burnt bones of one of the family. They stated what they needed through the burial of loamy soil. All this they sealed beneath a thick layer of gravel and it was upon this floor that their ceremonies were performed. The compacted turf, bits of charcoal and trodden-in pebbles around the entrance showed where they entered the ring.

Kealkil

***County Cork: W 054556.* 6 miles NNE of Bantry, 12 miles W of Dunmanway, alongside a minor road just S of Kealkil. (Oval, 3.1 × 2.9 metres; ring-cairn, circular, 6.6 metres.)**

Kealkil must be one of the smallest rings in the British Isles, a miniscule setting of five stones on the shoulder of Maughanclea Hill, from which the valley descends in a series of steps towards Bantry Bay.

This is one of many Five-Stone rings to be found in the inland regions of Cork and Kerry, built near patches of thin, light soil that Bronze Age people could cultivate with their primitive tools. The size and number of stones in these circles is so unusual that it is tempting to see them as versions of the Scottish Four-Posters, also very small, but here with a recumbent stone added.

The leprous-white stones of Kealkil are graded up towards the recumbent, itself of no great size but exceptional inasmuch as it was set at the exact north of the ring. To its north-east two pillars stand on an axis that points between the circle and the pillaged ring-cairn to its east. Excavation of the cairn produced little except three fragments of scallop shell, but the very presence of the ring-cairn is a reminder of the probable links between north-east Scotland and south-west Ireland in prehistoric times.

Kealkil was excavated in 1938 over a period of four weeks. The larger, writhing outlying pillar had toppled, breaking its top. It had virtually no stonehole and it must have been lowered into its clay-lined socket and then had a few stones packed round it at ground level. When it was re-erected in 1938 with the help of six labourers the task of heaving its four tons upright proved very difficult, even though it was shorter that it had been originally.

Nothing had survived in the acid soil inside the ring but two shallow ditches crossed at right angles near the centre, each over two metres long. It was supposed that these had held beams to support a central wooden post in the manner of an American Indian totem-pole. The irretrievable decay of such objects denies us all opportunity of re-creating them in our minds, leaving only romantic fancies as to what Kealkil had been used for.

Opposite Circle and standing stones at Kealkil.
Over Beaghmore, rings F and G.

Opposite Castleruddery, 'By Time's fell hand defac'd'. William Shakespeare.

Above Kealkil. The two pillars to the north-east of the stone circle.

The Lios

County Limerick: R 640410. 12 miles SSE of Limerick, 2½ miles N of Bruff, to E of the main road, T50A. (Circular, 47.6 metres.)

This immense and atmospheric ring, surrounded by trees, stands at the edge of one of the most important areas of prehistoric Ireland. Gathered around the shores of Lough Gur in a landscape of forested limestone hills are the remains of a Neolithic village whose timber-framed houses decayed five thousand years ago. There are field-systems, a wedge-shaped megalithic tomb, ring-cairns, standing stones, cairns, an artificial island of boulders amidst which Neolithic pottery was found, stone circles and there is the huge circle of the Lios itself.

Here, where the New Stone Age farmers had worked in fields walled with stones, people put up a slender pole and from it set out a ring whose circumference they marked with ten more posts. One opposing pair was aligned on the moon's minimum midsummer setting and this is where the entrance to the circle was to be. Twelve heavy stones of limestone or of volcanic breccia from a mile away were heaved upright around the perimeter, two at the entrance, two side by side opposite, the remaining eight replacing the posts. The result was a heavy but conventional stone circle. But then sections of bank were heaped up between the stones, built of clay carried in baskets from the nearby lough, with one narrow gap for the stone-lined entrance. To prevent the bank from collapsing inwards more stones were needed, laid upright along the ring's inner edge, forming a henge-like circle very similar to Castleruddery many miles to the east in County

Wicklow. The work took months and involved a hundred or more labourers. Coarse and fine pottery dating back to about 2500 BC was found broken under the bank during the excavation of 1939. The same styles of pottery, but accompanied by English ware and some early beaker vessels, were discovered inside the ring, suggesting that this magnificent circle was visited by traders and prospectors in the centuries that followed its construction. Another beaker, made as late as 2000 BC, lay smashed by the entrance. One wonders what these foreign visitors made of the massed lunar ceremonies that must have taken place here.

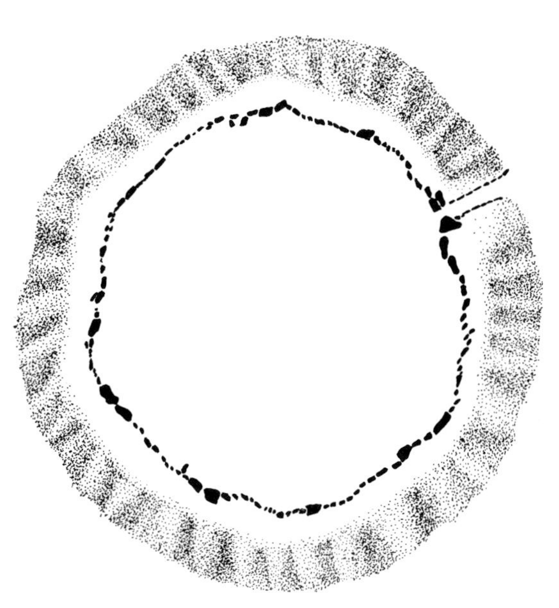

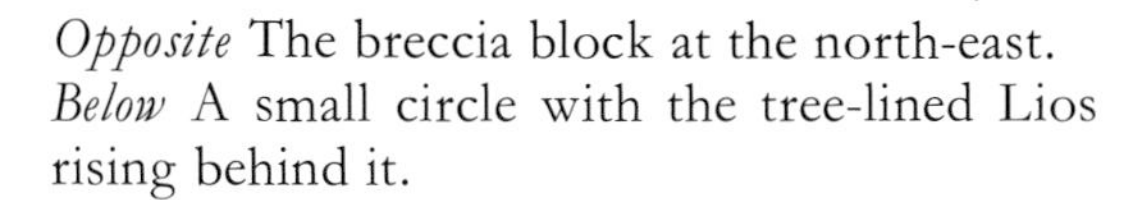

Opposite The breccia block at the north-east. *Below* A small circle with the tree-lined Lios rising behind it.

Lissyviggeen

County Kerry: V 997906. 2½ miles E of Killarney and ¼ mile from the main road, to the left after crossing Woodford Bridge. In State care. (Circular, 4.0 metres.)

This mysterious circle, hidden inside an earthen bank and with a pair of standing stones outside, may be not the simple monument it appears to be but two or three distinct structures of separate periods. As a unified complex it has no parallel.

Known also as the Seven Sisters, it was put up in an undulating landscape of gentle hills overlooking the waters of Lough Leane. With the river Flesk flowing only half a mile away the countryside must have been attractive to prehistoric people and to this spot they dragged seven boulders, none high, setting them in a ring with the broadest, its top hacked flat, at the west opposite the tallest stone. The wide boulder was probably the recumbent, hardly different from the others and quite unlike the distinctive slab at Drombeg or the colossal blocks in Scotland. Only its breadth and its orientations reveal its origins. The outlying pillars were put up at the same time.

At this stage Lissyviggeen was like other rings thirty miles to the east, where the tiny recumbent stone circle of Kilmartin Lower (W 455832) also had seven stones, including a recumbent at the west-north-west and an outlying stone near it. There are similar rings in these hills and the builders of Lissyviggeen may have wandered from the Boggeraghs, settling farther to the west at a time late in the

Bronze Age when the recumbent tradition was almost at an end.

If this is so then other people may have added the henge-like bank with its two entrances. As with the Lios to the north it had no ditch, and like that great enclosure it was put up in straightish sections around the stone ring, separating it from the standing stones, diminishing its power. That the two pillars do not belong to this phase is suggested by the fact that the southern entrance of the bank is not in line with them and that other small rings had similar pairs but no surrounding bank.

The date of Lissyviggeen is unknown. The ring's smallness, its remote position, its crude architecture suggest that even 1700 BC might not be too late.

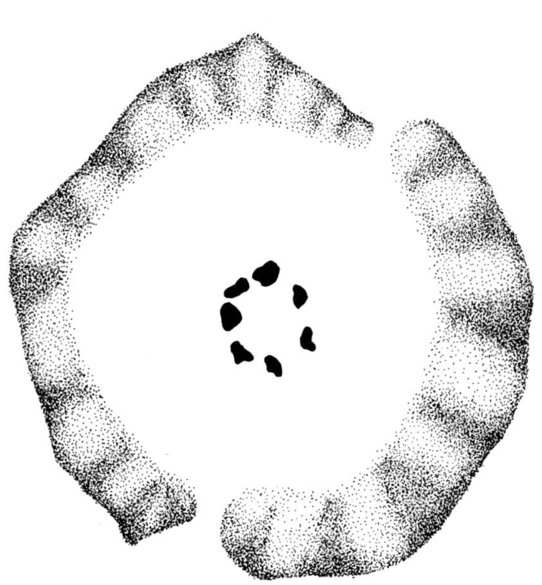

The tiny stones of the circle, daughters of the giants outside.

New Grange

County Meath: O 007727. **6 miles W of Drogheda, 26 miles N of Dublin, 3 miles ESE of Slane. In State care. (Stone circle, a flattened ring, 103.6 × 97.7 metres; chambered tomb, a flattened ring, 85.3 × 79.2 metres.)**

West of Drogheda is a charming reach of the river Boyne, one of the traditionally sacred rivers of the Celts. Here it bends to the south around a lovely expanse of fertile country just above its tidal limits, the low hills patterned with fields and oak copses. And here, thousands of years ago, Neolithic farmers lived, planting their crops, herding their cattle, burying their dead in one of the most magnificent cemeteries of prehistoric Europe.

Here, within an area of three square miles, are at least nineteen passage-graves, three of them, Dowth, Knowth and New Grange, stupendous mounds as large as hills, and as well as these burial-places there are standing stones, nine or ten henges, small barrows, possible house sites, all built near the river, where as early as the Middle Stone Age families may have fished, wandering along the banks in search of food. The very antiquity of the area may have attracted later people.

It was on a long ridge that the encircled tomb of New Grange was constructed, as early as 3250 BC if three radio-carbon assays from its mound can be trusted. Seven hundred years later Beaker groups were squatting in the shelter of its ruined sides.

The passage-grave was unusual because it had a great ring of standing stones around it. Almost certainly this stone circle was not later than the barrow but whether it was earlier is unclear. Both the ring and the mound have flattened arcs at the south-east, both have significantly larger pillars or kerbstones in that arc, and both seem to share a common centre. It is likely that both were raised by the same people.

This was one of the largest megalithic rings in the British Isles, maybe even the earliest, its stones of heavy grey wacke – a sandstone-like rock – and slate from nearby mixed with a few syenite blocks from the hills around Pomeroy in County Tyrone, some sixty miles away. These blocks were probably brought here by glacial action. The ring was graded in height with the most massive stones standing along the south-east arc where the passage-grave entrance was to be. The re-erection of one stone showed that its base had been shaped and that it had stood on a bedding of stones in a shallow socket, packing-stones keeping it upright. A deposit of flint tools lay by it. Another circle-stone had a row of cupmarks on its base where they could not have been seen.

Once this sacred enclosure was up a long, stone-built passage was erected, leading to a high, domed chamber with three small cells in its sides. The wonderful architecture of the corbelled chamber can instantly be appreciated but the careful construction of the passage roof is not apparent, the upper sides of its slabs grooved to run rainwater away.

While some people were building this internal structure other gangs were laying out a heart-shaped ring of ninety-seven kerbstones inside the circle with a long, flatter stretch at the south-east. A gap was left for the entrance and the kerbs here, like the circle-stones, were longer and heavier, some of them ten or more tons in weight, and every one of them meticulously chosen for its fine texture. Not until this ring was completed could the final mound be raised, a flat-topped and almost vertically sided drum of alternating layers of

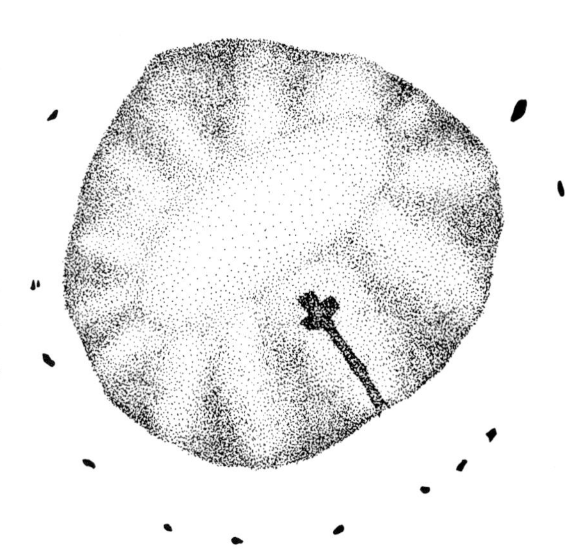

Below New Grange. The vast flat-topped mound of the passage-grave. A stone once stood upon this mound, just above the entrance.

small boulders and turves. This was coated with a wall of brilliantly white quartz stones. From a distance New Grange must have been as conspicuous as an iced cake on a contorted billiard-table.

The work was not over. The art that makes this chambered tomb and its fellows some of the marvels of our prehistoric past was to be carved on the passage and the chambers and on the kerbstones, laboriously pecked and scratched out with hard flints, tedious tappings and scrapings that resulted in a glory of triangles, chevrons, lozenges, meanders and spirals. Already the hidden surfaces of passage-stones had circles and cupmarks on them, but now the symbolism of these artists and priests burgeoned in compositions of solar and lunar motifs that astound our imaginations.

Each community had its own repertoire. At the Loughcrew passage-grave cemetery (N 585775) not thirty miles west of New Grange, the tombs were decorated with carvings of stars and rays and spokes quite unlike those of the Boyne mounds, although the underlying conceptions of sun, moon and death may have been the same. At New Grange the geometrical art covers kerb after kerb, especially the stone lying at the north-west at the back of the mound with its two splendid panels, one with spirals and latticework, the other with its three outlined cartouches, each

Opposite The carved north-west kerbstone at New Grange.
Below The rough, unshaped circle-stones standing ponderously outside the tomb entrance.

containing three cupmarks. At the entry to the passage itself is the amazing Entrance Stone, deceiving the eye with its five swirling, interlocking spirals bordered by a pattern of lozenges. The nearby tomb of Knowth (N 999738) has a similar stone at its entrance with elegant carved rectangles and an almost identical stone far down its passage.

Both Entrance Stones have grooves in them, pointing towards the passage. Here, at New Grange, are more ornate stones, dots, inset triangles, 'serpents' and spirals reaching out to the eye as the shadowed light animates them, and in the cells where the burnt bones of the dead were brought there are more still. These were the holy places and here there is a profusion of spirals on walls and roof where they looked down on the stone basins beneath them. There are four of these, one rectangular of sandstone in the west cell, another broken in the north, and two, one inside the other, in the east. The upper one, a beautifully circular granite basin, is particularly well made and has two cupmarks on it. It stands in a circular basin of slate. Here the dead were laid with their offerings of pots, bone pins, beads, flints. None of this survived at New Grange. The tomb had already been entered and robbed.

The visitor should not, probably will not be allowed to, miss the curious 'roof-box' over the entrance. This low and wide aperture, blocked by a stone which periodically was pushed aside, seemed to be purposeless and yet it had clearly been carefully designed. It was meant for the dead. Through here at sunrise on midwinter's day – and only then – the sun shone directly in a ray that reached to the very end of the passage and into the chambers, illuminating the bones of the dead in their rest.

Opposite Lissyviggeen.
Below New Grange. A carved roofslab.

NORTHERN ENGLAND

ARBOR LOW *Derbyshire*
BARBROOK *Derbyshire*
CARLES, CASTLERIGG *Cumberland (Cumbria)*
GREY CROFT *Cumberland (Cumbria)*
LONG MEG AND HER DAUGHTERS *Cumberland (Cumbria)*
SWINSIDE *Cumberland (Cumbria)*

There are two main regions of stone circles in northern England. In the Peak District there are just a few great rings in areas of Neolithic occupation, circle-henges like Arbor Low standing on ancient trade-routes from the Lake District to Wessex. Otherwise there are only the smaller rings and cairns like Barbrook that belong to the Bronze Age, put up on the poorer soils to the east of the limestone upland on which Arbor Low stands.

The other important region centres on the Lake District. Here are some of the most magnificent rings in the British Isles. They may also be the earliest, although the present lack of radio-carbon dates and pottery makes this impossible to prove. They are large, circular, of many heavy stones, and they surround open spaces capacious enough to accommodate huge assemblies. These were not family monuments but meeting-places for people coming from widely scattered homesteads for the seasonal ceremonies.

The earliest rings often have well-defined entrances that are all the more pronounced because the remainder of the ring is composed of closely set stones. Sometimes there is an outlier. A careful observer will also detect the traces of weathered earthen banks in which the stones once stood.

Later, at the beginning of the Bronze Age, the number of stones tended to become standardized and it is not unusual in the Lake District to find smaller rings with twelve stones set in a circle or an ellipse. Some possess avenues of spaced stones leading up to them.

Finally, almost at the end of the stone circle tradition, diminutive rings with burial-cairns were built on spurs and terraces of the lower fells. Rings like Lacra (SD 151812) or Moor Divock (NY 490227) have little in common with the proud stone circles that had been erected in the Late Neolithic a thousand years before them.

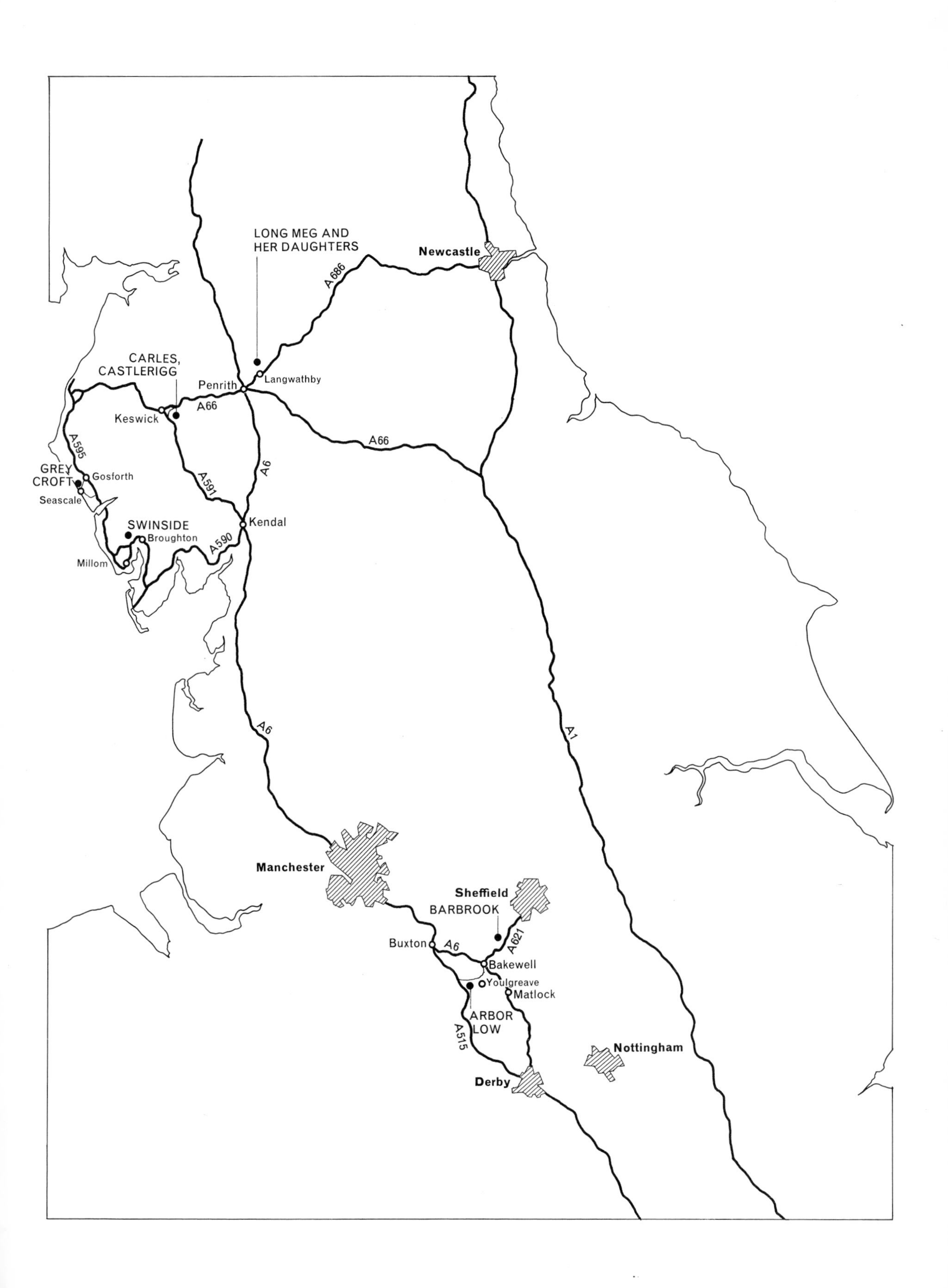
LONG MEG AND
HER DAUGHTERS
Newcastle
A686
CARLES,
CASTLERIGG
Penrith
Langwathby
Keswick
A66
A66
A595
A6
A591
GREY
CROFT
Gosforth
Seascale
SWINSIDE
Broughton
Kendal
A590
Millom
A6
A1
Manchester
Sheffield
BARBROOK
A621
Buxton
A6
Bakewell
Youlgreave
Matlock
ARBOR
LOW
A515
Nottingham
Derby

Arbor Low

Derbyshire: SK 160636. 9 miles W of Matlock on a minor road 3 miles W of Youlgreave. In State care. Signposted. Pay a small fee at farmhouse. (Egg-shaped, 41.5 × 37.2 metres.)
Although there are several megalithic tombs in the Peak District, there are very few Neolithic stone circles – Arbor Low, the Bull Ring and perhaps Ninestone Close (SK 225625), although the last is doubtful. The farmers of the New Stone Age preferred the rich limestone soils to the west of the Derwent and it was there that the two great circle-henges of the Bull Ring and Arbor Low were built, near the trackway which ran across the moor, reaching northwards to the Lake District and south to the Cotswolds and Wessex. The Bull Ring (SK 078783) has lost all its stones although its henge bank and ditch are still in good condition. Arbor Low is better.

It has many of the features of Avebury, and it seems probable that, like Stanton Drew in Somerset and Cairnpapple near Edinburgh, it was raised by people connected by trade to the inhabitants of Avebury and sharing their beliefs. It can hardly be a coincidence that at all of these monuments there is a henge with a stone circle inside it, that all of them had a Cove, which is a feature found in no other stone circle, and that three of them had forms of avenue.

The uneven bank of Arbor Low is broken at the north by an entrance where a causeway was left across a rock-cut ditch. Flints and some coarse sherds of pottery were found here during the excavations of 1901–2. On the central plateau stones lie tumbled. There has been much argument as to whether these limestone blocks ever stood upright, but one stone at the west is still not quite prostrate, showing that the rest fell because of the shallowness of their stoneholes in the bedrock.

At the centre of the ring there is a collapsed Cove that once faced the maximum midsummer setting of the moon. Such Coves are so like the entrances to chambered tombs where funerary rites were performed that it is likely that they were part of the same tradition. A man's skeleton was discovered buried alongside the Cove during the excavations here.

Perhaps because building-stone was scarce, Arbor Low's avenue, like that at Stonehenge, was composed of earth. A single low bank curves away from the southern entrance, petering out a field away in the direction of Gib Hill, a huge round barrow to the south-west that got its name from the gallows that once stood upon it. Although a massive cist of limestone slabs, scoured and bubbled by the weather, perches on its crest, this was a later addition to the mound, just as Food-Vessel people added a round barrow to the southern rim of the bank at Arbor Low. Gib Hill covered no original burial. Underneath the barrow were four clay mounds with some animal bones and burnt flints in them. In this

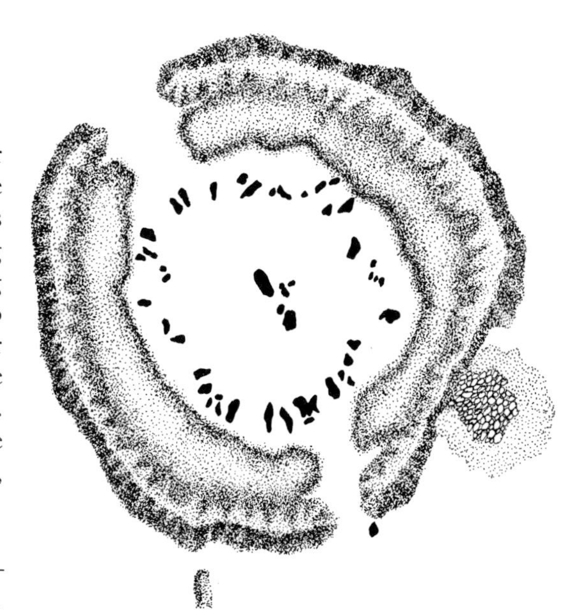

the barrow is similar to Silbury Hill near Avebury where repeated excavations have failed to find a single body. These enormous mounds may be territorial markers containing offerings of fertile soil and meat, standing conspicuously near the large circle-henges to which dozens of families came for trade, for meetings and for rituals in the years when the Neolithic was blurring into the Bronze Age.

(Finds from Arbor Low and Gib Hill can be seen in the City Museum, Weston Park, Sheffield. Closed Sunday mornings.)

Below Saxons called it *eordburh-hlaw*, an earthwork built by giants, who set the stones here.

Barbrook

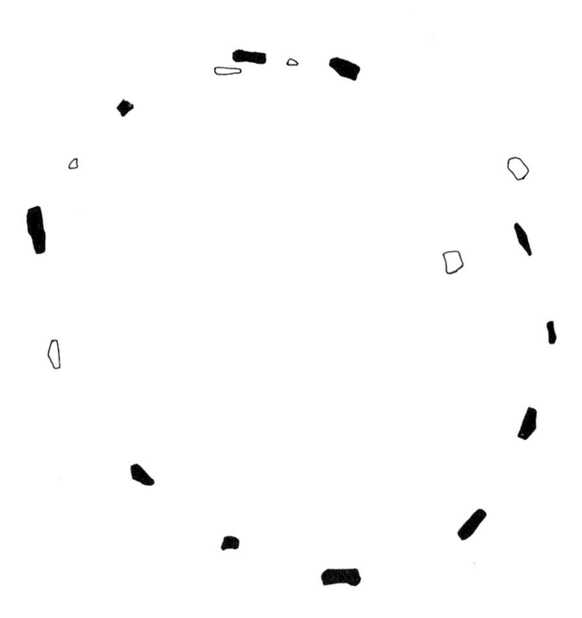

***Derbyshire*: *SK 278755*. 6 miles NE of Bakewell on Ramsley Moor to W of the A621. On Water Board property. (Flattened circle, 14.6 × 12.5 metres.)**

With an improvement in the climate in the later years of the New Stone Age, it became possible to farm land that previously had seemed unattractive. Around the beginning of the Bronze Age uplands like Dartmoor and the Yorkshire Moors were settled by families who cut down trees, dragged away stones and ploughed the thin soils, starting the processes which would transform these areas into the unfertile and treeless moors of today. This happened in the Peak District. East of the Derwent the limestone gives way to millstone grit where forests of oak, elm and alder grew thickly during the New Stone Age. Bronze Age farmers cleared much of this woodland, grazing their cattle on the new expanses of grass and sedge and weeds. Remains of their round, stone-walled huts can still be seen on the slopes, often near to stone circles of which the ruins of about forty survive.

A characteristic circle here has its stones set in a rubble bank with one or two entrances through it. These are not huge rings, rarely more than twenty metres across, nor are the stones great. In the central space it is not uncommon to find a small cairn with a cist containing a cremation. Regrettably, many of these cairns have been robbed and all trace of their contents has vanished. The smallness of the rings and their comparative closeness to each other suggest that, like those on Dartmoor, they were family monuments in which the cremations were offerings rather than burials.

Barbrook stands on a slope in the middle of dark moorlands just east of a gully through which a stream tumbles. At least one stone is missing but once there were twelve stones around the circumference of a ring which is clearly flattened at the south-west where the tallest stone, about hip-high, rises. It stands at one end of the short axis but its partner opposite has been removed. There are possible cupmarks on the flat-topped stone at the south.

Around these stones and just touching them the builders piled up a rubble bank whose inner edge they lined with a little drystone wall of which a few stones can still be seen today. It was a well-made ring, clearly visible from lower down the hillside even though it stands in a hollow. There are several standing stones on the moor around it, none tall, but it cannot be assumed that they had any direct connection with the circle.

About three hundred metres north of the stone circle is a similar embanked ring, Barbrook II (SK 277758), which also had a bank with inner drystone walling against which nine rough stones had been propped and wedged into place. The outer edge of the bank was supported by kerbstones of millstone grit.

A recent excavation revealed a cairn in the southern half of the circle. One of its kerbs had a cupmark on it. The cairn covered a pit in which there was a decorated coarse urn of the Bronze Age which contained cremated human bone. By it were two flint scrapers and a flint knife, all of them burnt from the heat of the pyre in which the corpse had been consumed. Near the cairn was another pit with a cremation. And towards the south of the central space there was a neat cist whose capstone had several cupmarks on it. Charcoal from the urn showed that the burial had been made around 1835 BC (1500 ± 150 bc), almost in the Middle Bronze Age and very late in the stone circle tradition.

(Finds from Barbrook II are in Sheffield City Museum. For details see Arbor Low.)

Opposite The tallest stone, at the south-west.

Carles, Castlerigg

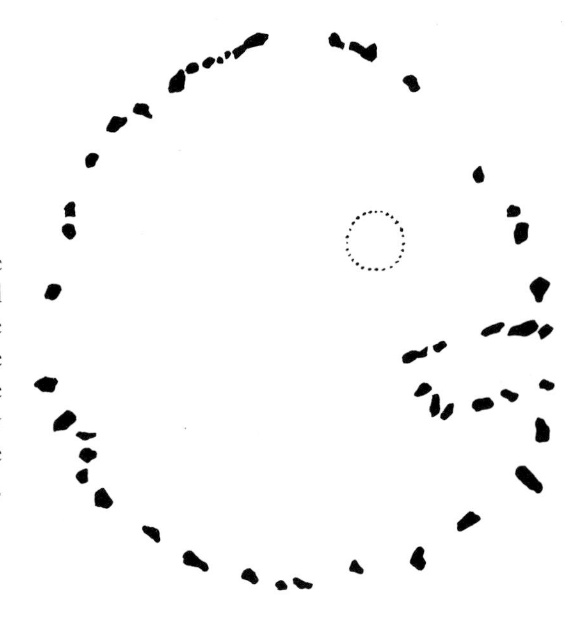

Cumberland (Cumbria) NY 292236. 1½ miles E of Keswick on Chestnut Hill. Alongside the lane. In State care. Signposted. (Flattened circle, 32.9 × 29.9 metres.)

Of all the superb rings in the Lake District, the Castlerigg stone circle is the most exciting and the most mysterious. Whether it is seen in the grey dampness of early morning mist or in the soft sunlight of an autumn evening when the stones seem luminescent, there is an intensity here that disturbs the day-dreaming of the romantic. Castlerigg is not gentle. It is hard, distant, deathless. Keats wrote of it:

Scarce images of life, one here, one there,
Lay vast and edgeways; like a dismal cirque
Of Druid stones, upon a forlorn moor . . .

Ley-liners have hailed it. Astronomers have aligned every stone upon every peak. Artists have painted it. Poets have sung it. Its photographs have vitalized the covers of many books. Yet no one seems to have said what it was. Its nickname, the Carles, comes from the legend that the stones are men petrified for their wrong-doing.

Castlerigg may be one of the earliest stone circles in the British Isles. It was built on a level stretch of land on Chestnut Hill in the very heart of the mountains with the Derwent, Lonscale and Castlerigg fells looming above it. It was put up where one of the good passes led down from Borrowdale and from the sources of fine stone for axes. To its north-west a broad valley of fertile land opened between the Derwent and Bassenthwaite lakes, making this an ideal area for prehistoric people.

All the circle-stones, of which there were originally about forty-two, are of the local metamorphic slate and none is of very great weight, although the high pillar set radially at the south-east was over sixteen bulky tons and must have needed several score of people to haul it upright into its prepared stonehole. The ring has a flattened arc at the north-east where the land falls away. It also has an entrance defined by two tall stones, smaller ones alongside them emphasizing their height, flanking a gap at the exact north where the far slope leads down to the river Greta.

Around the circumference are faint traces of a bank. Also just visible are the remains of a round cairn that has been practically levelled by nineteenth-century ploughing in the ring's interior. In 1856 Williams said there were three cairns here and that a stone club – probably one of the Cumbrian 'picks' of the Neolithic Age – and a greenstone axe had been found near the centre of the circle. An unpolished stone axe was found in or near the ring in 1875. If there were burial-cairns here it is quite possible that they were added by Bronze Age communities. This could also be true of the peculiar rectangle of stones jutting out from the eastern stones. Nothing like it is known in any other British stone circle. In 1882 Kinsey Dover dug into it but other than discovering a deep pit at its western end with charcoal in it he found nothing to explain it.

Against the hedge to the south-west of the circle is a plough-scarred low stone which is almost certainly not standing in its correct position. It may have come from the stone circle itself.

A hundred or more people may have used this Cumbrian ring, engaging in ceremonies of which no memory survives.

(An imaginative painting of the Carles is displayed in the Tullie House Museum, Castle Street, Carlisle. Open weekdays and also from June to August on Sunday afternoons.)

Opposite The wide north entrance of the Carles, Castlerigg stone circle.
Over Swinside, viewed from the south-east.

Opposite The attractive ring of Grey Croft on the coast of the Irish Sea. Its stones are boulders of volcanic lava.

Above Carles, Castlerigg. The stones are as worn by the weather as the hills and valleys behind them.

Grey Croft

Cumberland (Cumbria): NY 034024. **2 miles WSW of Gosforth and $\frac{3}{4}$ mile N of Seascale. A $\frac{1}{4}$ mile walk from the farm lane across private land. (Flattened circle, 27.0 metres.)**

This quiet and pleasant ring, which has been reconstructed, has a lovely but ironic situation in a wide, level field close to the coast. To its east the Lakeland fells can be seen, and to the west are the waters of the Irish Sea. It would seem that the landscape is much as prehistoric man saw it, but in contradiction of this pastoral scene the towers and blocks of the Calder Hall nuclear power station rise fast to the north.

The circle was erected on a rise in the ground which although very low did give it a conspicuous position. There were originally twelve stones, volcanic lava boulders brought down from the Lake District by glacial action. In the field walls of the neighbourhood are many other erratics, showing that the builders had no difficulty in finding suitable stones. Weighing up to four tons, the pillars have approximately level tops and care must have been taken in selecting the best stones. There is a tiny outlier to the north.

Because the stones were damaging his plough, James Fox, a tenant-farmer, toppled and buried every stone except the one at the

south around 1820, and for almost a hundred years only this stone marked the place where the ring had stood. In 1949 an excavation located nine of the stones and these were re-erected, using the original packing-stones where possible. An attempt to lift the stones with block and tackle failed and a 'tractor was used to drag the stones up a prepared ramp.' Experiments like this increase one's respect for the skill of the prehistoric workers.

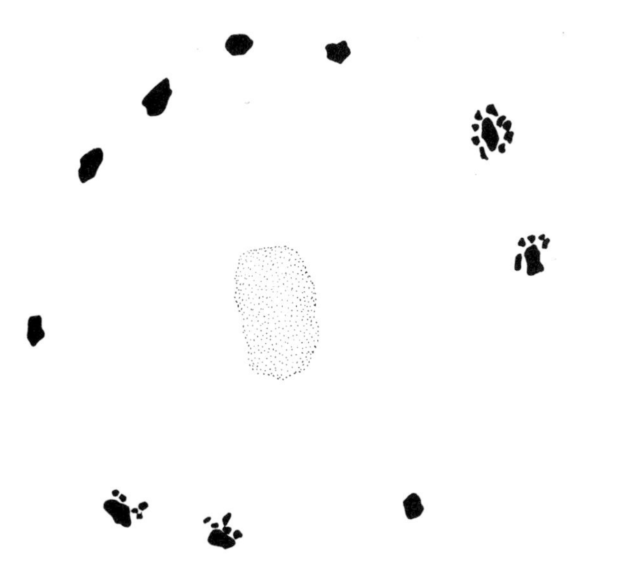

Opposite Blocks raised by men, millions of years after glacial ice brought them here.
Below The Grey Croft stones, from the east.

Close to the westernmost stone a broken Neolithic axe from the Lake District was discovered. The oval cairn inside the ring was found to be of particular interest. This can just be made out today. It had heavy stones around its base and when these were removed the excavators came upon a thin layer of ash in the sandy soil upon which the cairn had been heaped. Flecks of human bone lay in it. Under this layer were even thinner seams, black and sticky, containing fragments of charcoal, stems of grass or bracken, and six hawthorn berries. As some of the cairn-stones had been reddened by heat it is probable that a pyre had burnt here. The bracken and the berries show that this must have happened in autumn, and part of a jet ring lying under a large western kerbstone points to a date early in the Bronze Age, between about 2300 and 2100 BC, for the building of the cairn. Other finds of flint flakes and a scraper probably belonged to this period.

Grey Croft is not a large ring. Its size and the number of stones indicate that it belonged to a later age than the big circles like Castlerigg and Long Meg. Nor is the cairn enormous. The few scraps of human bone came from only one skeleton, making it unlikely that the stone circle was in any sense a burial-ground. The pyre was lit, presumably, when the ring was first erected, in a single act of dedication to hallow this new enclosure.

The outlying stone to the north is very low indeed and can hardly have had any practical use as a foresight on a heavenly body. It is interesting, however, that it stands very close to True North which, in times when there were no magnetic compasses and no Pole Star, means that the people probably observed the places where a star, or even the sun or moon, rose and set and then placed the outlier at a point midway between them. Why they did this is unknown, but cardinal positions are marked by special stones in quite a number of stone circles along the western coasts of Britain.

(The finds from this ring are in the Tullie House Museum, Carlisle. For details see Carles, Castlerigg.)

Calder Hall power station rising behind the quiet stone circle.

Long Meg and Her Daughters

Cumberland (Cumbria): NY 571373. **5½ miles NE of Penrith, 2 miles N of Langwathby. The farm lane passes through it. In State care. Signposted. Always open. (Flattened circle, 109.4 × 93.0 metres.)**

This is one of the largest rings in the British Isles, and must certainly have been intended for hundreds of people. Perhaps because of its size an entirely level clearing could not be found for it. For whatever reason, it was put up on land sloping appreciably down to the north where the ring has its flattened arc.

Some seventy stones line this ring, some of them of considerable bulk and weight, smooth and hard porphyritic boulders from the locality, standing in a wide bank only a few centimetres high today which can most easily be made out at the west. The heaviest of these stones, an immense thirty-ton block, squats at the east opposite another, almost as big, on the western axis of the circle. Two other enormous boulders stand at a south-west entrance which has been emphasized by two extra portal-stones just outside the circumference. Outside this entrance is Long Meg, an outlying stone twice as high as a grown man, whose thin shape is quite different from that of the muscular boulders of the ring. Presumably because they needed such a slender pillar, the people dragged this red sandstone column up from the

banks of the river Eden a full mile and a half away. There are carvings on this outlier though they have not been interpreted.

Wordsworth was astonished by Long Meg and Her Daughters.

A weight of awe, not easy to be borne,
Fell suddenly upon my Spirit – cast
From the dread bosom of the unknown past
When first I saw that family forlorn . . .

Many legends are attached to the ring. Some say that the stones are uncountable, others that they are protected by natural forces and that it

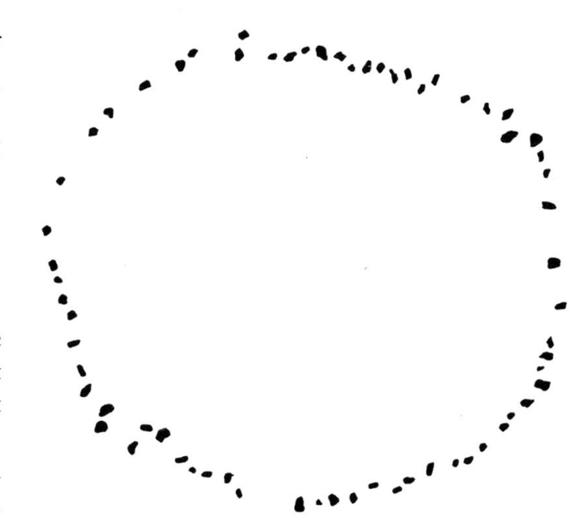

Below Long Meg overlooking her daughters. 'A faire felde ful of folke . . . .' William Langland.

was no coincidence that violent storms stopped Colonel Lacy from blasting the stones in the early eighteenth century. The ring is also supposed to be the petrified bodies of a witch and her daughters, and once again a stone is associated with dancing girls, the witch being the outlying stone. In 1702 Celia Fiennes wrote, 'the story is that these soliciting her to an Unlawfull Love by an enchantment are turned wth her to stone.' If a piece is chipped off Long Meg she is supposed to bleed. The most far-fetched belief, perhaps, is that she was a giantess who was buried on the south side of the cloisters of Westminster Abbey, probably to the consternation of the abbot and twenty-six monks who died in the Black Death and were buried under a large blue stone there. It also is known as Long Meg.

In the stone circle the great boulders at east and west mark cardinal points. From the centre of the circle Long Meg was aligned precisely on midwinter sunset. It could also have acted as a directional marker from the lower land to the south, from which it can be seen well before the circle itself comes into view. On its south-east face are several prehistoric carvings most easily seen in evening sunlight. Near the middle of the stone are a spiral, a cup-and-ring mark with a groove leading out of it and two concentric circles with two half-circles over them. Lower down, and almost weathered away, there are other circles and cupmarks. Such art can be seen at its best in the passage-graves such as New Grange in Ireland, and the magic symbols on Long Meg may have been made by people who had travelled across the Irish Sea during the Late Neolithic period four and a half thousand years ago.

In the seventeenth century John Aubrey wrote that two cairns stood at the centre of the ring where 'a Giants bone, and Body' had been found. In 1725 Stukeley noticed traces of these cairns as 'two roundish plots of ground' but they have gone completely today, leaving the vast interior of the ring empty and featureless. It is still one of the most impressive monuments of prehistoric Britain.

Long Meg – twice the height of a grown man.

Swinside

Cumberland (Cumbria): SD 172883. 5 miles N of Millom 2½ miles NW of Broughton. 1¼ miles along a private farm road. (Circular, 28.6 metres.)

Swinside, a delightful and almost perfect ring, stands on a gently sloping field with fells to its north and with the countryside falling easily to the south where the Duddo Sands three miles away offered easy beaching for travellers from Ireland. Swinside and the Irish circle of Ballynoe in County Down are so similar, both large, both of many stones, both with well-built entrances, that the people who built one must have known of the other.

Swinside stands in the south-west corner of the Lake District on the lower slopes of the fells. Its seal-grey stones of porphyritic slate came from the nearby hillsides where they are plentiful. Locally they are known as 'grey cobbles'. Over fifty stones stood here, and thirty-two are still erect, the tallest, a thin bent pillar, standing almost exactly at the north. There is an obvious entrance at the south-east marked by two additional portal-stones placed just outside the circumference.

Dymond's excavation of 1901 showed that each of these stones had been bedded on a layer of rammed pebbles. On the fallen stones one can still see how their bases were bashed into beaked shapes to make their levering upwards easier, and once they were upright in their holes packing-stones were jammed into the sides of the holes around them. The excavation discovered little to indicate the purpose of the

ring. Once down to the prehistoric ground level of yellowish marl know as pinnel, all that was found near the centre was a small lump of charcoal and a minute fragment of human bone alongside it, the usual evidence of dedicatory offerings when the ring was built.

Swinside is also known as Sunken Kirk, because in medieval times the stones were thought to be the foundations of a church being built during the daytime which the Devil would bury during the night.

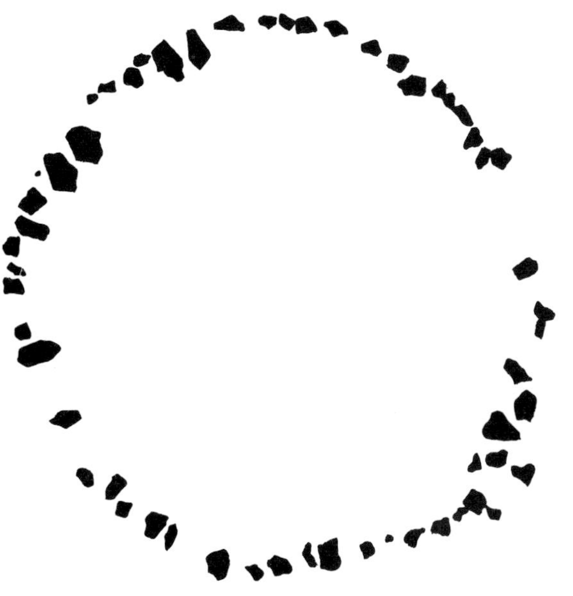

Left Swinside, the loveliest of all the circles, like a ring of dancers holding hands.
Right Seal-grey slate from the local hillsides.

SOUTHERN ENGLAND

AVEBURY *Wiltshire*
BOSCAWEN-UN *Cornwall*
DOWN TOR *Devon*
GREY WETHERS *Devon*
THE HURLERS *Cornwall*
MERRY MAIDENS *Cornwall*
ROLLRIGHT STONES *Oxfordshire*
SCORHILL *Devon*
STANTON DREW *Somerset (Avon)*
STONEHENGE *Wiltshire*
THE TRIPPET STONES *Cornwall*

The great rings of southern England with their dead, weathered stones are some of the best known of the British stone circles. Names like Avebury, Stonehenge, the Rollright Stones live in the memory. Yet, for the most part lacking burials, weapons and pottery, they remain the most mysterious of them all. Whether in Cornwall, Wiltshire, even as far north as Oxfordshire, the emptiness of these sacred enclosures challenges the imagination. Only on Dartmoor are there little cairns inside the circles, but even these have been rifled and few clues are left for anyone wanting to solve the puzzle of the stones. Elsewhere in the south, gaunt pillars stand outside the circles, or avenues reach from a river to the ring, or a thick stone, stained and clawed by centuries of rain, leans at the centre of the ring. And in each area, on Land's End, on Bodmin Moor, on Dartmoor and in Wessex, there is a complex of two or three rings that huddle closely together like gossips whose words have been worn away by the endless turning of time.

In the Land's End area it is noticeable that a stone circle is often close to a Neolithic chambered tomb, suggesting that prehistoric people occupied family territories of a few square miles that survived virtually unaltered for hundreds of years, the megalithic ring being built as a temple in the Bronze Age when the chambered tomb had fallen into disuse.

Another fact about these Land's End circles is that they were constructed of nineteen or twenty stones, whatever their diameter. Astronomers have speculated that this number was related to the number of years it took for the moon to pass from its maximum southerly position on the horizon to its minimum and back to its maximum again. The people of Bodmin Moor also had preferred numbers of stones for their circles, here of twenty-six to twenty-eight stones. It may be that the number was related to the number of nights in a lunar month, but this seems unlikely. The majority of the great Dartmoor stone circles consisted of thirty to thirty-six stones.

The rings now are hardly more than skeletons in a charnel-house, their flesh and life decayed before our memories began. It is no surprise that the romantic welcomes them and the curious visit them. They are worth exploring for their secrets.

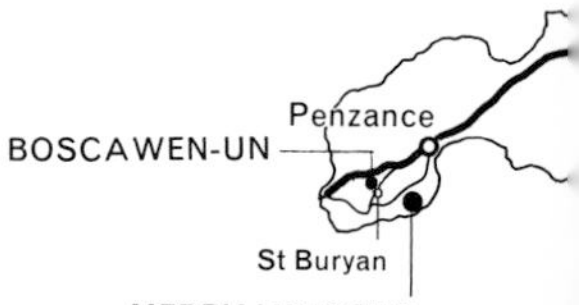

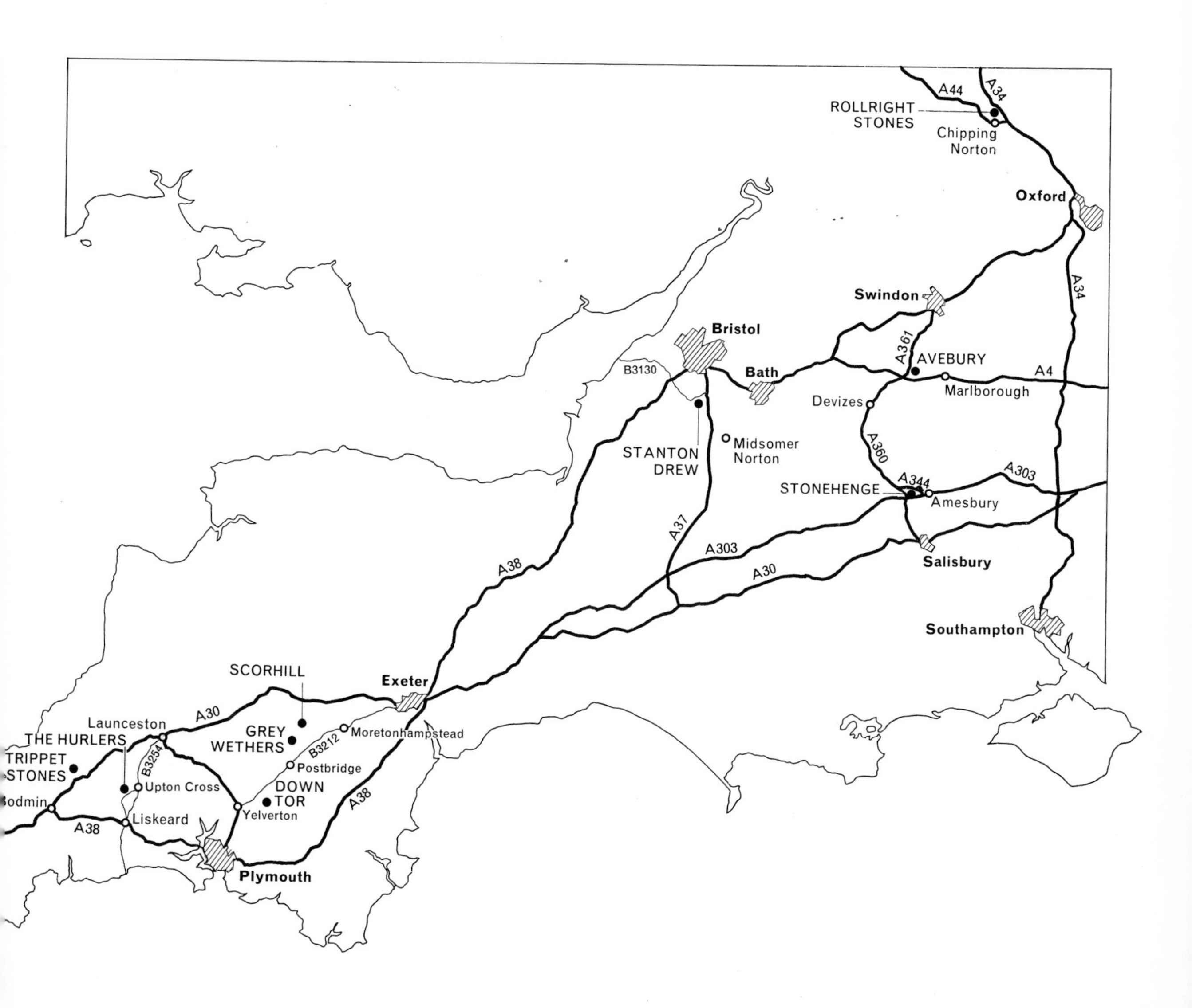

A44
A34
ROLLRIGHT STONES
Chipping Norton
Oxford
Swindon
A34
Bristol
A361
AVEBURY
Bath
A4
B3130
Marlborough
Devizes
STANTON DREW
Midsomer Norton
A360
A344
A303
STONEHENGE
Amesbury
A37
A303
Salisbury
A38
A30
Southampton
SCORHILL
Exeter
A30
Launceston
GREY WETHERS
Moretonhampstead
THE HURLERS
B3212
TRIPPET STONES
B3254
Postbridge
Upton Cross
DOWN TOR
Yelverton
A38
Liskeard
A38
Plymouth

Avebury

Wiltshire: SU 103700. **6 miles W of Marlborough, 8 miles NE of Devizes, on the A361 9 miles SSW of Swindon. National Trust. Always open. (Irregular circular bank, 427 metres; inner ditch, 351 metres; outer stone circle, 338 metres; S circle, 103.0 metres; N circle, 98.0 metres.)**

At Avebury stone-lined avenues from south and west led to a huge circular bank with an inner ditch. Inside was a great stone circle enclosing two smaller circles, each with internal features. Excavations have uncovered many objects of the Late Neolithic Age.

There was plenty of building stone on the Marlborough Downs, the chalk upland that borders the clay plains to the north and west of Avebury. Sarsens, thick weathered slabs of sandstone, lie on these downs and spread in spoke-like streams down their sides (see Lockeridge Dene, SU 145673). These stones were used by Neolithic families for their long burial-mounds and, later, for circles of stones, of which there were several here. It was an alluring region. The soils were easily tilled and were productive. Forests provided timber. Springs and streams gave water for the cattle. Valleys and ranges of hills created natural routes out of the area and soon tracks like the Ridgeway, of which miles can still be walked (SU 144764 to SU 119680 around Avebury), were being travelled by stone-axe traders from the Lake District, Wales and Cornwall. In later centuries luxuries of bronze and gold were carried along rivers and trackways into this populated metropolis of southern Britain.

The outer bank at Avebury is a vast body of chalk that curves in a grotesque ring around the outside of a ditch as wide as a castle moat. The ring is a quarter of a mile across, and two roads contort at its centre where the fringes of the modern village begin. Around the inner edge of the ditch, enclosing a central plateau, there are the remains of the outer circle, a ring of a hundred stones of which only two arcs survive, at the south-west and north-west. This was, by far, the largest stone circle in these islands and the one with the biggest stones. Inside it today there are other stones. One fine arc, south-east of the crossroads, shows where an inner circle once stood. There are sufficient sarsens left for one to imagine this ring. In a field of long grass in the north-east sector of Avebury there are four or five almost meaningless stones, all that have been preserved of a concentric circle with a Cove in it.

Four gaps in the bank, three still marked by gigantic stones, show where the original entrances were. That at the south leads to a double line of stones outside Avebury. This Kennet avenue rises over a ridge and then descends towards the Kennet valley. From Avebury's western entrance the village lane ends abruptly at a fence, but once a second avenue marched down here, passed over the Winterbourne stream, and extended at least a mile westwards to where two lonely stones still

stand, Adam and Eve or the Longstones, the smaller one a survivor of the avenue, the larger, Adam, all that is left of a three-sided Cove on a hillock near Beckhampton (SU 089693).

All this can be seen at Avebury. Many people will ask what it means, for the stones do not tell their own story.

People lived at Avebury long before the circles were raised and one of their magnificent chambered tombs at West Kennet (SU 104677) can still be entered. The largest man-made mound in Europe, Silbury Hill (SU 100685) was put up around the same time as Avebury

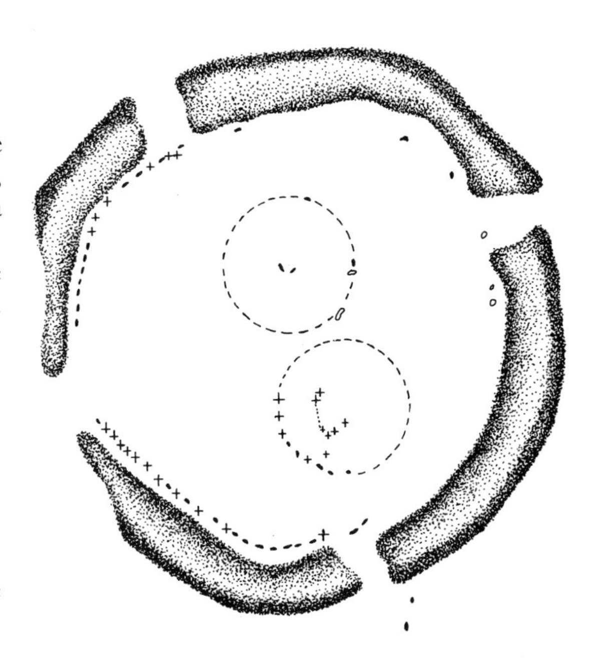

Below As a medieval Christian tried to bury the stone on the left it fell and crushed him.

and it seems likely that during later Neolithic times there was a settlement of round timber huts where Avebury village now stands. About 2600 BC its inhabitants, natives of the area from the evidence of their pottery, erected the south inner stone circle of thirty stones for ceremonies of fertility which included the use of human bones. Near its centre they raised a high stone known as the Obelisk, now indicated by a hip-high concrete marker. It may have served as the focus for an ancestor cult. Human bones were found at its base near little pits filled with rich, fertile soil. An unexplained rectangle of smaller sarsens known as the Z-Stones stood around the Obelisk. Some survive. Concrete markers show where the others stood.

A second circle was put up to the north of the first, this time a double ring, the outer of twenty-seven stones, the inner of twelve. Only two stones still stand. The novel architecture suggests that this ring was for rituals different from those in the south circle and it may be that corpses were brought here for funeral rites before burial elsewhere. At the middle of this ring three enormous slabs were heaved upright to make a Cove, apparently a replica of the one already standing to the west of Avebury. Two of its colossal stones still stand.

It is possible that the people even began to build a third circle. Places where a few of its stones stood are marked inside the north entrance. But the project was abandoned and, instead, a chasm-like ditch was dug out around the existing circles and the settlement. The chalk was piled up in a series of interlocking dumps and humps outside the ditch. The humps can still be seen along the bank, showing how unevenly it was built. Antler picks found in the ditch were the tools used by the builders of this fanatical structure. Such a massive undertaking must have been directed by a powerful chieftain whose kraal this was, and his power was emphasized by a new ring of stones that ran along the inner edge of the ditch, with gargantuan sarsens at the entrances. These sixty-ton slabs must have demanded the strength of every adult in the region.

Right Almost all these pagan stones were buried in the Middle Ages.

Huts probably stood inside this great ring of stones. Scaffolds for corpses exposed to the open air rose by the ditch, explaining why human jaws and long bones have been discovered deep down in the ditch where they had tumbled from the skeletons or been thrown by the living. By this time, around 2400 BC, Beaker people from the Continent were well established here and they joined the natives in the building of the Kennet avenue, where several of their burials have been found. The alternating pillar and lozenge shapes of the sarsens in this avenue have led to the hypothesis that these were 'male' and 'female' stones that reflected rites of fertility here.

Exactly where the destroyed Beckhampton avenue ended is uncertain. The Kennet avenue led southwards and then uphill towards the Ridgeway, where it terminated at a smaller concentric stone circle, the Sanctuary (SU 118679), the successor to a series of timber rings that may have been charnel-houses where corpses were stored until the flesh decayed, the avenue being the route along which dead bodies were carried. Avebury is a complicated site but the evidence suggests that rites of fertility and death were as usual here as in any other stone circle in the British Isles.

(Excellent displays of material from the region can be seen in the village museum behind the church, and in the marvellous museum of the Wiltshire Archaeological Society, Long Street, Devizes. Closed Mondays.)

Opposite These sarsens from the Marlborough Downs are among the heaviest stones in prehistoric Britain.
Below 'Male' and 'female' stones at Avebury.

Boscawen-Un

Cornwall: SW 412273. **1 mile N of St Buryan, ½ mile S of the A30, across rough ground and gorse. On private land. Unsignposted. (Flattened circle, 25.3 × 22.3 metres.)**

Unlike most stone circles in the south-west peninsula Boscawen-Un stands on lowish ground, and it cannot easily be seen from a distance when the gorse bushes are high and thick. It has been restored.

This fine ring has nineteen stones, one being of quartz, the others unshaped granite boulders, around the circumference of a flattened circle with a wide gap at the west. These stones, like those of Boskednan to the north, have their smoother sides facing inwards as though to add elegance to the ring. Well to the south-west of the ring's centre is a tall granite pillar which now leans considerably but which once towered higher than a man's head.

'Centre' stones are rarely at the exact centre of any stone circle. This could be because they were added later but, alternatively, it is possible that these high pillars, which may have been thought of as the embodiment of the spirits of ancestors, were put up to stand near but not over a central burial. Whether this was true of Boscawen-Un is not clear because although a trench was dug across the ring in 1864 no finds were recorded. However, a broken flat stone by the north-eastern perimeter may be the

possible remains of a cist-slab.

Two cairns near the circle have both been dug into and cremated bones, scraps of bronze and some Bronze Age pots taken from them.

Lockyer believed the quartz circle-stone, standing at the west-south-west of the ring, was 'placed in a post of honour', showing the place from which the May Day sun would have risen over the centre of the circle. As with other Land's End circles, the west-south-west does seem to have been important to the builders.

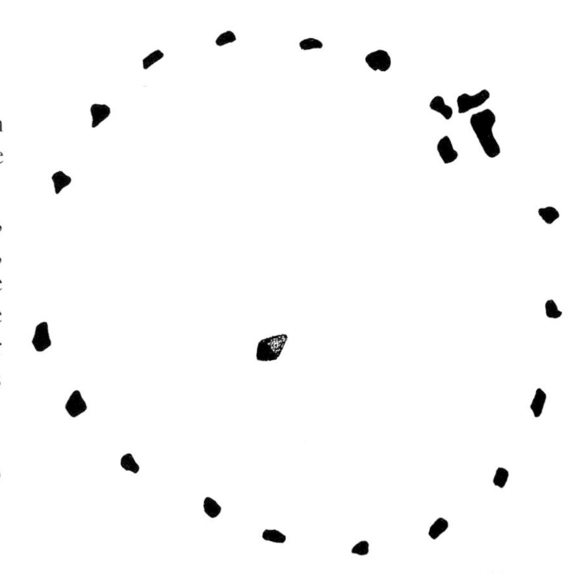

Opposite William Stukeley believed this ring to be the first erected by incoming Druids.
Below The south-western quartz stone.

Down Tor

Devon: SX 587694. On Hingston Hill, 4½ miles ENE of Yelverton and 2 miles E of Burrator reservoir. (Circular, 11.3 metres.)

Scattered about the south and east of Dartmoor, often well into the moor itself, are stone rows, often of quite small stones that do not merit the label of 'megalithic'. The rows are intriguing because of their great length. Over sixty are known, most of them single lines, some double and few treble. Here and there double and treble lines, rather like the fan-shaped settings of northern Scotland, lie side by side in bewildering confusion. It is not uncommon to find a stone circle with an internal cairn at the uphill end of such rows. Down Tor is one such site.

Here the ring of low granite stones encloses a grassed-over cairn with a wrecked cist at its centre where a cremation once rested. From this encircled cairn a single line of stones extends to the east-north-east for almost a quarter of a mile, descending a gentle slope and then climbing a short distance to a triangular stone set at right angles to the row. Many of the stones were re-erected in 1894 and it is possible that errors occurred in the reconstruction, but today one can remark on how the stones increase in height as they approach the stone circle until the final stone, a great pillar more than five tons in weight, is nearly three metres high. There are at least 174 stones in the row.

Away to the east a large cairn stands in line

with the row, and to the north-east is a pear-shaped walled compound where cattle may have been stalled.

It has been conventional to regard such Dartmoor rows as processional ways but some of the double rows are too narrow for human beings to walk along. Their frequent links with cairns and burials suggest that these may have been 'ghost-paths' along which the spirits of the dead could be summoned whenever the living needed them.

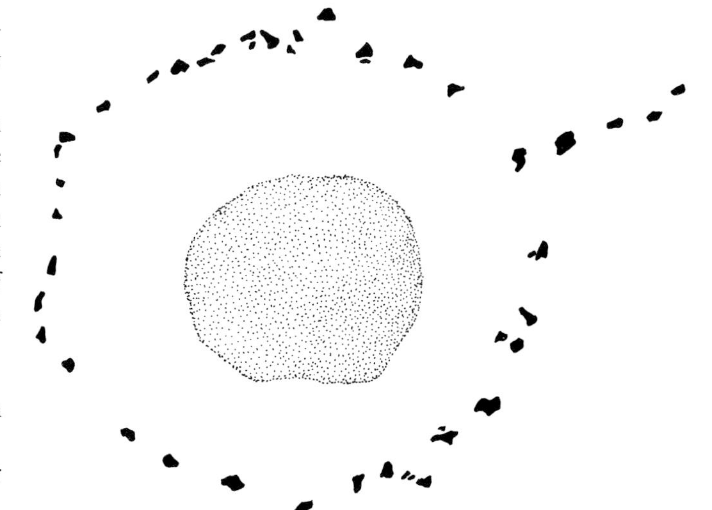

Opposite Nearer the circle the stones increase in height as they climb uphill.
Below This row may have been a pathway for the dead from the distant encircled cairn.

Grey Wethers

Devon: SX 638832. 2½ miles N of Postbridge. Either a 3 mile walk NNW from Merripit Hill by the B3212, or a rather shorter, maze-like stroll through Fernworthy Forest (Forestry Commission property) past Fernworthy circle, from the car park at the end of the reservoir road. An Ordnance Survey map is necessary. (N ring, circular, 32.0 metres; S ring, circular, 33.2 metres.)

The rings on Dartmoor can be divided into two main types. Around the eastern and southern edges of the moor are the large open rings, such as Scorhill, Brisworthy and Sherberton, built when people began settling around the borders of this upland as the climate improved towards the end of the Neolithic period. But in the centuries after 2300 BC more and more families moved on to the higher, unexploited lands at the heart of the moor, which in those prehistoric times was not a peat-deadened waste but forested and attractive, with animals to hunt, good land to clear and cultivate, and with plentiful building-stone lying on the slopes of shattered tors that today stub like egg-boxes out of the bare moorland. It was on these uplands, when the trees had been felled, that long lines of stones were constructed, often leading to little circles with

burial-cairns inside them, monuments quite different from the more traditional rings around the rim of Dartmoor.

The Grey Wethers is an evocative site to visit. It is in wild, uncultivated country below the littered hillside of Sittaford Tor from which the stones were dragged long ago. Because the rings were restored in the late nineteenth century, the determined visitor, prepared to walk a hardish mile or two, will be rewarded with the sight of two adjacent circles looking much as they did when they were first put up.

In some ways the Grey Wethers are similar to the Hurlers on Bodmin Moor, but the rings seem even more austere against the drab buffs and browns of the landscape and the rigidity of the bare slopes around them. There are two big rings, both circular, the southern rather larger than the northern. They stand on either side of a slight crest from which the ground falls away to north and south, and it is tempting to think that this fact might indicate the directions from which people came to the rings and also the reason why two circles were built, each standing at the very edge of a separate territory whose common boundary passed between the rings. But it is also noticeable that the larger ring, the southern, rests now on better-drained land than the northern. Its stones also seem better dressed and these may be indications that this was the first circle constructed here.

During the nineteenth-century excavations the diggers found that charcoal had been spread over the interiors of the rings. Charcoal was also discovered at another Dartmoor circle, Brisworthy (SX 565655), and the entire inner space of Fernworthy, a mile to the east of the Grey Wethers, was strewn with charcoal. Whether this came from pyres on which bodies had been burnt or from bonfires lit to clear stubble from autumn fields after the harvest is unclear, but two diminutive mounds near the Grey Wethers were examined and found to be untouched cairns covering pits in which charcoal had been deposited. It seems likely that fire and death were elements in the rituals that once took place at the Grey Wethers. Strangely, there appear to be no astronomical alignments here, even though the rings were laid out on an almost exact north-south axis.

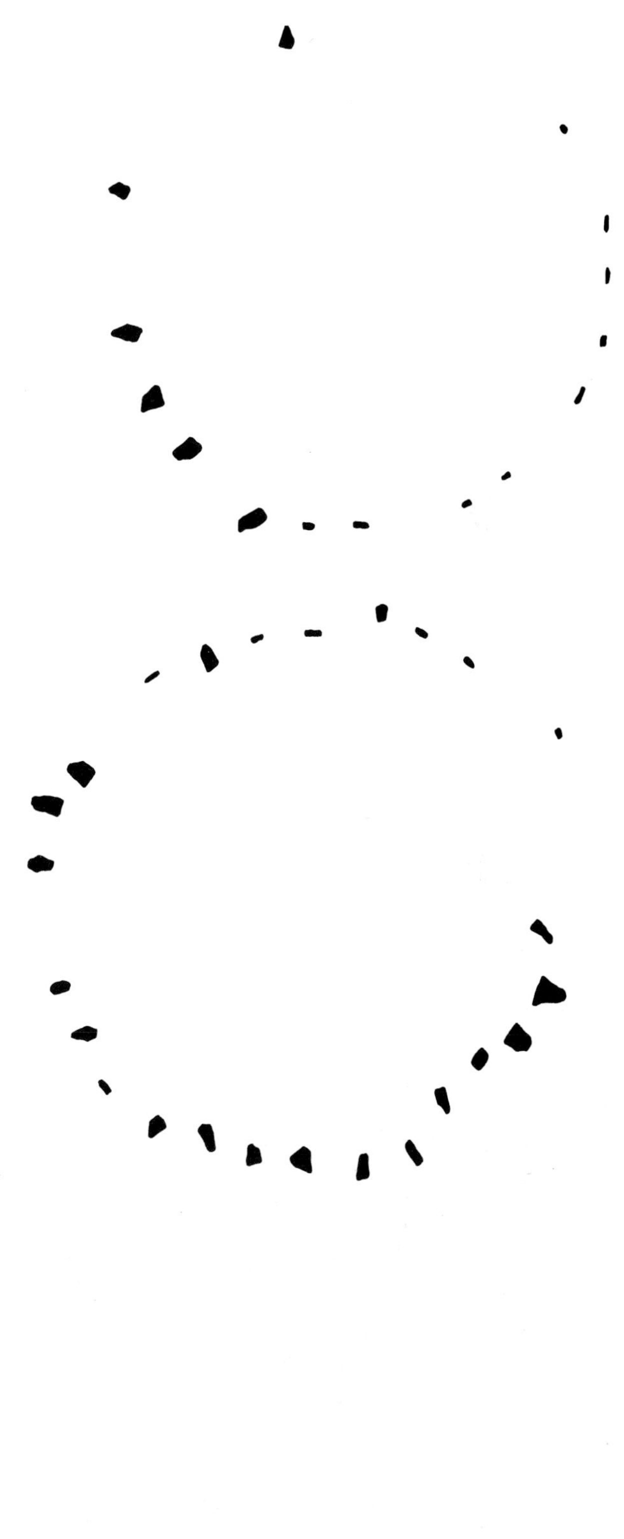

Opposite Legend claims that these sheep-grey stones slowly revolve in their holes at sunrise.

The Hurlers

Cornwall: SW 258714, $4\frac{1}{4}$ miles N of Liskeard and $1\frac{1}{2}$ miles W of Upton Cross. To N of the road as it proceeds W from the Minions. In State care. (NE ring, circular, 34.7 metres; centre ring, egg-shaped, 41.8 × 40.5 metres; SW ring, circular, 32.9 metres.)

Bodmin Moor seems to have been in prehistoric times a rather isolated area. A couple of small henges to its south, a ruined circle-henge, the Stripple Stones (SX 144752) and a delightful little ring of chunky quartz stones at Duloe (SX 235583) indicate some contact with the outside world, but otherwise the monuments on Bodmin Moor are bleak, native structures that fit well with the hard, uncompromising landscape.

There are enormous open rings here, Stannon and Fernacre to the north near Rough Tor with its possible Neolithic settlement, both of them flattened circles composed of many low, unobtrusive stones. Southwards is Leaze (SX 137773) with a modern wall through it, another broken ring near it, and further south still are other simple rings at Craddock Moor, the Trippet Stones and the Hurlers.

The name of the Hurlers stems from the legend that the three circles here were men turned to stone for sporting on the Sabbath. The three rings stand on a south-south-west / north-north-east axis on a pronounced slope of scrub and grazing land pocked and shabbied by past mining. The granite stones have been

dressed to shape and have roughly level tops. The two outer rings, both circular and very large, are ruined, the southern circle particularly so, but the central ring is still in good condition. Its tallest stones are at the south. There is a small stone near the centre.

Many stones were re-erected here in 1936 and partial excavation revealed where missing stones had stood. A 'floor' of granite crystals was discovered in the middle ring, probably made up of the chippings from the shaping of the stones. The northern circle also was paved and there was a crude stretch of pathway, about two metres wide, leading from it to the central ring. This suggests that people had passed from one to the other ring during their ceremonies. The excavators found only three crude flints which were of no value for dating.

A hundred metres west-south-west of the rings is a pair of tall stones called, not unexpectedly, the Pipers, showing that there was once a legend of music and probably of dancing attached to the Hurlers. The axis of these outliers points to the southern arc of the central circle.

The whole complex of rings and standing stones is an excellent example of the multiple rings that are characteristic of the south-west peninsula. All kinds of speculations have been made about them. We do not know, however, whether these three rings were put up as one monument or whether the circles were added successively, although the latter does seem more likely and might account for the fact that the central 'circle' with its little internal stone is larger than the others. The lesser north and south circles may have been added in later centuries as the rituals of fertility became more involved. Such an interpretation would be in keeping with the findings at Avebury.

A quarter of a mile north is the famous Rillaton Early Bronze Age round barrow, perched on the steep slope of a hillside overlooking what once must have been a low-lying expanse of forest. A magnificent gold cup, designed in imitation of a beaker, came from this barrow.

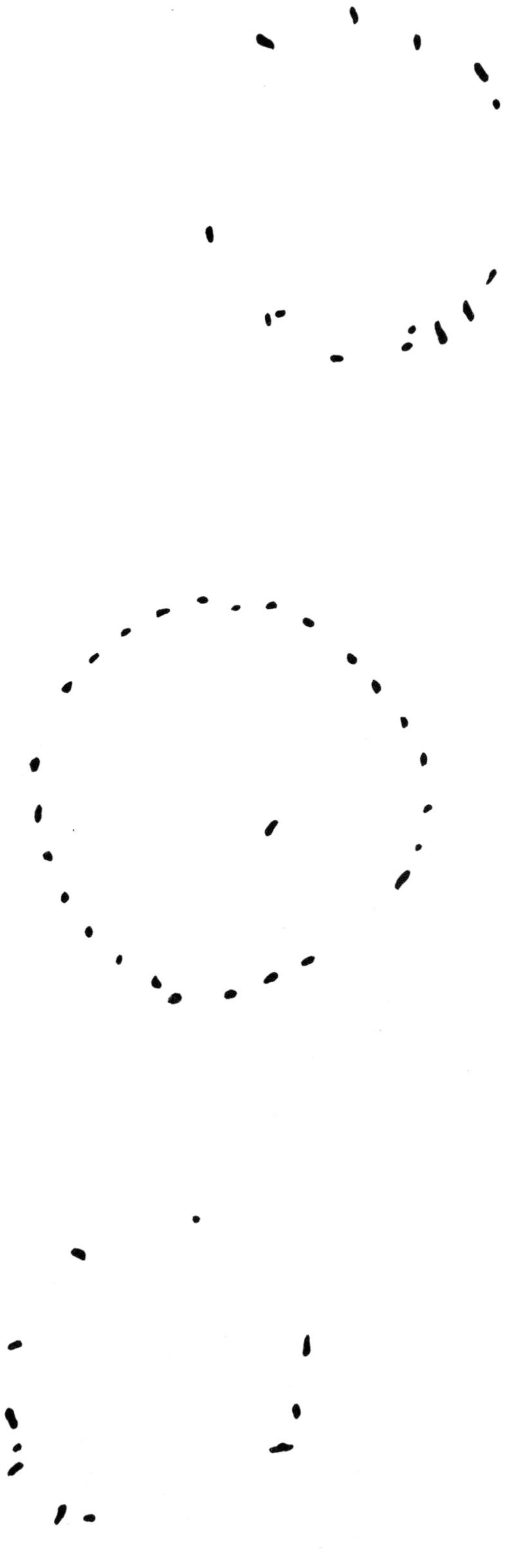

Opposite The granite columns of the central ring in a mine-scarred landscape.

Merry Maidens

Cornwall: SW 432245. **On E side of the B3315, 1½ miles SE of St Buryan, 4 miles SSW of Penzance. In a private field. (Circular, 23.8 metres.)**

The name of this ring with its legends of impious girl dancers seems to brush the fingertips of the past. Another name, the Dawn's Men, has nothing to do with astronomical alignments. It is a corruption of Dans Maen, the Stone Dance, telling the same story of a belief that people once danced inside the ring of stones.

The Merry Maidens circle was built on a slight slope down to the west-south-west where, only a short distance away alongside the road, Tregiffian chambered tomb with its charmingly cupmarked stone can be visited. From it the circle is visible one field away.

Like other Land's End rings, the Merry Maidens now consists of nineteen stones of local granite. The stones seem to have been 'dressed' to shape before their erection. Certainly the builders took care to keep the tops of the stones flat and level. Today there is a wide gap at the east and this may be the original entrance, just as other and larger rings of western Britain had well-defined portals through which people entered the ring. Again as usual in the Land's End circles, the tallest stone, not conspicuously bigger than the others, is at the west-south-west, perhaps acting as an astronomical marker on the minimum moon or showing where one

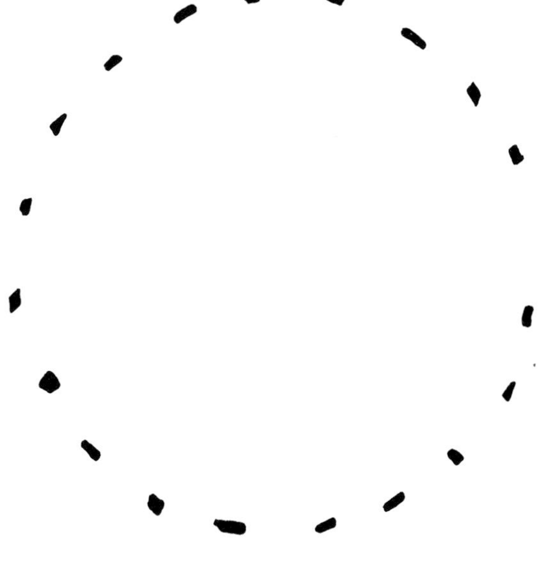

might stand to face the May Day sunrise.

Two immense standing stones, the Pipers, rise in separate fields a quarter of a mile to the north-east of the circle, and another pillar, the Goon Rith, can be seen to the west. Attempts have been made to relate them to the circle by astronomical explanations, but no convincing alignments have been detected. Such outlying stones may well have been territorial markers or even 'ancestor' stones whose real significance is now lost to us.

Opposite Irreverent girls, who danced on the Sabbath and were turned to stone.
Below The tops of the stones were levelled.

Rollright Stones

Oxfordshire: SP 296308. 2¼ miles NW of Chipping Norton, on a lane from A34 leading SW to Adlestrop. On private land but admission allowed. Photographs available. (Circular, 31.6 metres.)

The Rollright Stones were mentioned despairingly by a Cambridge clerk as long ago as the fourteenth century. 'In the Oxford countryside there are great stones, arranged as it were . . . by the hand of man. But at what time this was done, or by what people, or for what memorial or significance, is unknown.'

Today seventy-seven ravaged limestones stand closely grouped around the circumference of this open ring. They are not all original. Some are the tops of broken stones, replaced wrongly about a century ago. A drawing by John Aubrey shows some twenty-five stones standing in the seventeenth century, the tallest at the north-west with two more at the south-east just outside the ring, as though forming a double entrance like that in some of the Lake District rings.

Whether any excavation has taken place here is debatable. Stukeley said that an antiquary, Ralph Sheldon, had dug at the centre but had failed to find any bones. Yet John Aubrey, whose friend Sheldon was, said he 'told me he was at some charge to digge within this Circle, to try if he could find any Bones: but he was sure that no body was buried there: but had he digged without the circle, and neer to it it is not unlikely he mought [might] have found Bones there. . . .' Even if Sheldon did not disturb the centre modern picnickers and witch-covens have, and there is probably little left for the archaeologist to discover here.

Just outside the ring to the north-north-east is an outlier, the King Stone, hunched like a puff-adder at the shoulder of the long steep spur where the circle stands. It has been as deformed by people as by weather. So magical was it supposed to be that 'people from Wales kept chipping off bits to keep away the Devil', a nice relic of the fertility legends attached to these rings.

In a long flat field away to the east are the tall, denuded stones of a chambered tomb, the Whispering Knights, whose role as a shrine and temple may have been taken over by the later stone circle early in the Bronze Age.

It was not an observatory. Attempts have been made to find an alignment from the ring to its outlier, but even the most recent and accurate, by Alexander Thom, can offer no more than an orientation towards the rising of the star Capella about 1750 BC, far too late and too dim to be persuasive.

The legends are more informative. The circle is said to be a king and his army turned to stone as they moved towards the edge of the ridge. Other stories say that here a witch turned herself into an elder tree, a tree renowned for its healing properties; and that the stones go down the hill to drink water from a spring on New Year's Day. Infertile women can be

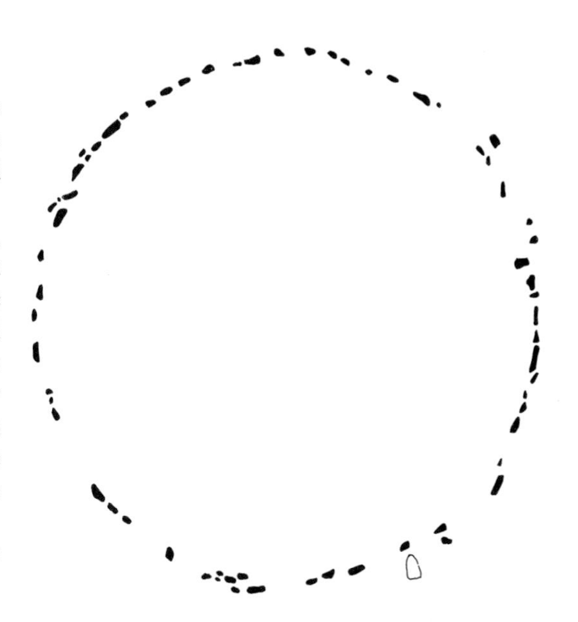

cured by touching the stones. And as late as the eighteenth century youths and girls visited the Rollright Stones at midsummer, feasting and merrymaking as tradition said they should.

The water, the healing powers, fertility, midwinter, midsummer, all these combine in legends and folk-memories that perhaps more than any excavation tell us 'for what memorial or significance' this isolated ring, far away from any other stone circle, was put up so many centuries ago alongside the trackway from Wessex northwards to the Peak District. Some people will doubt the usefulness of such stories

Below A mixture of tops and stumps with the Whispering Knights chambered tomb behind.

but the words of John Aubrey, that tireless collector of gossip, are worth remembering.

> I know that some will nauseate these old Fables: but I doe profess, to regard them as the most considerable pieces of Antiquity, I collect: and that they are to be registred for Posterity, to let them understand the Encroachment of Ignorance on Mankind: and to learne what strange Absurdities Man by Custome and education be brought to believe.

Below An army of warriors turned to stone by witchcraft.
Opposite The heavily weathered Rollrights.

Over left The Merry Maidens.
Over right The Trippet Stones, another circle connected by legend with dancers.

Opposite A winter view of a sarsen and trilithon at Stonehenge.

Above Rollright Stones. A limestone pillar, one of the few original stones.

Scorhill

Devon: SX 655874. **$6\frac{1}{4}$ miles W of Moretonhampstead. A $\frac{1}{2}$ mile walk WSW on the moor from the corner of the lane from Berrydown to Scorhill farm. (Circular, 26.2 metres.)**

Early in the nineteenth century the Reverend Samuel Rowe described Scorhill as 'by far the finest of the rude but venerable shrines of Druidical worship in Devonshire', and there are few who would disagree with him.

Situated at the north-east corner of the moor, the ring stands on a wide expanse of open country with the long ridge of Hangingstone Hill outlined in the far distance. Traces of an old cart-track can be seen across the ring.

Like most of the great Dartmoor stone rings Scorhill consisted of some thirty-six stones, though some have been robbed in modern times for building purposes. The stones are of local granite and were erected in their natural state without any shaping or flattening of their tops. Holes in two or three fallen pillars at the south of the perimeter are the relics of stone-breaking and have nothing to do with prehistoric activity. One especially high stone, thin and tapering, rises markedly above the others at the north-west, though it does not appear to have any astronomical purpose.

It can be presumed that Scorhill, like many other open rings of southern England, was used by several families for rituals connected with the fertility of the land. Nearby are several other antiquities. A mile to the north are the

almost unrecognizable ruins of the Buttern circles, and to the south across the river Teign are the fields and hut circles of the Batworthy settlement. Farther south still is the Shovel Down complex, where single and double rows converge on cairns, one with a triple ring of stones around it. Near the Batworthy clapper bridge, only a short distance from Scorhill circle, is the legendary Holed Stone. This granite block was once thought to be a 'Druidical' stone but, as it lies in the Teign, probably flowing water created a natural hole.

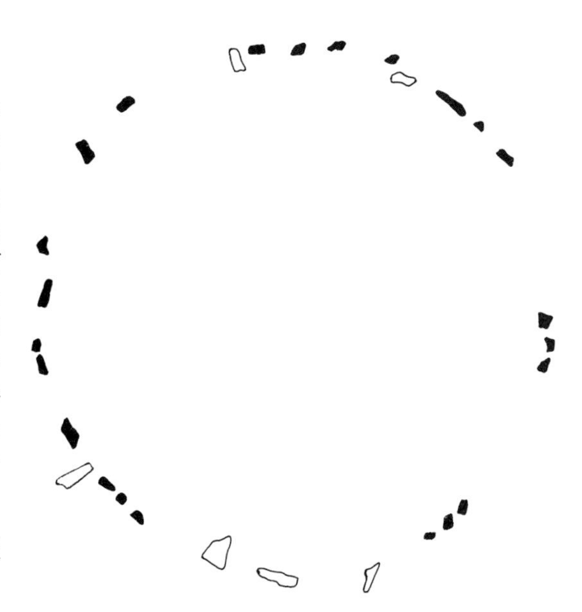

Opposite Scorhill, in the Dartmoor landscape. *Below* Riders have said that their horses shy and refuse to enter this eerie ring.

Stanton Drew

Somerset (Avon): ST 603630. **9 miles W of Bath, 6 miles NW of Midsomer Norton. Best approached along the B3130. Partly in State care. Circles closed on Sundays. The Cove, near the Druids' Arms, is open daily. (NE ring, elliptical, 32.3 × 29.8 metres; centre ring, circular, 113.5 metres; SW ring, elliptical, 42.9 × 39.9 metres.)**

The site at Stanton Drew is another example of the multiple complexes of the south-west peninsula, with three stone circles, two avenues, an outlying stone and a Cove. All these features are duplicated at Avebury, thirty miles to the east, and it is likely that Stanton Drew is a variation of Avebury, put up by a smaller community whose beliefs were similar to those of the inhabitants of the Marlborough Downs.

The three open rings, all ruined, stand on a bent north-north-east / south-south-west axis on low land with hills around them. This choice of a valley setting near water is typical of the large Late Neolithic rings. Bronze Age circles were more often built on higher land. The presence of chambered tombs near Stanton Drew and the relative absence of Bronze Age round barrows supports the belief that these great rings were put up around 2500 BC by people of the late New Stone Age.

The stones, many of them very large, came from a variety of sources, some from Harptree four miles to the south, some from Broadtree Down, some from Dundry Hill only four miles north-west but high and steep-sided. If people brought stones from here it can only have been with much difficulty and it is possible that glacial action had carried stones much closer to Stanton Drew than geologists think at present.

The central ring is by far the largest.

Below Stanton Drew, a multiple complex of three stone circles. The stones were brought from a number of different areas.

Its great stones of sandstone, limestone and breccia now lie unobtrusively in the meadow grass. To its north-east is a smaller ring, much better preserved, whose stones are all breccia, coarsely pebbled pillars of thick and heavy proportions against which human beings are dwarfed. There were eight of these monsters. Four still stand. From the central and north-east rings short avenues converged to the east, probably directed down the slope to where the river flowed. The association of avenues and water is customary.

The south-west circle is separated from the others and is on private land. All its stones are fallen, breccia and sandstone alike, and turf is creeping over them. No excavations have been recorded at Stanton Drew. A seventeenth-century report said that when a stone fell, 'in the Pitt in which it stood were found the crumbes of a man's bones, and a round ball, like a large horse-bell, with a screwe as the stemme of it.' It hardly sounds prehistoric.

The plan of Stanton Drew is teasing. A line drawn through the centres of the south-west and centre circles points to where an outlier once stood on a ridge five hundred metres northwards. This stone, known as Hautville's Quoit, originally three metres high, lies tumbled and broken by the hedge alongside the B3130. In 1906 Lockyer suggested it was a foresight on the rising of Arcturus in 1690 BC, but this is too late a date.

A line extended through the centres of the north-east and centre rings leads to the three-sided Cove, erected at the edge of a slight ridge. This setting of limestones has a fallen back stone. The side-slabs came from one stone. As at Avebury, this Cove may be a representation of a chambered tomb entrance to which human bones were brought. It is interesting that the Christian church was interposed between the Cove and the stone circles as though to stop continuing pagan activity there.

As with other rings, there are legends of fertility at Stanton Drew. The rings are said to be a wedding party turned to stone for continuing their celebrations into the Sabbath.

Right The church interposes between the frowning block and the Cove, behind its tower.

Stonehenge

Wiltshire: SU 123422. **2 miles W of Amesbury on S side of the A344. In State care. The stone circles are closed but access is provided around the perimeter of the monument. Guide-books and explanatory models. (Ditch, circular, 106.0 metres; sarsen ring, circular, 29.6 metres.)**

The visitor will see first a ditch, then a bank, a wide space, a lintelled circle of sarsens, a circle of bluestones, a horseshoe of sarsens, another of bluestones, and a tall bluestone near the centre of the monument. Many of the stones are now fallen or have been removed.

There is no evidence of there having been any other stone circle within twenty miles of Stonehenge. Salisbury Plain, a scoured and windblown plateau of chalk, has very little natural building-stone and what prehistoric monuments were here were made of earth with frameworks of oak or other timber. Of over fifty long burial-mounds only one had stone-built chambers. Any rings would have been of wood and their posts would have long since rotted. It would only be by a fortunate chance of weather that their filled-up holes would appear on an aerial photograph. In 1925 Woodhenge (SU 150434), less than two miles from Stonehenge, was detected in this way. Its concentric ovals of holes, now displayed by concrete markers, are warnings that many more such timber settings were probably put up in this stoneless region. Stonehenge is not a typical stone circle but is an imitation, erected in stone, of these vanished wooden settings.

For nearly a thousand years before any building took place at Stonehenge, Neolithic farmers had been living on Salisbury Plain. At its centre twenty-nine of their long barrows cluster around the waters of the Christchurch Avon, dry dead bones stored in the wooden mortuary rooms. Only Tidcombe at the extreme north had stone chambers.

As societies grew and trading networks expanded, these long shrines, adequate for single families, were supplemented by circular earthworks, known as henges, where assemblies of people could meet not only for trade but for seasonal rituals of fertility that involved both burial rites and the use of human bones. For obvious reasons such centres were built at the heart of the region and it was this consideration and not astronomy that, late in the Neolithic period, decided the location for the centre at Stonehenge.

Stonehenge I. This first structure was no more than a circular ditch, dug in straightish sections by work-gangs. A chalk bank, high as a man, was heaped around its inner edge by Grooved Ware communities whose bits of pottery have been found in the ditch and in the gigantic settlement of Durrington Walls two miles to the east. A date of about 2800 BC (2180 ± 105 bc) from an antler pick shows when this work took place.

A gap was left at the north-east where the crude sarsen of the Heel Stone was raised outside the entrance in line with the sun as it rose above the horizon on midsummer's day. Other sight-lines seem to have been taken on the maximum rising of the moon at midwinter. From the centre of Stonehenge, where there may have been a hut, two standing stones at the entrance defined these alignments, one on the lunar position, the other marking the sun's midsummer rising. Today only the fallen Slaughter Stone survives of these megalithic portals. Four much smaller sarsens, the Four Stations, were set up in a rectangle just inside the bank. Two remain, one of them prostrate. The short sides of this rectangle pointed towards midsummer sunrise, the long ones to the midwinter setting of the moon, which, perhaps by coincidence, in this latitude occurred at approximate right angles to midsummer sunrise. The west-north-west diagonal of the rectangle indicated May Day sunset. Midwinter, midsummer, May Day were all times of importance to herdsmen and farmers and these orientations helped the Neolithic people to determine when their festivals should be held.

These ceremonies included offerings to the forces that they feared, and rituals of death. Fifty-six pits, first noticed by John Aubrey in the seventeenth century and named the Aubrey Holes after him, were dug around the perimeter of the plateau and libations were poured into them. Then they were backfilled. Later they were reopened and human cremated bone and personal possessions such as battle-axes, bone pins and flints were placed in them. A date of about 2300 BC (1848 ± 275 bc) shows that such burials may have continued over several centuries. Other cremations were placed in the ditch. In keeping with the long burial-mounds around it, Stonehenge, therefore, maintained a funerary tradition.

Stonehenge II. About 2200 BC intrusive Beaker people became dominant in the region and it was they who decided to erect a stone circle inside the henge. One of their burials has been discovered in the ditch. Stone for battle-axes had long been imported from South Wales and it was from there that bluestones were carried by water, four-ton blocks of dolerite from Carn Meini in the Preseli mountains. An avenue lined with earthen banks led up to

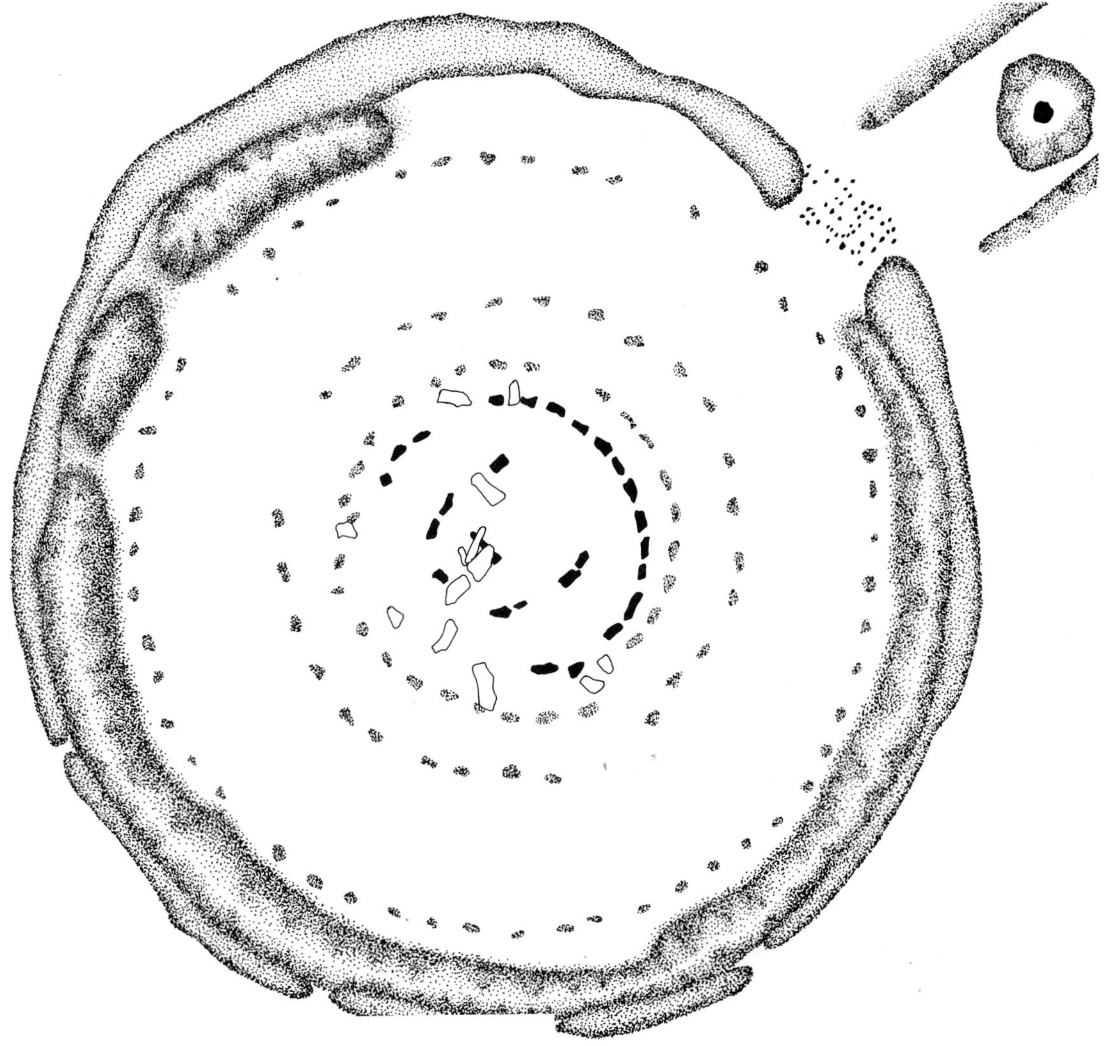

Stonehenge's entrance. A protective bank and ditch were constructed around the Heel Stone and two of the Station Stones, and one by one the bluestones were dragged up to the henge. Two rings were planned, one inside the other, but they were never completed. The work was abandoned around 2100 BC and the bluestones were removed.

Stonehenge IIIA. This, the world-famous sarsen monument, still stands today. It consisted of five trilithons (two stones supporting a third laid on top of them) in a horseshoe setting open to the north-east but rising in height towards the south-west and the midwinter sunset. A burial was placed exactly on the axis of this horseshoe. Around the trilithons a circle of thirty sarsens was raised, each stone over twenty tons in weight. Thirty heavy lintels crowned this ring.

The sarsens were brought twenty miles from the Marlborough Downs and each must have taken months to transport. Once there the stones were smoothed with mauls, the tops of

Opposite The trilithons.
Below Stonehenge seen from the north-east entrance. The leaning pillar on the left is at the exact south.

the standing stones were hacked away, leaving projecting pegs; corresponding sockets were cut in the underside of the lintels to receive the pegs; and the ends of each lintel were shaped to give a neat fit with abutting lintels. Every stone was fashioned. It was a carpentry design and we must assume that this was a project of people native to Salisbury Plain who for centuries had traditionally worked in wood.

Bronze Age cemeteries of round barrows were grouped around the ancient long barrows. Rich graves of chieftains whose followers built Stonehenge lay under them. Bush Barrow (SU 118413) is hardly a mile away from the circle. Beneath it an elderly man with his bronze weapons and gold ornaments was buried within sight of Stonehenge. Other cemeteries at Lake, Lake Down, Wilsford Down and Winterbourne Stoke (SU 101417) can still be seen nearby. It is probable that the bodies in them were first taken to Stonehenge for funerary rites before their burial in these barrow cemeteries.

Stonehenge IIIB. Centuries later it was decided to return the bluestones to Stonehenge. Two rings of stoneholes were prepared for them outside the main sarsen circle, but in the end this idea was rejected.

Stonehenge IIIC. Around 1550 BC (1240 ± 105 bc), well over a thousand years after the henge was built, the final modification began. A circle of bluestones was raised inside the sarsen ring. A horseshoe of nineteen shaped bluestones was set up inside the trilithons. One taller bluestone was erected near the centre of the monument.

Carvings of bronze axes and daggers, symbols of the sun, were pecked into the sarsens. 'Boats of the Dead' were battered on to the faces of western stones. Much of this can still be seen today. What cannot be seen are the ceremonies of death and supplication that took place in the living heart of Stonehenge.

(Many of the finds from the monument, and some interesting displays, can be seen in Salisbury Museum, St Ann Street, Salisbury. Closed Mondays and Sunday mornings.)

Like burnt-out house timbers, the central area is now a confusion of stones.

The Trippet Stones

Cornwall: SX 131750. **6 miles NE of Bodmin and 1 mile N of the A30 on Manor Common. (Circular, 33.0 metres.)**

Even in ruins and with cattle browsing between the stones, this remains one of the most attractive circles in the British Isles, its smooth grey pillars set on a wide moorland against a background of slopes, shallow valleys and jagged tors. Three-quarters of a mile to the east the wreckage of the Stripple Stones is silhouetted on the side of Hawk's Tor. This circle-henge with its central stone has been almost entirely despoiled in modern times.

The ring of the Trippet Stones encloses a broad flat space, as featureless as the moor around it. Originally it probably had twenty-six stones of local granite, all of them larger than in most Cornish rings, but the site has been so damaged by stone-breakers that today only twelve survive.

The name derives from the legend that this was a ring of petrified dancing girls, and the level, uncluttered interior of the circle would have been perfect for ritual dances, although at what time of the year these took place can only be guessed. Nor is the date of construction known. Lockyer believed that there was a north-north-east alignment from the circle to the peaked mass of Rough Tor, orientated on the rising of the star Arcturus about 1700 BC,

and Alexander Thom suggested an alternative alignment of a small outlying stone to the north-north-west on the setting of Castor in 1840 BC. Both dates, however, seem too close to the very end of the Early Bronze Age for such an imposing megalithic monument as the Trippet Stones. The spacing of the other circles on Bodmin Moor in 'territories' of about four square miles suggests that this ring was put up by a group of farming people. It probably was built within a century or two of 2300 BC.

Opposite The circle stones now lean gently. *Below* The legend runs that these stones were once dancing girls.

Glossary

Barrow An artificial mound of earth, chalk or turf built to cover burials. Long barrows, often with timber- or stone-built chambers at their eastern ends, were customary during the Neolithic period in many parts of Britain. Round barrows, circular mounds with no entrance or chamber, slowly replaced the long forms after 2500 BC and remained popular throughout the Bronze Age.

Beakers These were fine pots made by people from the European mainland who first entered this country around 2600 BC. The pots were flat-based, sinuous in outline, and decorated all over their bodies with cross-hatched patterns. Like most early prehistoric pottery in the British Isles, the vessels were coil-built. There was no wheel-turned pottery in Britain until the Late Iron Age. Beakers were almost certainly drinking pots.

Bluestones The name given to a variety of rocks, mainly doleritic, to be found near Carn Meini in the Preseli mountains of south-west Wales. It is thought that Beaker people transported some of the bluestones to Stonehenge.

Boulder-tomb An above-ground burial-place constructed of lumpish boulders. Boulder-tombs are to be found mainly in south-west Ireland. They may have been built as late as the Early Bronze Age, between about 2500 and 2000 BC.

Breccia A rough conglomerate stone composed of angular rock fragments cemented together by calcite or silica.

Bronze Age *Early* About 2300 to 1700 BC. Period when metallurgy was first introduced into the British Isles. Great bronze daggers and knives became the regalia of rich chieftains. Cemeteries of round barrows and cairns slowly developed during this time.

Middle About 1700 to 1300 BC. A period of more intensive farming by family groups in upland regions. Flanged bronze axes known as palstaves were widely used.

Late About 1300 to 800 BC. Period when smiths learnt to mix lead with copper to make sheets of bronze for shields and cauldrons. A time of unrest as the deteriorating climate caused more competition for good, well-drained land.

Cairn Long and round mounds of smallish stones, the equivalents of barrows in the highland areas of the British Isles where stone is plentiful.

Cairn-circle A low round cairn with standing stones set in its inner edge. Probably of the Early Bronze Age, such monuments are a combination of cairn and stone circle.

Capstone A heavy, flattish stone placed on top of a cist or forming the roof of a burial chamber.

Chambered tomb A Neolithic barrow or cairn which contained one or more stone-built rooms in which dead bodies were laid. Long chambered tombs were popular in England and parts of Wales and Scotland but in Ireland and western Britain round chambered tombs known as passage-graves were more common.

Circle-henge A henge which had a stone circle on its central plateau. Avebury and Stonehenge are good examples of this type of monument, which can be found along the hilly spine of Britain from Aberdeen down to Cornwall.

Cist A grave lined with stone slabs and covered with a capstone.

Cist-slab The capstone of a cist.

Cove A setting of three large stones like an unroofed sentry-box. It may have been an imitation of the entrance to a chambered tomb where funerary rites took place. No undamaged Cove survives but there are ruined versions at Stanton Drew, Avebury and Arbor Low.

Cupmark An artificial, circular depression, the size of a cup but not so deep, ground into a rock or on to a standing stone. Cupmarks are frequently associated with burials and may be symbols of the sun or moon.

Earthwork A construction of soil. Circular earthen banks, piled up from ditch material, were frequently built in the Neolithic and Early Bronze Ages for a variety of purposes, including defence, occupation and ritual.

Flanker One of the two tall stones that stood on either side of the prostrate recumbent stone in the circles of north-east Scotland.

Flat-rimmed ware Poorly made, flat-based and unpatterned pottery common in northern Britain during the Neolithic and Bronze Ages. Instead of curving the rim over, or decorating it, the potters were content to smooth it flat.

Food-vessel An Early Bronze Age ware with a variety of forms. Food-vessels were particularly common in Yorkshire and in Ireland and were presumably made by native people. Flat-based and lavishly decorated, the pots have thick sides, heavy rims and often several lugs around their bodies. They are frequently found with burials and may have contained food for the dead person.

Gneiss 'Sparkling' metamorphic stone, often with grey or pink bands caused by the presence of quartz or feldspar.

Grooved ware Flat-based pottery whose origins are not yet known. It was formerly known as Rinyo-Clacton ware because it had been found both at the Neolithic village of Rinyo in the Orkneys and at

Clacton in Essex. The pots often have incised, zoned decoration on their bodies. Plain forms also are known. Grooved ware was used by the inhabitants of the famous Skara Brae village in the Orkneys. It also occurs in henges and in some large stone circles.

Henge A large circular earthen enclosure consisting of an outer bank and internal ditch and with one or more entrances. As with all prehistoric monuments, every henge is different. Double-ditched forms occur in eastern England. Stonehenge has an outer ditch. Some cobble-built henges in western Britain have no ditch at all. Not to be confused with the massive earthwork enclosures for occupation, like Durrington Walls near Stonehenge, henges were meeting-places for trade and ritual. They were built in lowland areas and they belong to the Late Neolithic to Early Bronze Age period, about 2900 to 1700 BC.

Kerbstone One of a series of contiguous heavy stones, set on their sides, that lined the bases of some barrows and cairns.

Megalithic 'Big Stone'. A term applied to stone circles and chambered tombs, some of whose stones weigh many tons.

Neolithic The New Stone Age from about 4500 to 2250 BC, during which farming was introduced into the British Isles. Pottery was another innovation. It was also the time of the chambered tombs and earthen long barrows and, later in the period, of the first henges and stone circles.

Passage-grave A chambered tomb, generally circular, with a long passage of stones leading to one or more central chambers. Cremations are rather more common than inhumations in passage-graves. Two large groups of passage-graves in Ireland have superbly decorated kerbstones and internal stones with abstract motifs of triangles, spirals and lozenges pecked into the stones with flints and other hard stones.

Quartz A very hard silicate, found particularly in areas of granite and gneiss. It has many varieties. In stone circles the quartz fragments often occur in the form of attractive large white crystals. Feldspars, the most widespread of all minerals, contain crystals very similar to quartz.

Radio-carbon dating A method of determining the amount of radio-active Carbon-14 that survives in dead organic material such as charcoal, bone and antler. By contrasting the proportion of the dissipating Carbon-14 with that of the stable Carbon-12 in a sample physicists can estimate the time at which the sample died.

Because of past fluctuations in the carbon content of the earth's atmosphere Carbon-14 dating is less accurate than was anticipated and its 'dates' have now to be recalculated using tables obtained from the more reliable tree-ring chronology. It is conventional for archaeologists to write 'bc' after a radio-carbon date, and to indicate a recalculated date by the use of 'BC'. The 'BC' dates in this book have been recalculated and are therefore 'real' dates.

Recumbent stone In north-east Scotland this was the massive block, often of a different stone from the pillars of the circle, that lay flat between its flankers somewhere between south-west and south-south-east on the circumference of a recumbent stone circle. In south-west Ireland the recumbent was often a thin slab set on edge. It had no flankers. Instead, the tallest stones were placed on the opposite side of the ring and seem to have acted as portal- or entrance-stones.

Ring-cairn A low, round cairn with an open circular space at its centre where burials were placed. Ring-cairns were common to many upland areas but it was only in north-east Scotland that they were integrated with stone circles.

Ringwork A circular bank of earth or stones.

Sarsen A block of tertiary sandstone from the chalk downs of north Wiltshire. Sarsen, perhaps a corruption of 'saracen' or 'foreign' stone, was frequently used in the construction of chambered tombs in Wessex. The stone circles of Avebury and of the final phase of Stonehenge were built of sarsen, which is extremely hard.

Sherd A broken piece of pottery.

Sondage pit A pit dug during an excavation to find out what the underlying layers of undisturbed soil look like.

Trilithon 'Three Stones'. A setting of two upright stones with a lintel-stone placed on top of them. Of British prehistoric monuments today only Stonehenge has trilithons but it is probable that there were many timber versions in the lowland regions of the British Isles, all of which have long since vanished.

Wedge-grave A wedge-shaped chambered tomb with an entrance facing between west and south-west. They were quite common in Ireland. They may have been quite late forms of megalithic monuments.

Index

Figures in **bold** type refer to colour illustrations. Those in *italic* refer to black-and-white illustrations.

Reading list

For readers wishing to learn more about the megalithic rings of the British Isles there is only one comprehensive book with a full list of stone circles and their grid references: Aubrey Burl, *The Stone Circles of the British Isles* (Yale University Press, New Haven and London, 1976). Other works of interest are listed below, under the section headings.

Introduction

Hadingham, E. *Circles and Standing Stones* (Heinemann, London, 1975 and Doubleday, New York, 1976).

MacKie, E. *Science and Society in Prehistoric Britain* (Elek, London, 1977).

Clues to the past: recumbent stone circles

Much information about these sites comes from a series of papers by F. R. Coles, published between 1900 and 1907 in the *Proceedings of the Society of Antiquaries of Scotland*, XXXIV to XLI. Other material appears in:

Browne, G. F. *On Some Antiquities in the Neighbourhood of Dunecht House, Aberdeenshire* (Cambridge University Press, Cambridge, 1921).

Keiller, A. *Megalithic Monuments of North-East Scotland* (Morven Institute, London, 1934).

The people

Ashbee, P. *The Ancient British: a Social-Archaeological Study* (Geo Abstracts, University of East Anglia, Norwich, 1978).

Branigan, K. *Prehistoric Britain* (Spur Books, Bourne End, 1976).

Forde-Johnston, J. *Prehistoric Britain and Ireland* (Dent, London, and W. W. Norton, New York, 1976).

The stone circles

There are a few books devoted to individual rings. Among those accessible to the general reader are the following works.

Burl, A. *Prehistoric Avebury* (Yale University Press, New Haven and London, 1979).

Ponting, G. and M. *The Standing Stones of Callanish* (Stornaway, 1977).

Ravenhill, T. H. *The Rollright Stones and the Men Who Erected Them*, second edition (Cornish, Birmingham, 1932).

Bones and burials

Ashbee, P. *The Bronze Age Round Barrow in Britain* (Phoenix, London, 1960).

Ashbee, P. *The Earthen Long Barrow in Britain* (Dent, London, and University of Toronto Press, Toronto, 1970).

Grinsell, L. V. *Barrow, Pyramid and Tomb* (Thames and Hudson, London, and Westview Press, Boulder, Colorado, 1975).

Henshall, A. S. *The Chambered Tombs of Scotland*, I and II (Edinburgh University Press, Endinburgh, 1963 and 1972).

Art and the Other World

Hadingham, E. *Ancient Carvings in Britain: a Mystery* (Garnstone, London, 1974).

Morris, R. W. B. *The Prehistoric Rock Art of Argyll* (Dolphin, Poole, 1977).

Astronomy: science or symbolism?

Brown, P. L. *Megaliths, Myths and Man* (Blandford, Poole, and Taplinger, New York, 1976).

Lockyer, N. *Stonehenge and Other British Stone Monuments Astronomically Considered*, second edition (Macmillan, London, 1909).

Thom, A. *Megalithic Sites in Britain* (Oxford University Press, Oxford and New Jersey, 1967).

Thom, A. and A. S. *Megalithic Remains in Britain and Brittany* (Oxford University Press, Oxford and New Jersey, 1978).

Wood, J. E. *Sun, Moon and Standing Stones* (Oxford University Press, Oxford, 1978).

A useful account of the background to archaeo-astronomy and the origins of ley-lines and other extreme views about stone circles can be found in:

Brown, P. L. *Megaliths and Masterminds* (Robert Hale, London, 1979).

Stonehenge: bones and batter-dashers

Atkinson, R. J. C. *Stonehenge* (Hamish Hamilton, London, 1956).

Hoyle, F. *On Stonehenge* (Heinemann, London, and W. H. Freeman, San Francisco, 1977).

Stover, L. E. and Kraig, B. *Stonehenge: the Indo-European Heritage* (Nelson-Hall, Chicago, 1978).

Lunacy, leys and legends

Bord, J. and C. *Mysterious Britain* (Garnstone, London, 1972).

Grinsell, L. V. *Folklore of Prehistoric Sites in Britain* (David and Charles, Newton Abbot, 1976).

Michell, J. *The View over Atlantis* (Sago, London, 1969).

Visiting the circles

ENGLAND

Dyer, J. *Southern England: an Archaeological Guide* (Faber and Faber, London, 1973 and Noyes Press, New Jersey, 1974).

Hawkes, J. *A Guide to the Prehistoric and Roman Monuments in England and Wales* (Chatto and Windus, London, 1973).

Thomas, N. *A Guide to Prehistoric England* (Batsford, London, 1976).

Wainwright, R. *A Guide to the Prehistoric Remains in Britain, I: South and East* (Constable, London, 1978).

There are also useful pocket-books in the 'Discovering Regional Archaeology' series, published by Shire Publications, Princes Risborough.

Dyer, J. *The Cotswolds and Upper Thames* (1970).

Grinsell, L. *South-Western England* (1970).

Grinsell, L. and Dyer, J. *Wessex* (1971).

Marsden, B. M. *Central England* (1970).

Marsden, B. M. *North-Eastern England* (1971).

Marsden, B. M. *North-Western England* (1971).

IRELAND

Evans, E. *Prehistoric and Early Christian Ireland. A Guide* (Batsford, London, 1966).

O'Riordain, S. P. *Antiquities of the Irish Countryside* (Methuen, London, 1964).

SCOTLAND

Feachem, R. *A Guide to Prehistoric Scotland* (Batsford, London, 1963).

MacKie, E. W. *Scotland: an Archaeological Guide* (Faber and Faber, London, and Noyes Press, New Jersey, 1975).

WALES

Anthony, I. *Discovering Regional Archaeology: Wales* (Shire, Princes Risborough, 1973).

Houlder, C. *Wales: an Archaeological Guide* (Faber and Faber, London, 1974 and Noyes Press, New Jersey, 1975).

Acknowledgments

The publishers would like to thank the following for their assistance:
Artwork John Shipperbottom 92, 99, 109, 111, 113, 121, 125, 127, 131, 132, 135, 139, 140, 150, 153, 159, 160, 169, 171, 173, 175, 177, 181, 183, 185, 188, 193, 195, 197, 198, 205, 207, 209, 217, 218, 220, 227, 231, 235, 239, 245, 247, 249, 251, 253, 255, 263, 265, 269, 275; Arka Graphics 91, 119, 149, 167, 179, 187, 214, 236–7; Jim Marks 34, 35, 66; Richard Phipps 13.
Photography Aubrey Burl 28, 124, 125; Crown Copyright: reproduced by permission of the Scottish Development Dept. 168–9.